ADDITIONAL PRAISE FOR *ALLIES AT ODDS?*

"Even before the Iraq War, the transatlantic relationship was adrift on stormy seas. In *Allies at Odds?*, Thomas S. Mowle uses realist, institutionalist and epistemic international relations theories to explain why the United States and Europe increasingly are at odds, and to predict the future course of the relationship. Given the real-world events that are the backdrop to this study, *Allies at Odds?* is a timely and useful analysis that is both theoretically rigorous, and policy relevant."

—Christopher Layne, Visiting Fellow in Foreign Policy Studies at the Cato Institute

"Finally, amidst the numerous recent works aspiring to tell the story of transatlantic security relations, a major monograph that compares the utility of various theoretical lenses in explaining these relations across a broad swathe of issue areas. Recommended reading for all those who wish not merely to know what has happened, but also to start thinking about what it all means for our understanding of international relations more generally."

—Anand Menon, Director, European Research Institute, University of Birmingham

"This is an excellent analysis of a topical issue. The dispute over policy on Iraq has turned into the most serious transatlantic dispute since the days of Vietnam, and raises important questions about the values and goals of Americans and Europeans. Thomas Mowle provides illuminating insight into differences over arms control, the environment, human rights, and military cooperation, and offers some thought-provoking conclusions about the way that Americans and Europeans view each other, and about how they see their own place in the global system."

—John McCormick, Indiana University, Indianapolis

ABOUT THE AUTHOR

Major Thomas S. Mowle is an Associate Professor of Political Science at the United States Air Force Academy, and Director of the Center for the Study of Defense Policy. He holds a Ph.D. in Political Science from The Ohio State University and has also taught at St. Mary's University in San Antonio. He is also a fellow with the European Union Center at the University of Oklahoma. In recent years, he has participated in the Salzburg Seminar, the Manfred Worner Seminar, and the European Union Visitors Programme. Most of his research focuses on international relations theory and foreign policy, with a special interest in recent years on trans-Atlantic relations. Recent publications include "Arms Control after the Cold War" in James M. Smith and Gwendolyn M. Hall, ed., *Milestones in Strategic Arms Control 1945–2000: United States Air Force Roles and Outcomes* (Montgomery, AL: Air University Press, 2002, pp. 179–208) and "Worldviews in Foreign Policy: Realism, Liberalism, and External Conflict," *Political Psychology* 24, No. 3 (2003).

ALLIES AT ODDS? THE UNITED STATES AND THE EUROPEAN UNION

Thomas S. Mowle

palgrave
macmillan

First published 2004 by
PALGRAVE MACMILLAN™
175 Fifth Avenue, New York, N.Y. 10010 and
Houndmills, Basingstoke, Hampshire, England RG21 6XS
Companies and representatives throughout the world

PALGRAVE MACMILLAN is the global academic imprint of the Palgrave Macmillan division of St. Martin's Press, LLC and of Palgrave Macmillan Ltd. Macmillan® is a registered trademark in the United States, United Kingdom and other countries. Palgrave is a registered trademark in the European Union and other countries.

ISBN 1-4039-6650-8 hardcover
ISBN 1-4039-6653-2 paperback

Library of Congress Cataloging-in-Publication Data
Mowle, Thomas S.
    Allies at odds? : the United States and the European Union /
by Thomas S. Mowle.
        p. cm.
    Includes bibliographical references and index.
    ISBN 1-4039-6650-8 — ISBN 1-4039-6653-2 (pbk.)
    1. European Union—United States. 2. European Union countries—Foreign relations—United States. 3. United States—Foreign relations—European Union countries. I. Title.
    D2009.M68 2004
    327.7304'09'0511—dc22   2004041596

A catalogue record for this book is available from the British Library.

Design by Newgen Imaging Systems (P) Ltd., Chennai, India.

First edition: October 2004
10 9 8 7 6 5 4 3 2 1

Printed in the United States of America.

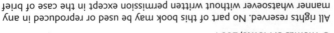

CONTENTS

To Jan, Elyse, and Adrien

Acknowledgments

This book developed from a question asked by Sir David Hannay, former British ambassador to the United Nations, at Salzburg Seminar 385, "Europe in the Global Community," in March 2001. Sir David posed a question to our study group that remains almost unchanged as the guiding question in this research: *Why, despite their professed similarity of goals, do the policy preferences of the European Union (EU) and United States diverge on so many multilateral issues?* I had the good fortune to be a rapporteur for the subject of the EU and multilateral institutions; three years later, I have this book. My first thanks must go then to Sir David and the organizers of the Salzburg Seminar, Tim Ryback and Ben Glahn in particular, for maintaining that hothouse of intellectual stimulation, as well the other faculty of that session, especially Philippe de Schoutheete and John Richardson.

I cannot list all the other Seminar attendees who have contributed to my understanding of the EU, so I will single out those whose contributions are most concrete. One is Elisabeth Johansson, my co-rapporteur at Salzburg, who helped me shape my initial concepts and approach, thus getting the book off the ground. Also invaluable were Catherine Gegout's assistance with finding EU foreign policy documentation and the hospitality of Jorge-Manuel Bento-Silva in Brussels, who helped me set up contacts with the Directorate-General for External Relations. The Salzburg connection also introduced me to Jonathan Davidson in the European Commission's Mission to the United States, which in turn linked me to the European Union Center at the University of Oklahoma and The Right Honourable Henry McLeish, Member of Scottish Parliament.

I also must acknowledge the help provided by Julianne Smith of the German Marshall Fund of the United States and the Manfred Wörner Seminar on German-American Understanding. Anthony Cary from the Commission, Carolyn Leddy from the Senate Foreign Relations Committee, and Damon Wilson of NATO all helped to arrange interviews. Wendin Smith's hospitality in Washington was very helpful in allowing me to conduct a series of interviews in summer 2002.

These interviews were conducted in support of a separate research grant, encouraged by Jim Smith and Hal Bidlack of the Institute for National Security Studies. Little from that series of interviews found its way directly into this book, since the interviewees generally preferred not to be quoted by name, but that separate research helped to deepen my understanding of the cases. Not all interview subjects wished to even have their assistance acknowledged. In the United States, these interviews included Jim Burger, Brian Butcher, Guy Roberts, Jim Roberts, and Brian Wilson in the Department of Defense; Mark Lagon from the Senate staff; Mark Richard from the Department of Justice; and David Bowker, Maryruth Coleman, Ed Cummings, Richard D'Andrea, Rosemary DiCarlo, Richard Figueroa, Fred Fleitz, Bill Grant, Doug Hoyt, Edward Ifft, Tony Kolankeiwicz, Ambassador Don Mahley, Peter Martin, Steve Mouton, Peter Mulrean, Chris Murray, Charles Ries, Robert Simmons, and Curtis Stewart from the Department of State. In the EU, interview subjects included Marie-Annick Bourdin, Fraser Cameron, Paul Clairet, Chris Kendall, Michael Köhler, Edward Llewellyn, Lars-Erik Lundin, Yves Mollard La Bruyère, Diederik Paalman, and Gunnar Wiegand in the European Commission; and Jim Cloos, Frank de Wispelaere, Mark Otte, Terkel Petersen, Ana Ramírez Fueyo, and Antonio Tanca, from the European Council Secretariat. Additional interviews were conducted with persons not currently associated with governments, including Loretta Bondi of The Fund for Peace, Tamar Gabelnick of Federation of American Scientists, Heather Hamilton of World Federalist Association, Tom Malinowski of Human Rights Watch, Michael Moodie of Chemical and Biological Arms Control Institute, Amy Sands of Center for Nonproliferation Studies at the Monterey Institute of International Studies, Rachel Stohl of Center for Defense Information, John Washburn of American Non-Governmental Organizations Coalition for the International Criminal Court (ICC), and Gillian Woolett of Pharmaceutical Research and Manufacturers of America.

Many people have reviewed parts of this draft. I appreciate the substantive comments made by Hal Bidlack, Marie-Annick Bourdin, Nick Carrera, Damon Coletta, Brad Gutierrez, Jolyon Howorth, Henrike Paepcke, Fran Pilch, Lance Robinson, Amy Sands, Randy Schweller, and Jeremy Zucker. I did not always adopt their comments, so full responsibility for any errors of fact or interpretation rest with me. Furthermore, it must be stated very clearly that the views expressed in this book are those of the author and do not necessarily reflect the official policy or position of the United States Air Force, Department of Defense, or the U.S. government.

I would also like to thank the Pikes Peak Library District for a staggering amount of Inter-Library Loan materials, and PepsiCo for keeping me awake via massive quantities of Diet Mountain Dew.

Finally, I would like to acknowledge the love and support of my wife Jan, and my daughters Elyse and Adrien, who put up with my long hours and lack of sleep during the writing process. Thank you.

List of Acronyms

ABM	Anti-Ballistic Missile
AFSOUTH	Allied Forces South
AHG	Ad Hoc Group
AOSIS	Alliance of Small Island States
ASPA	American Service-Members' Protection Act
AWACS	Airborne Warning and Control System
BTU	British Thermal Unit
BTWC	Biological (Bacteriological) and Toxin Weapons Convention [EU acronym]
BWC	Biological (Bacteriological) and Toxin Weapons Convention [U.S. acronym]
CAT	Convention Against Torture
CCW	Convention on Conventional Weapons
CD	Conference/Committee on Disarmament
CEDAW	Convention for the Elimination of All Forms of Discrimination Against Women
CFCs	Chlorofluorocarbons
CFSP	Common Foreign and Security Policy
CJTF	Combined Joint Task Force
CMA	Chemical Manufacturers Association
CoE	Council of Europe
COP	Conference of the Parties
CRC	Convention on the Rights of the Child
CSCE	Conference for Security and Cooperation in Europe
CTBT	Comprehensive Nuclear Test Ban Treaty
CWC	Chemical Weapons Convention
DoD	[U.S.] Department of Defense
EC	European Community
ECHR	European Court of Human Rights/European Convention on Human Rights
EDC	European Defense Community
EEC	European Economic Community
EIF	Entry Into Force
EP	European Parliament
ESDP	European Security and Defence Policy (EU)
ESDI	European Security and Defence Initiative (NATO)
EU	European Union

EURATOM	European Atomic Energy Community
FCCC	Framework Convention on Climate Change
GHG	Greenhouse Gas
HBA	Helms-Burton Act
HRC	[UN] Human Rights Commission
IAEA	International Atomic Energy Agency
ICBL	International Campaign to Ban Landmines
ICC	International Criminal Court
ICCPR	International Covenant on Civil and Political Rights
ICJ	International Court of Justice
ICTY	International Criminal Tribunal for the former Yugoslavia
IFOR	Implementation Force
ILC	International Law Commission
ILSA	Iran-Libya Sanctions Act
IPCC	Intergovernmental Panel on Climate Change
ISAF	International Security Assistance Force
JNA	Yugoslav National Army
KFOR	Kosovo Force
LCPD	Large Combustion Plant Directive
LRTAP	Convention on Long-Range Transboundary Air Pollution
MBT	Mine Ban Treaty
NAC	North Atlantic Council
NATO	North Atlantic Treaty Organization
NGO	Non-Governmental Organization
NIEO	New International Economic Order
NNWS	Non-Nuclear Weapons States
NPT	Nuclear Non-Proliferation Treaty
NRF	NATO Response Force
NWS	Nuclear Weapons States
OECD	Organization for Economic Cooperation and Development
OPCW	Organization for the Prohibition of Chemical Weapons
OPEC	Organization of Petroleum Exporting Countries
OSCE	Conference for Security and Cooperation in Europe
PhRMA	Pharmaceutical Research and Manufacturers Association
PNET	Peaceful Nuclear Explosions Treaty
PrepCom	Preparatory Committee
POW	Prisoner of War
QMV	Qualified Majority Voting
RRF	Rapid Reaction Force
SACEUR	Supreme Allied Commander in Europe
SAM	Surface-to-Air Missile
SEA	Single European Act
SFOR	Stabilization Force
SOFA	Status of Forces Agreement
SST	Supersonic Transport
TEU	Treaty on European Union

TTBT	Threshold Test Ban Treaty
UCMJ	Uniform Code of Military Justice
UDHR	Universal Declaration on Human Rights
UN	United Nations
UNDP	United Nations Development Programme
UNEP	United Nations Environment Programme
UNGA	United Nations General Assembly
UNHRC	United Nations Human Rights Commission
UNMIK	United Nations Interim Mission in Kosovo
UNMOVIC	United Nations Monitoring, Verification, and Inspection Commission
UNPROFOR	United Nations Protection Force
UNSC	United Nations Security Council
UNSCR	United Nations Security Council Resolution
UNSCOM	United Nations Special Commission
U.S.	United States
USA	United States of America
VerEx	Verification Experts
WEU	Western European Union
WMD	Weapons of Mass Destruction
WTO	World Trade Organization

1

The United States and the European Union: On the Brink of the Transatlantic Rift?

In 2002–3, the Iraqi crisis made clear that the United States and its allies in Europe are increasingly at odds. Germany and France were the most vocal opponents of American policy, with Chancellor Gerhard Schröder winning reelection in September 2002 largely due to his firm opposition to German participation in any war in Iraq, and President Jacques Chirac vowing on 10 March 2003 to veto UN approval for an attack.[1] While Prime Minister Tony Blair sent troops in support of Saddam Hussein's overthrow, and many European governments offered at least rhetorical support for the operation, public opinion in Europe strongly preferred maintaining inspections rather than using military force to achieve regime change in Iraq.

If this clash with respect to Iraq were an isolated event, then one could disregard it as merely a difference of opinion over a very difficult decision. If it were merely a few European countries opposing U.S. policy, then one could concur with U.S. Secretary of Defense Donald Rumsfeld's distinction between an "Old Europe" that opposes the United States and a "New Europe" that supports the United States.[2] Neither view would be accurate. Disputes have erupted over many different issues, and the Iraqi case is unusual in that some members of the European Union (EU) sided with the United States rather than against it.

This is the puzzle at the root of this book: *Why, despite their professed similarity of goals, do the policy preferences of the European Union and United States diverge on so many multilateral issues?* The EU—acting as one or simply as the collection of its member states—and the United States have disagreed on a wide range of subjects, especially since 1997. These include the Kyoto Protocol on climate change, the Mine Ban Treaty, the International Criminal Court (ICC), the future of the North Atlantic Treaty Organization (NATO), and the Comprehensive Nuclear Test Ban Treaty (CTPT). All of these standoffs became apparent while Bill Clinton was president. Since the inauguration of George W. Bush, and continuing after the terrorist attacks of 11 September 2001, the list of differences has grown to include verification provisions for the Biological (Bacteriological) and Toxin Weapons Convention (BWC), a Small Arms Program of Action, and policy toward Iraq. Many of the differences between the United States and the European Union can be seen in their interaction with multilateral institutions, often working on global issues. In general, the EU has supported the multilateral solution, and the United States has not.[3]

This series of disputes seems odd because the United States and the European Union profess to share many of the same values and interests: democracy, human rights, peace and stability. The original Treaty on European Union (TEU), signed at Maastricht on 7 February 1992, stated:

> The objectives of the common foreign and security policy shall be:
>   to safeguard the common values, fundamental interests and independence of the Union;
>   to strengthen the security of the Union and its Member States in all ways;
>   to preserve peace and strengthen international security, in accordance with the principles of the United Nations Charter as well as the principles of the Helsinki Final Act and the objectives of the Paris Charter;
>   to promote international cooperation;
>   to develop and consolidate democracy and the rule of law, and respect for human rights and fundamental freedoms.[4]

The Treaty of Amsterdam in 1997 left these words substantially intact, only dropping the reference to "Member States," adding safeguarding "the integrity of the Union" and strengthening security "on external borders." In June 2000, EU External Relations Commissioner Chris Patten described "the projection of stability as the EU's essential mission," with a focus in neighboring regions on "peace, prosperity and security...rooted in free trade. We seek to promote human rights, democracy and the rule of law."[5]

The 1999 *National Security Strategy of the United States* listed three similar goals: "to enhance America's security, to bolster America's economic prosperity, [and] to promote democracy and human rights abroad."[6] Elaborating, it stated that the American vision was for a

> stable, peaceful security environment—one in which our nation, citizens and interests are not threatened; the health and well-being of our citizens are enhanced by a cleaner global environment and effective strategies to combat infectious disease; America continues to prosper through increasingly open international markets and sustainable growth in the global economy; and democratic values and respect for human rights and the rule of law are increasingly accepted.[7]

In November 2001, the State Department's Director of Policy Planning, Ambassador Richard Haass, listed the Bush administration's "important foreign policy tasks" as including "stymieing the proliferation of weapons of mass destruction...promoting world trade...[promoting] good governance, rule of law, and democracy...integrating new countries and peoples into the global economic order . . . and coping with state failures."[8] In April 2002, he repeated these sentiments and added "limits on the power of the state, respect for women, private property, equal justice, religious tolerance" to the "consistent body of ideas and policies that [guide] the Bush Administration's foreign policy."[9] Each of these concepts, along with "strengthen alliances to defeat global terrorism" and "work with others to defuse regional conflicts," were incorporated as primary goals in the September 2002 *National Security Strategy of the United States*.[10] This document is notable, on the other hand, for its rejection of multilateral measures such as the ICC and arms control treaties in favor of reserving the right to independent action.[11] It thus brought American policy rhetoric in line with established American practice.

Policy disagreements despite agreement over basic goals are not unusual. There may be many means to the same end. It is nevertheless difficult to overcome such a divergence unless you understand its sources. This book describes the history of these differences between the United States and the European Union and assesses what factors seem to best explain them, allowing us in the end to make some projections regarding the future of transatlantic relations. Before further laying out the plan and approach of this book let us first review some vignettes that capture recent trends among these allies.

The divergence between the United States and Europe came to public attention, briefly, on 3 May 2001, when United Nations Economic and Social Council voted the United States off the UN Human Rights Commission (HRC) for the first time since it was founded in 1947. The *New York Times* blamed the vote on "rising resentments abroad" over American nonpayment of UN dues, its position on the death penalty, and its rejection of agreements including the Mine Ban Treaty and the Kyoto Protocol. Others saw a closer link to the politics of human rights. William Safire saw it as punishment for criticizing China and not Israel.[12] Amnesty International USA, on the other hand, said it was "due in part to an effort by nations that routinely violate human rights to escape scrutiny of their human rights' records."[13] Since the policies of states like Sudan and Sierra Leone (both elected to the HRC at the same time) had not changed, the lost votes were attributed to a new suspect: the EU. As Joanna Weschler of Human Rights Watch noted, "It wasn't just enemies. It was friends as well who voted the United States out of the commission."[14] Senator Jesse Helms (R-NC) observed that it was "no surprise that a few European countries maneuvered . . . to eliminate the United States from the United Nations Human Rights Commission seat."[15] *The New Republic* editorialized, "The European countries . . . resent America's public commitment to human rights because it gets in the way of business . . . Many European governments view moral questions as a bothersome distraction from the *realpolitik* that dominates the European diplomatic tradition."[16]

This dispute put a spotlight not only on transatlantic differences, but also on the EU itself. The Union had evolved over 50 years from the European

Coal and Steel Community through the European Economic Community (EEC) until it took its current name at Maastricht in 1992. It had grown from six original members seeking peace through economic development and interdependence to include 15 European states, from Finland to Portugal and from Ireland to Greece. The Union also had deepened cooperation among its members to the point where it was ready, at the end of 2001, to discard the currencies of 12 of its members in favor of the common euro. This is not the place to describe either the history of the EU, which has been presented in great detail elsewhere, or the mechanics of its governance, which continue to change through the 2004 Constitutional Treaty.[17] Instead, let us focus on the EU as an actor in the global community.

This book takes the EU seriously, which has been unusual outside the realm of economic and trade policy. At one level, the EU is simply an intergovernmental organization, a group of sovereign states who work together to achieve common goals. In some areas, however, the Union has established supranational authority over its member states. European Monetary Union is the most visible of these, but the principle was established as early as 1964. In a case comparable in significance to *McCullough v. Maryland* (1820) in the United States, the European Court of Justice ruled, "The Member States have limited their sovereign rights, albeit in limited fields...the Treaty [of Rome] carries with it a permanent limitation of their sovereign rights."[18] In essence, the member states of the EU have agreed to share their sovereignty with each other, while retaining the legal right to reassert their individual sovereignty by withdrawing from the Treaties.[19] The EU might best be described as a confederation: a grouping of political actors in which clear delineations are made between areas of unit sovereignty and areas of central sovereignty.[20]

The European Community (EC) had competence over matters of trade and economics. As the history of the U.S. Constitution's commerce clause would predict, this power created an incentive to coordinate in other areas, including foreign policy in general. A Common Commercial Policy and Common External Tariff affected more than just trade. European Political Cooperation remained informal until the 1986 Single European Act (SEA). The Treaty on European Union formally established a Common Foreign and Security Policy (CFSP) "pillar" alongside the existing Community and a third pillar for Justice and Home Affairs. The CFSP was to be the province of the European Council, composed of the heads of government of all member states. This was in contrast to the Community pillar, where an appointed Commission took the lead in developing policies for approval by the Council (or rather, by the appropriate Council of Ministers, such as the Environment Council, composed of each member state's Minister of the Environment). The Commission did not fully stay away from foreign policy, as it created its own commissioner for External Relations in 1993. The Council followed up with its High Representative for the CFSP, established in the Treaty of Amsterdam in 1997. Presidency of the European Council, and leadership of the Councils of Ministers, rotated every six months among the member states. The elected European Parliament (EP) appointed the Commission President and the other Commissioners. The EP had budgetary power, as well as the ability to block or delay decisions of the Council in some areas and to set a public agenda for the Union.

The CFSP aimed at having EU member states coordinate their positions in international organizations and to vote as a bloc as much as possible. Even when the members do not formalize their agreement by taking a Common Position, they generally vote together. By 2001, this tendency had been observed many times, which led to suspicion that much the same thing had happened with regard to the HRC. Despite the bluster over that election, there was little anyone could do, so the issue dropped from the public eye almost as quickly as it entered it. One year later, the United States returned to the HRC as one of four candidates for four open seats—Spain and Italy agreed to withdraw from the competition to ensure the United States would be elected along with Australia, Germany, and Ireland. The Western European and Others Group in the United Nations worked to rotate future membership so the United States will almost always be a member of the HRC.[21]

This election represented a longer trend, and foreshadowed deeper disputes that would link human rights and traditional national security issues. One such dispute surrounded the treatment of detainees from the war in Afghanistan, who were being held at the U.S. Naval Base in Guantánamo Bay, Cuba. A photo of shackled and hooded prisoners prompted an outcry in Europe, which was further excited by Secretary of Defense Donald Rumsfeld's statement, "I do not feel even the slightest concern about their treatment. They are being treated vastly better than they treated anybody else over the last several years and vastly better than was their circumstance when they were found."[22] He later noted that the detainees' handling was "humane and appropriate and consistent with the Geneva Convention for the most part."[23] This did not satisfy Europeans. The High Representative for the CFSP, Javier Solana, replied, "The Geneva Convention must be applied to everyone who is detained in similar circumstances."[24] Dutch Foreign Affairs Minister Jozias van Aartsen warned, "In the fight [against terrorism] we need to uphold our norms and values. That applies to prisoners, too."[25] British Foreign Secretary Jack Straw added, "The British government's position is that prisoners—regardless of their technical status—should be treated humanely and according to customary international law."[26] German Foreign Minister Joschka Fischer said, "Regarding those under arrest in Guantánamo, we are of the view that, regardless of any later definition of their status, they are to be treated as prisoners of war. That means in accordance with international law and in a humanitarian way, as written in the Geneva Convention."[27]

Reacting to this criticism, the United States modified its interpretation slightly—agreeing that the Geneva Conventions applied to the Taliban forces, but not to al-Qaeda members. Nevertheless, since Taliban forces violated provisions of the Conventions, they were unlawful combatants since "they had not carried arms openly or been part of a recognisable military hierarchy" and thus were ineligible for status as Prisoners of War (POWs).[28] Later in 2002, the Department of Defense (DoD) further modified its stance, to become, "DoD is treating all of the detainees under its control humanely and in a manner consistent with the Third Geneva Convention of 1949."[29] The United Kingdom disagreed with this interpretation and decided that it would not turn captives over to the United States, but would grant POW status to Taliban forces.[30] Nevertheless, this bow to international law, combined with no evidence of mistreatment beyond the initial photos— which DoD officials concede may have violated Geneva restrictions against using captives for publicity—calmed this dispute. Even if the Conventions were applied to al-Qaeda, they would remain unlawful combatants and not POWs, so nothing about their treatment would change. The deeper lesson of this episode lies in the quick assumption of European leaders that the United States was casting aside international law.[31]

A dispute over the ICC in the UN Security Council (UNSC) in summer 2002 replaced Afghan detainees at the nexus of human rights, American military policy, multilateralism, and transatlantic relations. On 30 June, the United States vetoed renewal of the UN police-training mission in Bosnia because it did not have blanket immunity from the ICC (which is fully discussed in chapter 5). U.S. Ambassador to the United Nations John Negroponte said, "With our global responsibilities, we are and will remain a special target, and cannot have our decisions second-guessed by a court whose jurisdiction we do not recognize."[32] Europeans saw this step as extreme. The French Ambassador to the United Nations, Jean-David Levitte, said "what is at stake is the very capacity of the United Nations to continue peacekeeping operations. For the United States the simplest thing is to withdraw the 46 U.S. police. There is simply no need to kill off [the mission]."[33] Per Stig Møller, the Danish foreign minister speaking for the EU Presidency, "deeply regret[ted] this dramatic step," while Commission President Romano Prodi said "This complicates the situation and is another example of the divisions between the United States and Europe."[34] As the deadlock went on, the EU investigated whether it could accelerate its planned assumption of the police-training mission.[35]

To resolve the dispute, the United States suggested giving each UNSC permanent member veto power prosecutions of its own citizens—a provision the United States had advocated unsuccessfully in the ICC's Rome Statute. UK Prime Minister Tony Blair said the U.S. worry was "perfectly legitimate [since] they do massive amounts of peacekeeping in the world and don't want their peacekeepers to be subject to some political prosecution."[36] At the time, the United States had 702 participants in UN peacekeeping, out of total UN forces of 47,000. Despite Blair's sympathy, France and Britain proposed a compromise in which the UNSC would vote one year of blanket immunity for U.S. peacekeepers, as arguably provided for in Article 16 of the ICC Statute, with a promised intent to renew each year. To further legitimize this agreement, the UNSC would extend immunity to all non-ratifiers

in peacekeeping missions, a privilege already granted to states that had ratified. For nearly two weeks, the United States held out for the indefinite
renewal, but conceded on 12 July. Negroponte said this "first step" would
be acceptable for now, and that the United States would next try to work out
bilateral agreements under Article 98 of the Statute, to win immunity.[37]

In the midst of these efforts to ensure its exemption from the ICC, the
U.S. Congress passed the American Service-Members' Protection Act
(ASPA), signed into law on 3 August 2002. While subject to Presidential
waivers, the bill states U.S. government agencies may not, among other
things, "cooperate with the International Criminal Court, . . . extradite any
person from the United States to the International Criminal Court, . . . [or]
provide support to the International Criminal Court." It tells the President
to continue keeping American forces out of peacekeeping operations unless
exempted from the ICC or justified by an overriding national interest, and
prohibits military aid to non-allied ICC states parties unless they agree to
Article 98 exemptions. Finally, the ASPA states, "The President is authorized
to use all means necessary and appropriate to bring about the release of any
[American or allied person] who is being detained or imprisoned by, on
behalf of, or at the request of the International Criminal Court" for activities
related to their "official actions."[38]

The EP responded to the impending ASPA on 4 July 2002 with its own resolution in opposition. The EP argued that via ASPA "the United States [denies]
itself two of the principal weapons—military and intelligence cooperation—
of the global coalition against terrorism and deals a damaging blow to a third
element of that coalition—international goodwill" and called on Congress
"to reject the unilateralism which the ASPA represents." Citing the NATO
principle that members should "[abstain] from violence in resolving conflicts
between the partners," the EP resolution repeated the Dutch Parliament's
13 June concern over provisions "which would give the U.S. President the
right to authorise the use of force against the Netherlands to free members
of the U.S. armed forces, civilians and allies held captive by the ICC."[39]
This led to the ASPA's colloquial label, the "Hague Invasion Act." The
U.S. Embassy in The Hague had, on 12 June, reassured its hosts that
"The ASPA . . . does not require or suggest that any particular means be used
to address this issue. Obviously, we cannot envisage circumstances under
which the United States would need to resort to military action against the
Netherlands or another ally."[40]

Meanwhile, the United States used ASPA provisions on withholding
military aid to seek bilateral immunity agreements. Under Article 98 of the
Rome Statute,

> The Court may not proceed with a request for surrender which would require
> the requested State to act inconsistently with its obligations under international
> agreements pursuant to which the consent of a sending State is required to sur-
> render a person of that State to the Court, unless the Court can first obtain the
> cooperation of the sending State for the giving of consent for the surrender.

To the extent the United States could obtain such bilateral agreements, it would achieve parts of what it had not achieved via the UNSC. John Bolton, undersecretary of state for arms control and international security, said "this issue is one that directly affects individual Americans and quite possibly the highest decision-makers of our country who could be hauled before this court." Furthermore, he said, it was the EU members who suggested using Article 98, "a process expressly contemplated by the Rome Statute."[41]

The European Commission, however, issued a finding in August 2002 that compliance with U.S. requests for a new agreement "acts against the object and purpose of the statute."[42] Swedish Foreign Minister Anna Lindh said, "It is not reasonable to exempt a country, and it is fundamentally strange and wrong for the USA to try to stay on the sidelines and exempt its own citizens."[43] After Romania became one of the first countries (along with Israel) to sign a bilateral agreement, Prodi advised other aspirants for EU membership to delay signing until the EU had reached a final position. Bolton responded, "We're not applying any pressure on countries to sign these agreements, and we don't think it is appropriate for the European Union to prevent other countries from signing them."[44] American Secretary of State Colin Powell urged such states to disregard the EU and sign on "as soon as possible," while Pierre-Richard Prosper, U.S. ambassador for war crimes, said that if the EU member states would not agree, this "would obviously pose a fundamental problem in aspects of our relationship, in as far as military engagement in Europe and elsewhere."[45] By the end of August, the European Council had asserted that it, not the Commission, would reach the final decision on the Article 98 agreements, and implied that it might agree to the U.S. position rather than risk creating a rift within the EU. The Council was not unified: Britain and Italy appeared ready to support the U.S. request, while Germany, France, and Austria were among those supporting the Commission's interpretation.[46] On 30 September, the EU foreign ministers proposed a compromise: members could sign agreements with the United States as long as they fell within what Møller referred to as "red lines": the immunity would only apply to Americans "sent" to EU countries in their official duties, would require the United States to agree to prosecute those accused itself, and must be nonreciprocal (the EU member's citizens would not be immune from the ICC).[47]

Despite these and many other disagreements, and the increasing bitterness of their tone, some European and American officials have discounted the notion that there is some sort of a transatlantic "crisis." Solana has criticized "obituaries" about transatlantic relations because "Europe and the United States are natural partners, linked by common values and interests."[48] Haass assures us "our relationship with Europe is not at risk."[49] Many officials interviewed in the course of this research, as well as NATO Secretary General Lord George Robertson, have suggested that these disagreements are a sign of a strong and healthy partnership. They may be correct. Certainly the relationship has survived deep rifts in the past: American nonsupport of the British–French–Israeli attack on Suez in 1956,

France's decision to withdraw from the NATO integrated military command structure in the 1960s, reaction to the Yom Kippur war in 1973, Soviet natural gas pipelines and the Olympic boycott in the early 1980s, the "double-track" policy of arms control and deployment of Ground Launched Cruise Missiles and Pershing IIs later in the 1980s, and different approaches to addressing revolutions in Central America and apartheid in South Africa. This book does not begin from the debatable premise that there is a "crisis," across the Atlantic but rather from the indisputable observation that these allies have recently been at odds over a long and consistent series of issues. Nevertheless, dismissing the issue seems rather cavalier.

Unlike in past "crises," the strategic environment no longer drives the United States and Europe together to the same degree. Until 1989, the Atlantic Alliance was based on a shared perception of threat from the Soviet Union. This limited the extent to which European and American interests could diverge. Realists could point to the Soviets' military power, massed along the intra-German border; liberals could point to the nature of communism as a threat to human rights and freedoms. Soviet actions regularly reminded the alliance of these dangers, particularly in its interventions to prop up communist governments in Hungary, Czechoslovakia, and Afghanistan. In the 1990s, that common threat vanished, and with it the common security vision that bound the two sides together. As the United States became preoccupied with Iraq and the rise of Chinese power, Europe focused its attention on the Balkans and economic difficulty in the former Soviet bloc. The al-Qaeda terrorist attacks have not re-created the same level of unity that the Soviets did. When European leaders discuss their security priorities, it seems clear that neither 9/11 nor the 11 March 2004 bombings in Madrid "changed everything" for them: terrorism has long been a greater danger in Europe than in the United States. No strategic consensus on terrorism replaces containment in binding NATO together. The "root causes" of terrorism, and even the possibility that U.S. policy may have motivated what all agree were absolutely unjustifiable attacks on New York and Washington, are more openly considered in Europe than in America. Seen in that way, the conduct of the "war on terrorism" becomes yet another source of disagreement rather than a source of unity. Without the shared assessment of threat, there is no intrinsic limit to how far the United States and the European Union could drift apart. This structural change drives the time frame of this book: it looks at issues that are detached from the bipolar era. Primarily, this means events since 1990, although it steps further back in time to provide context for environmental and human rights issues.

The other structural change, making the current disagreements different from those of the Cold War era, is that Europe exists. During the Cold War, the EC was primarily economic. Rudimentary political cooperation existed from the 1970s, which resulted in some common European diplomacy on issues like Israel, Central America, and South Africa.[50] The Soviet Union had already dissolved by the time the member states agreed at Maastricht that the EU would "assert its identity on the international scene, in particular through the implementation of a common foreign and security policy including the eventual framing of a common defence policy which might in time lead to a common defence."[51] As European integration has proceeded over the ensuing years, European states have been better able to develop unified political positions that contrast with the U.S. position. As shall be seen throughout this book, the EU has been willing and able to successfully negotiate as a bloc in contrast to U.S. preferences. If the end of the Cold War provides the context for this study, the beginning of the EU provides the content. This book hypothesizes that explanations for these disagreements might be found in the growing awareness of the gap between European and American power, in the differences between American and European cultural values, or in the effects of European institutions themselves.

The final reason not to be complacent about transatlantic relations is the complacency itself. Some persons interviewed on both sides of the Atlantic compared the relationship to a family, whose members may disagree about many issues without threatening the bonds. Some even cited the disagreements as proof of the strength of this "marriage," noting that only partners with a deep and close relationship could feel free to openly disagree about so many issues. This book does not try to follow that analogy to a potential Atlantic divorce, but no, constant disagreements are not proof of a healthy relationship, and citing bickering as proof of affection seems like an attempt to avoid the problem. The long series of disagreements may well be creating "noise" or "static" that erodes the quality of the relationship.[52] In such an environment, small actions take on greater significance and may be seen as gratuitous slights by the weaker partner (Europe). One example was the United States formally withdrawing its signature from the Rome Statute, as opposed to just not ratifying it. Another example was not mentioning European contributions to the war on terrorism during the 2002 State of the Union address.[53] A third example—and this list could continue indefinitely— was trying to end all work on a BWC Verification Protocol, as opposed to continuing to work within the framework. Frequent disagreement can lead to a habit of disagreement, and perceptions that a bullying and controlling United States is undermining sincere European efforts to address serious global security issues can lead to a sense of bitterness, anger, resentment, and frustration. Without the Soviet Union to provide a reason to keep the transatlantic alliance close, and with a growing realization in Europe that it has strength and ability, complacency about the future seems inappropriate.

Despair about the relationship is not appropriate, either. Even if ties of necessity have been loosened, political leadership can maintain the relationship. The term "rift" has often been used to describe transatlantic relations, but this is not an unstoppable geologic force. As manifested in Iceland, Europe, and North America are quite literally drifting apart, and generating enough heat to power that country in the process. Politics is not geology. While structure no longer drives the allies together, there are not yet structural forces driving them apart either. When disagreement is more over means than ends, there is room for political agency to find a way to work together. The issues discussed in this book retain global importance even if the United States and the European Union are unable to work together. And that is the final reason why we need to look closely at the differences between the two: these problems can only be resolved through the cooperative efforts of the allies. If they remain at odds, the problems will only get worse. If the partners can reconcile, then progress can be made.

This book, however, is political science, not an attempt at marriage counseling. It chronicles the recent history of transatlantic relations to test hypotheses that might explain why the United States and the European Union have disagreed so frequently on multilateral issues even though they profess the same goals. It does not advocate that either side should change its position on any particular issue: whether the United States should ratify the ICC or whether the EU should have tried to bring developing states into the Kyoto Protocol is a question for the politicians, not the political scientists. Nevertheless, the patterns found here may have policy implications. If one's goal is to preserve or even strengthen the bonds between the world's great economic and democratic powers, which certainly seems a worthy goal, then these patterns may suggest courses of action that could be taken by either side.

Chapter 2 sets forth hypotheses taken from three major approaches to international politics: the realist, liberal institutional, and epistemic. Hypotheses deduced from preexisting approaches allow us to make stronger conclusions about the evidence, and also help signal what evidence is most significant for each approach. This assessment of hypotheses deduced from existing theory also allows this book to speak to academic debates beyond the specific puzzle of transatlantic relations. Using well-established tools of international politics allows us to consider a variety of cases in a systematic manner.

There are other ways in which one could look at these cases, but they would not help us solve the puzzle. For example, some studies look very deeply at the details of an issue to try to understand precisely why different negotiating positions were taken or why agreement could not be reached. The references cited throughout this book guide the reader to these details if they are desired. This is good and valuable research as public policy study, but it does not help answer the puzzle because it is difficult then to sort out the significant trends from the disagreements rooted in personalities or peculiar combinations of events. Another way to address this puzzle would be from the field of comparative politics. One could examine differences in institutional structures, the manner of decision-making, domestic interest groups, history, the economic situation, and similar factors to try to understand the divergence between the United States and the European Union on these issues. This approach is not adopted because once again there are so many differences between the United States and the European Union in these areas that it would be difficult to isolate the most significant factors. Instead, each of the four substantive chapters describes a group of cases in their historical context, with enough detail for the reader to understand what is happening, focusing attention on the elements that are most relevant to the hypotheses deduced from existing theory.

One of the first indications of the growing political differences between the European Union and the United States came on 18 September 1997 in Oslo, with the adoption of the Convention on the Prohibition of the Use, Stockpiling, Production and Transfer of Anti-Personnel Mines and on their Destruction, more simply known as the Mine Ban Treaty (MBT) or the Ottawa Convention after the site of its inspiration and signature. At the time, the salience of this agreement was less than apparent: the ban on anti-personnel land mines had been promoted by a transatlantic coalition of non-governmental organizations (NGOs). The state support for the treaty had largely come from Canada, and from the personal agenda of Lloyd Axworthy, the Canadian Minister of Foreign Affairs and International Trade. While members of the EU came to support the treaty, the EU itself took only the most tepid position of support, out of deference to Finland. The key axis for the "human security" campaign ran between Canada and the Norway; neither of which were members of the EU.

In retrospect, however, the events of 1997 marked a turning point in American diplomacy, particularly in its relationship to the states of Europe. For the first time since the end of the Cold War, and indeed for the first time since its rise to superpower status at the beginning of the Cold War, the United States made nonnegotiable demands at an international security conference—and saw its demands set aside. The other states concluded that amending the treaty to accommodate American preferences would undermine their achievements, and thus chose to accept the treaty without U.S. participation. Its opening for signature in Ottawa on 3 December 1997 would not be an isolated event. A week later, on 11 December 1997, the Kyoto Protocol to the UN Framework Convention on Climate Change (FCCC) was adopted without including all the provisions demanded by the United States. Less than a year after Oslo, on 17 July 1998, the Rome Statute establishing an International Criminal Court (ICC) was approved, again in explicit rejection of the American preferences. Finally, on 4 December 1998, British Prime Minister Tony Blair and French President Jacques Chirac agreed at St. Malo to work toward a European defense force. In the space of a year, American friends and allies, demonstrating their independence from the United States, had reached four significant international agreements. These four events serve as the fulcrums of chapters 3–6, which consider in turn arms control, the environment, human rights, and military cooperation. These chapters are ordered chronologically according to these four key agreements.[54]

Before moving on to the conclusion, we should bound the scope of the issues included in this study. Previous sections referred to "multilateral" institutions and solutions, and "global" issues. "Global" refers to issues that are diffuse in their causes and effects. Examples include environmental protection, human rights, and non-proliferation of all sorts of weapons. Such problems generally cannot be resolved through the actions of a single state; indeed, attempts to do so fall into the problem of collective goods. The benefits of acting on these problems are not excludable: they must be shared broadly by all interested parties, without regard to the contribution they made to obtain them.[55] In this situation, there is a great temptation to free-ride on others' efforts, with the result that no one acts. Progress toward such goals requires the cooperation of many states, acting multilaterally. Multilateralism often, but not always, implies a diffusion of authority so that no single state directs the action.[56]

Both terms—multilateral and global—are at times misleading. Describing an approach as multilateral does not specify the number of states involved. Both the 2003 war in Iraq and the 1999 war in Kosovo could accurately be described as multilateral, although neither had the explicit sanction of the United Nations. Sometimes the difference between the United States and Europe is over the degree of multilateralism involved, rather then the principle that many states should help achieve the goal. Likewise, most global issues have local manifestations. War crimes may be a global issue, but the crimes are committed by specific people against specific victims in a specific place. Acid rain may damage Bavarian and Adirondack forests, but it remains a local case of a global problem with trans-boundary pollution. The most debatable issues thus included in this book fall in the chapter on military cooperation (chapter 6). Operations in the Balkans responded to a local violation of global principles regarding aggression and human rights. Operations since 1991 in Iraq responded to a local example of weapons proliferation; after 2001 this became wedded to global concerns with international terrorism. NATO and EU military restructuring are relevant to this discussion because they are two multilateral institutions that involve themselves in these security issues, and most of all because NATO is what makes the United States and members of the EU allies.

In keeping with the definition, this book excludes some transatlantic issues that would distract from its focus on multilateral agreements. It will not address the Helms-Burton Act (HBA), which excludes corporate officials who "traffic" in expropriated Cuban property from travel to the United States, and also allows Americans to sue such foreign corporations. Europeans see such extraterritorial extension of U.S. law as illegal, but there are no multilateral negotiations on the issue.[57] Clinton signed the HBA on 12 March 1996. French President François Mitterrand called the law "stupid," and the EU threatened to take the case to the World Trade Organization (WTO). At the same time, however, the European Council warned Cuba that it must make progress on human rights and political rights before it gets a cooperation agreement with the EU. Bilateral EU–U.S. discussions led to a compromise on 18 May 1998. The EU would not take the Act before the WTO and would also discourage investments in expropriated property. Clinton would "neutralize the application of the Helms-Burton legislation" by continuing to waive the application of the lawsuit provisions.[58] George W. Bush, as president, has continued this policy. Cuba is not the only such case: similar problems arose in the early 1980s with respect to

Iran and the Siberian gas pipeline, and the EC objected to those U.S. policies as well. On the other hand, Denmark and Sweden implemented extraterritorial provisions as part of their sanctions against South African apartheid, and the European Commission has at times tried to extend its reach to the parent corporations of European subsidiaries.[59]

In addition, the conflict between Israelis and Palestinians will not be addressed, because it does not involve multilateral efforts to address a global problem—the repeated efforts in international organizations to define Zionism as a form of racism will be mentioned, however, in chapter 5. U.S. policy toward Iraq in 2002–3, on the other hand, existed in context of UN resolutions as well as global concerns about terrorism and the proliferation of weapons of mass destruction. That aspect of the Middle Eastern crises fits the book's focus on global issues in a way the Israeli situation does not.

Finally, this book does not look at trade issues, even though they are both global and multilateral. Trade issues have been thoroughly covered in other works.[60] More importantly, disputes over trade are not very puzzling: the United States and the European Union compete in trade, so one expects to find conflict. The EU's External Economic Policy aims both at promoting free trade and at protecting internal interests, and U.S. priorities have also long balanced the principle of open markets against American jobs.[61] So the two have clashed over issues such as preferential trade in bananas and possible health risks associated with hormone-treated beef.[62] Steel was the major trade dispute of early 2002, as the United States imposed 30 percent tariffs on many imported products effective 20 March. EU Trade Commissioner Pascal Lamy called this "unjustified and unfounded," and vowed to "do everything we possibly can to protect our own industry and our own jobs."[63] As the EU considered retaliation against the tariffs, Commission President Romano Prodi said, "We are thoroughly disappointed at the decision of the U.S. government to further protect the U.S. steel industry through tariffs . . . Now we have no other choice: We must take action." The United States, for its part, insisted that its action fit within WTO safeguard procedures and that any compensation to the EU would need to be seen in context with the EU's restrictions on U.S. beef.[64] Finally, trade is not included because these disputes are less pervasive than sometimes believed. Even the steel dispute affected only approximately 1 percent of the $220 billion annual total transatlantic trade flow.[65]

Chapter 7 concludes the book by assessing which theoretical approach, or combination of approaches, better explains this puzzle. U.S. positions throughout this period are strongly consistent with realist expectations: the United States supports noneconomic multilateral institutions only when they restrict other states at least as much as they restrict itself. Surprisingly, much the same conclusion can be reached regarding the EU. We find little evidence to support epistemic hypotheses of European or American behavior. In the area of human rights, EU behavior is consistent with institutionalist hypotheses, as its members have accepted jurisdiction of institutions over itself despite the United States not being bound strongly by those institutions.

In other issue areas, however, EU behavior is more consistent with realist expectations: the EU has not restricted its own freedom of action in significant ways unless the United States is also bound. Even with the ICC, the most noteworthy example of transatlantic behavior in conformance with institutional expectations, the United States is bound to some extent along with the EU member states.

This conclusion is not meant to suggest that realism offers the best explanation for all of international politics. Nevertheless, since European–American relations seem to be a difficult case for realism, as explained in chapter 2, this result is significant for what it says about the continuing robustness of the realist approach. Over time, the EU may begin to behave more as the institutionalist approach would expect. It seems likely, however, that concerns for autonomy of action and relative power will continue to be relevant to EU foreign policy and transatlantic relations. One can expect that relationship to continue to slowly deteriorate from its Cold War security community into a looser partnership, in which the United States maintains its position of greater capability and influence and the EU and many of its member states maintain their unhappiness with the situation. This at least describes how Iraq was handled in 2003. Further discussion of these findings, however, must wait until after we understand these approaches and the recent history of U.S.–EU relations.

2

INTERNATIONAL RELATIONS
APPROACHES AND TRANSATLANTIC
RELATIONS

With our puzzle defined and described, we now develop a roadmap with which to find an explanation of the source and future of U.S.–EU divergence. One approach to this quest would be to evaluate a single hypothesis against a series of selected cases. Following that route, much would rely on the selection of cases. At the end of the journey, however, a definitive answer would not likely be found: even if the hypothesis appears to be supported, we still would not know if there are other, better, explanations that have not been explored; if not, then we would have no answer at all. A better method would be to examine the question using several hypotheses from within a single approach to international politics. This path would be richer than following a single hypothesis, in that we could now compare our evidence against different explanations.[1] Nevertheless, the approach still might push our analysis toward certain facts at the expense of others. Furthermore, in the end, all we could say is that we have found the best explanation from within that approach: we still would not know if other approaches offer a stronger explanation. The best way to assess the source and future of U.S.–EU divergence is to use hypotheses from several approaches to international politics.

This book follows this more ambitious strategy, looking at three major approaches to international politics. The two best-known approaches are realism and liberalism. Both approaches focus on the interaction between state actors. Realism emphasizes the importance of material power for sovereign states coexisting in an international anarchy. Liberalism does not refute realism as much as it modifies it, proposing that some political or economic mechanism can mediate the effects of anarchy.[2] Different scholars have proposed different third approaches, including radicalism[3] and constructivism.[4] This book uses the term "epistemic" to describe approaches to the study of foreign policy that emphasize the role of ideas in policy-making, which seems more useful than the other approaches to the question examined here.[5]

The first section of this chapter, on realist approaches, advances hypotheses that focus attention on power derived from material capabilities. These hypotheses consider whether the divergence between the United States and the European Union is related to the dominant position of the United States in the world. Europeans must address American power either by trying to balance against it or bandwagon with it. The United States, in turn, would try to reduce the European incentive to balance while seeking to maintain its own power. Since realism looks only at "rational unitary political units in anarchy,"[6] the EU poses an immediate problem for realists. By applying at least a veneer of hierarchy to intra-European relations, the presence of the EU may reduce the applicability of realist theory among those states. On the other hand, since the members of the EU do retain sovereignty, albeit constrained by costly-to-break treaties, it is unclear if one can legitimately treat the EU itself as a rational unitary political unit acting within the larger systemic anarchy. Rather than make an arbitrary choice between the two, and rather than staking these findings on such a choice, this chapter introduces hypotheses that treat both the EU and its members as actors.

The second section looks at the institutional variant of the liberal approach, which "stress[es] the role of international institutions, norms, and information."[7] This approach does not treat institutions as a mere tool, as realists do. Instead, institutional theories suggest that formal agreements can transform the relationships between states, leading to policies different from those the states would have followed had they been acting alone. This chapter suggests hypotheses describing two ways institutions could explain the divergence: first, European institutions will encourage the adoption of a common policy, one that will tend to be more supportive of multilateral regulation than the United States would prefer. Second, institutionalists would support the development of a web of rules and procedures that would reduce the importance of raw material power. As European institutions grow stronger, institutionalists would expect this tendency to become more common.

The third section addresses the epistemic approach, which looks at "the role of collective beliefs and ideas on which states rely in calculating how to realize their underlying goals."[8] Prime among these are theories that address culture. While Europe and America may hold similar material interests, differences linked to culture might lead them to interpret those interests in different ways. This chapter advances hypotheses suggesting that cultural values should be manifested most clearly in the specific terms of the dispute. Each side would advocate an international policy that reflects its own domestic preferences, unless clear national interests override them. Once again, these hypotheses examine both member state and EU policies, as appropriate.

Before beginning to describe the hypotheses derived from these three approaches, let us take a moment to reemphasize the overall goal of this book. It addresses a reality of international politics, without trying to establish the general supremacy of any theoretical approach to international politics. The failure of any of these approaches to explain the divergence does not mean that approach is without value in addressing other issues. It may be that the preconditions of the approach are absent: just as one would be unlikely to expect that institutional theory would have much to say about the outbreak of the Spanish–American War, it may be that realism has little to say about relations between postindustrial market democracies where the cost of coercion is very high relative to the degree of conflict of interest.[9] It also may be that each approach fits some issue areas better than others. While the final chapter (chapter 7) takes up these issues, it only does so in a suggestive way. No single case, or even a collection of cases between a pair of actors, could establish the supremacy of an approach or theory.

REALIST HYPOTHESES: BALANCING AND BANDWAGONING

The realist approach, as described in this section, suggests the following hypotheses:

H1A: The United States will support multilateral agreements only if they limit other states' ability to challenge the United States at least as much as they limit American capabilities or autonomy of action.

H1B: When European states act in unison, they will accept multilateral agreements if they have a negative impact on American relative power or autonomy of action, as long as the United States has also agreed to follow them. When European states adopt policy as independent states, they will support or bandwagon with the U.S. position on multilateral agreements, which in practice means that once again they support such agreements if the United States agrees to them.

These hypotheses are appropriate for realists, who expect state behavior to mirror the world of Hobbes's *Leviathan*. Since there is no international government, states exist in an anarchy. They must plan strategically to ensure their minimum goal of survival. All states have some inherent capability for offensive action, so pose a possible danger to your own state. Since states can never know each other's intentions with certainty, realists expect states to exist in mutual fear, forming alliances that are merely "temporary marriages of convenience" as states "aim to maximize their relative power positions... [and] would like to be the most formidable military power in the system because this is the best way to guarantee survival in a world that can be very dangerous."[10]

This description of international politics does not seem at first glance to describe the transatlantic relationship very well. The United States and the countries of Europe have not feared military attack from each other, and NATO alliance has run much deeper than mere convenience. Some scholars argue that realism does not apply among certain countries, such as the industrialized democracies.[11] Since realists consider neither economic nor political system relevant to understanding international politics, they must find another basis for such long-term cooperation. Realists assume that states behave rationally, so they would suggest that Europeans and Americans may continue to cooperate simply because the cost of military or economic coercion is too costly a way to resolve the conflicts of interest between them.[12]

Ruling out realism in that way begs the question of why the cost–benefit ratio should be consistently high between certain countries. If state preferences are fixed and conflictual, then the possibility will always remain that rational actors may conclude that the benefits of coercion outweigh the costs. In fact, there *are* points of material conflict between the United States and the European Union. The most obvious is in global trade, where both actors have an interest in greater share of individual markets. More broadly, the United States and the European Union have an interest in their own economic performance; a realist would argue that each seeks to grow at a faster rate than the other. In the material realm, the United States and Europe could come into conflict regarding contributions to NATO and the use of NATO resources. The two also face differing vulnerabilities to ballistic missiles, and differing dangers from a possibly resurgent Russia.

Nevertheless, transatlantic relations seem to be a fairly hard test of realism. The conflicts of interest do not seem very severe compared to the benefits all sides receive from cooperation. If realist hypotheses are not supported, it would not be a devastating failure for the approach. On the other hand, if we find evidence that supports realist hypotheses even in this puzzle, the realist approach would be enhanced.

The realist vision described here is derived from the theories of Kenneth Waltz.[13] Waltz argued that state behavior can be explained by the structure of international politics itself. International politics is distinct from other political systems because it lacks a formal hierarchy: all states are sovereign, and thus none has authority to direct any other. But just as none could rule over others in this anarchy, none could rely on others for aid. In this self-help system, each state must fulfill the same functions of governance, unable to specialize as units could in a hierarchy. With the structure an unchanging anarchy, and the states functionally equivalent, variation in behavior must be due to the only independent variable remaining: the distribution of capabilities in the system, which may be unipolar, bipolar, or multipolar.

This structural version of realism complements a classical form of realism, which is based on "interest defined in terms of power."[14] In the classical realist tradition Morgenthau thus harvested—a tradition Doyle describes as rooted in Thucydides, fertilized by Hobbes and Machiavelli, and brought to fruition by Carr—the quest for power is the basis for understanding international politics.[15] Since rational actors—states, in the modern era—need power to achieve their ends, whether to maintain the status quo or overthrow the world order, they must seek it where they can. While the underlying source of power may change over time, states will compete with each other for the scarce resource of power: a resource made scarce in part by the competition itself. Morgenthau sees this system existing outside of, or apart from, morality or ideology: "prudence...[is] the supreme virtue in politics." Morality or ideology leads to a belief that one's own preferences are morally superior, which in turn will "engender the distortion in judgment which, in the blindness of crusading frenzy, destroys nations and civilizations."[16]

This classical realism of the Cold War era was critiqued on several grounds. For one, the critical concepts of "power" and "balance of power" were poorly defined and difficult to measure. For another, its reliance on human nature as a driving force made it difficult to explain variation in state behavior. Furthermore, focusing analysis on the state made it difficult to explain the recurring patterns of state behavior. In sum, classical realism offered great qualitative richness, but did not seem to form a solid foundation for a science of international politics.[17] Waltz's structural realism intends to correct these flaws, but its expectations are in no way alien to classical realism.

Indeed, both forms of realism share three core assumptions. First, the relevant actors in international politics are "rational unitary political units in anarchy"; in other words, states. This assumption means that international organizations are agents of their member states, not independent actors. Moreover, realists do not look within the state at domestic forces, ideology, or the type of government. States rationally set goals, strategically assess their options, and then pursue the policies that are most likely to succeed. Second, state preferences aim at "fixed and uniformly conflictual goals." While states will behave as if their preferences are in conflict, this does not mean actual state policies will always be in conflict—as rational actors, the states may be "deterred or dissuaded" from directly pursuing their preferences in the face of superior power. Third, material capabilities are the prime factor in how conflicts between states are resolved.[18]

Within these assumptions of realism, we must define the nature of state goals. "Offensive realism" argues that states' goals tend to be expansionist: they either seek domination outright, or they expand their power to take advantage of opportunities.[19] "Defensive realism," in contrast, argues that states are most concerned with avoiding losses of power relative to other states, and so prefer the status quo.[20] Waltz himself suggested that state preferences may vary between security and domination.[21] In all cases, states will seek to maintain their freedom of action—their sovereignty—because they cannot be sure of the future, or even current, intentions of other states.

A key theoretical debate centers on these three alternatives. The idea of variable preferences is difficult to sustain, since there seems to be no material basis for the variation and realism excludes regime type, ideology, domestic interest groups, and leaders' preferences as factors because they violate either the assumption of unitary actors or of material primacy. If state preferences are fixed in favor of the status quo—defensive realism—then the Hobbesian vision would not come to pass. Lacking any rational basis for suspicion, over time hostility would dwindle away and states would be able to cooperate.[22] This book adopts the offensive version of realism since it seems to be the most consistent with its own terms. Offensive realism does not mean all states are actively expanding their power: some may not have the means, others may not have the opportunity, and still others may conclude that the costs of expansion exceed the expected benefits. Some states, due to either their geographic isolation or due to the balance between the cost of fielding offensive and defensive forces, may for long periods of time appear to be merely security seekers because the cost of expansion materially exceeds any benefits.[23] States will, however, want to expand their power when they expect to gain from doing so.[24] In the meantime, they will at least seek to maintain their power and the capacity to increase it at a later time.

For realists, states may choose between two basic approaches when confronted with superior power. The first is to balance against it in an attempt to maintain one's survival, and thus maintain the possibility of future gains. Waltz suggested that balancing may occur either through an internal build-up of one's capabilities, which would reduce the relative gap in capabilities, or through external means. External balancing can include cooperation or alliances with other states and attempts to reduce the capabilities of the stronger state.[25] Steven Walt amended the notion of balancing power, suggesting rather that states balance against the greater threat.[26] While "threat" may not seem to be an entirely measurable concept, threat includes factors that can moderate power, such as geography, reconnaissance, and the type of weaponry deployed.[27]

The other behavior states may adopt is to bandwagon, or to ally with, the greater power (or threat).[28] Bandwagoning states are not capitulating to the stronger state, but are seeking gains in hopes of being part of the dominant force in world politics.[29] The clearest recent examples of such bandwagoning are the rush of former Soviet allies to join the West, both NATO and the EU, and in general the turn in the 1990s toward market economies and more democratic forms of government. With "the West" having conclusively demonstrated its superiority over communist models, states concluded their best hope for future gain was to imitate success. Ultimately, this emulation may form the foundation for future balancing: if weaker states adopt the policies that led to the powers' strength, they may eventually become strong enough to balance their power.[30]

Now that the immediate post–Cold War turbulence has ended, the question for the realist approach is to assess which behavior, balancing or bandwagoning, is most likely to occur. The first step is to define the distribution of capabilities (power). For much of modern history this distribution was multipolar. Many states competed for power; coalitions and counter-coalitions formed, sometimes going to war, sometimes not. This was the golden age of *realpolitik*, but it ended with World War II.[31] The bipolar era that followed provided clarity and focus to international politics; some argue it also brought stability and peace.[32]

While there are those who disagree,[33] today we find a unipolar distribution of material power among the states in the international system. A quantitative assessment shows that the United States stands far above any other state by any material measure of power: economic, military, or technological.[34] The qualitative assessment is simpler: if the world was bipolar in 1988, then the total collapse of the Soviet Union and the failure of any other power to rise to take its place so far also brings us to a unipolar system.[35] Scholars differ over whether unipolarity can last. Some argue that it could be durable and peaceful because the fate of any challenger to the United States would seem to be preordained. Any state undertaking the difficult task of trying to achieve the stature of a rival would, in Thucydidean fashion, provoke fear and balancing among its nearer neighbors, and suffer from that as well as American resistance.[36] Others argue that unipolarity cannot last. Other states cannot live in a world dominated by another state, so they will take advantage of technological diffusion and emulate American success.[37] Anything the United States does to try to deter balancing would prompt a backlash, as was seen in reaction to the draft *Defense Planning Guidance 1994–99*. That leaked document stated: "We must account sufficiently for the interests of the large industrial nations to discourage them from challenging our leadership or seeking to overturn the established political or economic order...We must maintain the mechanisms for deterring potential competitors from even aspiring to a larger regional or global role."[38]

One need not resolve the issue of unipolarity's durability in order to develop clear realist hypotheses about American and European behavior.[39] In either case, the realist expects the United States to prefer that other states bandwagon with it rather than balance against it. Following benevolent policies will benefit the United States, either by prolonging unipolarity by reducing the incentive for others to balance it or by making the ensuing multipolarity less hostile toward the United States.[40] Implementing "benevolence" is difficult, however, because it conflicts with the realist focus on power and threat. The offensive realist expects the United States to take advantage of opportunities to expand its power when it is able to do so. By expanding its power, the United States may encourage bandwagoning by demonstrating that joining the United States provides a better hope for gain than challenging the United States. On the other hand, such a "resistance is useless" strategy may well backfire since it gives others a rationale for trying to resist American hegemony.[41] Furthermore, even a more defensive strategy of simply maintaining the status quo will require intervention on its behalf. This will remind potential challengers that the United States is a potential danger to them as well. The interventions themselves will be costly for the United States, reducing American relative power, and thereby making resistance seem not only advisable but also possible.[42]

As an alternative, the United States could follow policies designed to discourage balancing. If stronger states exercise restraint, weaker states may elect to use their resources for purposes other than balancing the United States.[43] Such restraint could be similar to the decisions made by Bismarck and George H.W. Bush at the end of the Austro-Prussian and Persian Gulf Wars, when both declined to fully exploit a decisive victory. Bismarck's advice was not followed after the Franco-Prussian war, which contributed to the development of a balance against Germany.[44] The United States could show restraint by signaling its preference for the status quo and its willingness to deal with others as equals. An example of such is the inclusion of Russia in the G-8 economic club, despite the fact that the Russian economy is not stable enough, large enough, nor capitalist enough to have earned membership. The United States could demonstrate its benign intentions by exercising moderation, agreeing to bind its own actions, adhering to multilateralism and by "reliance on consensual forms of international governance."[45] Unilateral behavior is particularly dangerous, because it would tend to provoke the security dilemma—one's own efforts to improve one's security leads other states to conclude that they must take action to improve their own security; in the end no one is more secure and all are more suspicious.[46]

Nevertheless, a realist would not expect the United States to accept relative losses willingly as a result of such steps. Only agreements that proportionately affect the material capabilities of all sides would be acceptable, given the preexisting U.S. dominance.[47] The United States should particularly favor agreements that would tend to reduce the ability of potential challengers to harm the United States. On issues that do not directly affect material factors, the United States should take the easy step of compromise with others, to reinforce its nonthreatening image without cost. In trying to maintain unipolarity, the United States should "manage . . . the arrogance of power. The dominant state in any international order faces strong temptations to go it alone, to dictate rather than consult, to preach its virtues, and to impose its values . . . In a unipolar setting, the dominant state, less constrained by other great powers, must constrain itself" lest it undermine its position.[48] Putting it a bit more bluntly, "if the façade of multilateralism renders the rule of an extraordinary power more palatable to ordinary powers, as it did during the Gulf War, international organizations are a strategic asset."[49] This is the first realist hypothesis: that the United States will support multilateral agreements only if they affect others' capabilities at least as much as they affect American capabilities. Capabilities in this sense may mean either actual material factors or a second-order capability, that of being able to act freely as a sovereign state without being subject to others' oversight.

For the states of Europe, realism also makes a clear prediction. A rational state does not engage in futile balancing, so weak states will see more benefit from bandwagoning with the United States rather than trying to balance its power.[50] If we take the states of the EU as individual actors, none of them with the possible exception of Germany could hope to balance American power by acting alone.[51] The others would need to bandwagon with the United States in hopes of thereby gaining through association. Even in the German case, the scenario of regional counterbalancing seems most likely to hinder any overt German attempts to rise to become a great power. Intra-European balancing against Germany would be further enhanced by other European states' bandwagoning with the United States. So we would expect a competition among European states for favor with the United States, as long as we are able to ignore the EU as an actor, as many realists do.[52] These states would generally follow the Americans' lead, supporting what it supports and opposing what it opposes.

The only alternative for Europe would be if they agreed among themselves to consolidate their power—in other words, bandwagon with each other at the regional level. Once they did so, they would at least have the potential to challenge the United States. Only in this way can the urge to deepen the Union can be comprehended by a realist, although it remains difficult for a realist to explain why states would agree to bargain away so much of their sovereignty.[53] Nevertheless, the deepening has occurred, and we need not explain that puzzle in realist terms here. If we assume that the EU can be an actor in a realist approach, a slightly different hypothesis results.

The EU, acting as one, would be strong enough to rationally consider options other than bandwagoning. Indeed, a fully united Europe would produce a bipolar distribution of capabilities.[54] And bipoles do not bandwagon with each other. They compete for influence and take steps to limit each other's power. A power-seeking EU would aim at enhancing European capabilities at the expense of the American. The EU would also aim to increase its own capability to act independently of the United States.

Multilateralism can be used as a tool for balancing. If an agreement is proposed that would tend to restrict American capabilities or freedom of action, then the United States is in a dilemma. If it accepts the agreement, then it will suffer a loss of relative power. On the other hand, if it opposes the agreement, the United States will be defying "world opinion," increasing the prestige of the EU relative to the United States. This technique of establishing European power as more legitimate than American could pay off in material resources, if other states begin to develop a preference for bandwagoning with the EU in trade and transnational matters. Furthermore, it may create a habit in those states of siding with the EU, rather than with the United States on multilateral issues, which could create material gains in negotiations where the United States cannot block the final accord.[55]

Such an instrumental use of multilateralism would have its limits. The EU could not afford to limit its own power through multilateralism unless the United States agrees. In practice, then, the realist hypothesis for European behavior is not so different whether the Europeans act as states or as a Union. In either case, the Europeans will tend to follow the same direction as the United States. The primary difference when acting as a Union is that the Europeans would more strongly promote an agreement and try to persuade the Americans to join—or, failing that, make it clear that it is the Americans who are to blame. In a few rare cases, the Europeans may conclude that the loss of relative economic or military power incurred via a multilateral agreement without the United States would be sufficiently balanced by gains in diplomatic power.

LIBERAL INSTITUTIONAL HYPOTHESES: THE EU EXPERIENCE

The institutional approach, as described in this section, suggests the following hypotheses:

H2A: EU institutions, especially as the Union deepens its decision-making into a formal CFSP process, will lead the Union to favor regulation and multilateralism more than the United States does.

H2B: EU support for a multilateral solution will be unrelated to whether
        or not the United States agrees to be bound by it as well.

We turn now to the second approach, liberalism. There are several varia-
tions of liberalism, which overlap with each other in that they all have at their
root some sort of mechanism that either moderates state preferences or
constrains state actions.[56] Setting aside Wilsonian liberal idealism, which
Carr labels as mere utopianism, we can define commercial, democratic,
sociological, and institutional versions of liberalism.[57] Both commercial and
democratic liberalism would expect cooperation among states with similar
economic or political structures. Sociological is the least common and least
well defined of these, having something in common both with the functional
project of the EU itself and the epistemic exchange of beliefs described in the
next section.

The institutional version of liberalism, however, speaks directly to the
problem described in this book. Realists recognize that institutions exist as a
way of channeling state interests and making cooperation a bit easier.
Stephen Krasner broke with this interpretation of institutions when he
argued that, at times, the institutions he called regimes can have a feedback
effect on state preferences. They may " 'alter actors' calculations of how to
maximize their interests,... may alter interests themselves,... become a
source of power..., [or] alter the power capabilities of different actors."[58]
Such institutions can have two types of effects. The first is that states will
apply the institution, once it is created, to serve new purposes, as we see with
NATO in the 1990s.[59] This is not entirely at odds with realism, since the
institution is not so much changing preferred goals but rather altering the
cost–benefit ratio associated with different strategies. The only meaningful
change in preferences would be a certain reluctance to dismantle an institution that seems to have outlived its original purpose, since it might turn out
to be useful in the future.[60] The second effect is that the institution may constrain action, and perhaps even consideration of options, to such an extent
that its members become self-bound by the institution.[61] If this occurs, then
nonmaterial factors would be explaining a part of international behavior.[62]
This second effect is the primary means by which institutions moderate
anarchy and provide an alternative to realism.

Much of the divergence between the United States and the European
Union involves the establishment or strengthening of multilateral institutions. In particular, the EU has tended to favor such institutions, which
include "a relatively stable set or 'structure' of identities and interests,"[63]
whereas the United States has tended to oppose at least the particular institution being created. Furthermore, the divergence has developed or become
apparent synchronously with the strengthening of the EU, itself a multilateral institution. While correlation does not indicate causation, causation
without correlation is even more unlikely. So we shall focus our attention on
multilateralism as a potential source of our puzzle: first, does the deepening
of the EU lead to a deeper preference for multilateral solutions; second, does

the structure of the deepened EU itself lead to European preferences that pull the continent away from the United States?

Both multilateral solutions and multilateralism as an approach have become more prevalent since the end of the Cold War, but theories of international relations have continued to neglect the topic. This seems odd, for even in the early 1990s there were reasons to believe that multilateralism could explain some of the puzzling events of the early post–Cold War—continued peace in Western Europe, as opposed to a return to the bad old days of balance of power rivalry;[64] the contrast between the cooperation seen in Europe and the tension seen in East Asia;[65] and even the resilience of NATO.[66] Multilateralism is "an institutional form which coordinates relations among three or more states on the bases of 'generalized' principles of conduct."[67] The states share normative beliefs about what should be done, and will evangelize these beliefs to the world at large. Multilateralism is a means or instrument for achieving certain goals, but also can become an end in itself—an expression of how the world should be ordered.[68] This transformation from strategy to goal bears some resemblance to what E.H. Carr disparaged as the utopian illusion of harmony of interests—the assertion by the powerful that their interests are in fact the interests of all. In reality, Carr wrote, the norms asserted for all serve only to aid the powerful and to mask how a certain world order directly serves their own immediate interests.[69]

Multilateralism moves beyond Carr's critique by adding two additional properties to the generalized principles of conduct: indivisibility and diffuse reciprocity.[70] The notion of indivisibility is closely related to generalized principles of conduct. The benefits of the multilateral approach would go to all, irrespective of any given state's contribution to the effort. The norms of conduct attempt to guard against the problem of free riders—states that gain the benefits of, for example, a global reduction in greenhouse gas emissions, without themselves suffering the cost of reducing their own emissions. Unanimity of agreement, encouraged by norms of conduct, may enhance each state's willingness to bear some share of the costs for the benefits received. If others are "defecting," then the states inclined to be cooperative are reluctant to maintain a slightly higher cost for slightly reduced benefits, since others are gaining the same benefits at no cost.[71]

The third property of multilateralism, diffuse reciprocity, is also born of the generalized principles of conduct. Diffuse reciprocity is the relationship one would see among friends or colleagues, as opposed to the more distant, contractual relationship of specific reciprocity. In the latter, a specific dyad of actors executes discrete transactions, which they have determined create an equivalence of value. Such "balanced reciprocity provides an unsatisfactory basis for long-term relationships."[72] Diffuse reciprocity, on the other hand, is less concerned about the equivalence in any immediate exchange, as each actor (not limited now to a dyad) assumes that after many interactions the costs and benefits will roughly even out.[73] Furthermore, diffuse reciprocity suggests that the states have an interest in contributing to and maintaining the group relationship, beyond immediate self-interest.[74]

This definition of multilateralism perhaps helps explain why realist theories have not treated it as a concept in its own right. Modern realist theories avoid using norms to explain cooperation: states pursue their own individual goals in an anarchy, in which they must strategically consider the actions and goals of the other states with whom they interact. As Robert Jervis puts it, "neoliberals think that establishing an institution can increase cooperation. Realists believe this is not so much a false statement as a false remedy, because the states will establish an institution if and only if they seek the goals that the institution will help them reach."[75] Scientifically, he and the other realists have a valid point: cooperation is easier to explain if you assume that states have a separate interest in cooperation.[76] We can proceed without that "crutch," and find that multilateral cooperation may develop when the goal is simply to coordinate on a common policy.[77] If collaboration is required, as illustrated by Prisoners' Dilemma, multilateral situations are likely to result in defections by a rational actor trying to receive the benefit without paying the cost.[78]

So a realist would conclude that multilateral cooperation is very difficult to achieve, and American and European failure to achieve it is no mystery at all. But this does not account for the reasonable success the United States and the European Union have had in certain areas, particularly in defense, nor does it account for the EU's clear enthusiasm for it. The institutionalist, in contrast, would see the EU as creating the kind of diffuse relationship that allows cooperation to become imbedded in how the states regard each other.[79] Ultimately, "actors invoke norms as shortcuts to their decision problems."[80] Thus multilateralism becomes self-reinforcing, and the presence of the EU encourages its members to prefer multilateral solutions.

If institutions moderate anarchy, the Union's preference for multilateralism should not be conditioned on others accepting them. Liberals would not argue that the Union should place itself at a clear disadvantage compared to other states, but it should not hold out for universal acceptance either. EU deepening is based on a presumption of benefit for its members, even though most of the world does not participate. Likewise, an institutionalist would prefer to join and adhere to an institution made up of several like-minded states, even if other states did not. American agreement should not be a prerequisite for European participation. This is not altruism: the Europeans benefit from the arrangement, and so should not forgo the advantages of institutionalism even if Americans do not join it immediately.

A second way the institutional experience of the EU could lead to a divergence with the United States regarding multilateral solutions is via its decision-making mechanisms.[81] When multilateral international negotiations are conducted, "the European Union affects international outcomes by concentrating the weight of its 15 member states on a single substantive position and rendering that position critical to any internationally negotiated agreement."[82] Effectively, the CFSP allows the EU to have 15 times the voting power of any state. Member states cannot legitimately break from the common position, even if they would prefer to do so. Furthermore, the EU cannot bargain like a state can. An individual state could change its negotiating position with much greater ease than the EU could, since change would require the Council to change as a group.

In itself, this would not necessarily explain the divergence with the United States. If the United States and the European Union have similar interests (goals) and similar preferences (means), then the greater weight of the EU should not matter very much. But it would be heroic to assume similar interests and preferences for any two states, let alone 16. One can show mathematically that under qualified majority voting, the Union will tend to adopt positions that favor more international regulation than the median European state would adopt on its own. This follows from an assumption that the Commission will tend to advocate increasing regulation for bureaucratic and ideological reasons, although even if the Commission is in the moderate range of state preferences, its policy proposal would be adopted over the objections of the status quo states. The weight of the EU will be shifted away from the status quo toward increased regulation.[83]

This result, flowing from the workings of the institution, will tend to place the European Union and United States at odds. Since the United States is in a dominant international position, on the other hand, it tends to favor the status quo, *ceteris paribus:* increasing international regulation will reduce American freedom of action. Any change to international norms would be scrutinized for possible negative consequences to the United States. Where the United States favors the status quo, or a position closer to it than the EU, then they will find themselves in conflict. Moreover, since the EU is acting with greater weight than it did as individual states, the EU's common and fixed position is somewhat more likely to win external international support. The United States would then be forced to choose between vetoing the agreement (where that option is present), declining to conform to the global position, or accepting a position at odds with American preferences.

EPISTEMIC HYPOTHESIS: CULTURAL DIFFERENCES

The epistemic approach, as described in this section, suggests a single hypothesis applicable to both parties:

H3: In both the United States and the European Union, support for multilateral policies will reflect their congruence with national policies already adopted.

The epistemic approach argues that ideas and values held among one group can influence the ideas and values held among other groups. The contrast with both realism and liberal institutionalism (and liberalism in general) is stark. Unlike realism, material sources of power are not decisive. Unlike liberalism, the nature of mediating institutions is not decisive. Unlike either of the other approaches, states need not be the primary actors. Epistemic approaches anticipate cross-national networks of experts, often under the auspices of NGOs influencing state decisions. As we shall see in the following chapters, such groups have often been part of these multilateral issues. Ultimately, however, it is states that have the resources and legal standing to address these issues, and it is states that are the focus of this book. If epistemicism is correct, states will seek to internationalize or export the ideas and values they hold. NGOs, in this conception, are both a channel for states to do this and independent actors influencing states for their own reasons.[84]

Epistemicism could operate at many levels. As shall be explained later, for our purposes we must look at a very deep layer, that of values: the meanings that each state places on concepts like security, democracy, sovereignty, rights, and capitalism. If we speak of collective values, then we are speaking of a persistent culture, which is the "source of a people's reality."[85] Culture here is meant to be similar to Samuel Huntington's well-known description of a "civilization" as "the highest cultural grouping of people and the broadest level of cultural identity people have short of that which distinguishes humans from other species."[86] This use of culture and values makes some scholars, even advocates of this approach, nervous, since research often relies on single-case studies and unclear variables.[87] For that reason, we will not try to measure ideas and values directly. Instead, this book assumes that national values are reflected in the laws and policies adopted by the state. Laws regarding capital punishment, environmental standards, and exporting weapons exemplify this. Epistemicism may explain why a state brings its policies into accord with others, as NGOs influence new states. If epistemicism underlies the transatlantic divergence, then it should parallel differences in domestic policies.

Epistemicism provides an opportunity to explain why state preferences may differ. The influence of cultural habits are seen even by some liberals as part of the explanation for why democracies do not seem to go to war with each other, and further that they tend to line up on the same side in major wars.[88] Other research has shown that democracies very rarely launch preventive wars. They tend to accommodate a rising power if it is also a democracy, or develop a collective response to it if it is not. Nondemocracies, on the other hand, more commonly launch preventive wars.[89] Another way to look at this same issue is to note, with Wendt, that U.S. power has a different meaning for Cuba than for Canada, just as Iraqi possession of nuclear weapons would have different meaning for Americans than would Israeli.[90] Looking at World War II, one leading realist argues, "interests, values, ideology, and strategic beliefs are, in many cases, just as important as imbalances of power or threat in determining how states choose sides and why they wage war."[91] The very concept of balancing threat rather than power has an epistemic, nonmaterial component.[92]

Many of these epistemic concepts, however, cannot be applied to explain our puzzle. Whatever the differences between the United States and the European Union, they are all liberal democracies, so the broad level of "ideology" does not fit. We find at least a rough congruence in their general "interests" in stability and predictability and in concern for human rights.

It is worth noting that the transatlantic divergence emerged last in the security realm, which deals most directly with traditional notions of "national interests." "Strategic beliefs" seem to be that instability in the areas around Europe should be minimized, and that NATO itself should continue to exist, with a modified mission. We are left then with cultural values, reflected in laws, as a hypothetical source for the transatlantic divergence.

Using culture in this way is problematic, as we must assume that a European culture exists: it cannot be German culture, or Catalan culture, or Finnish culture that explains a transatlantic divergence. Such an assumption fortunately only requires support, not proof. One can argue, for example, that an EU culture can be found in the EU's "liberal norms of domestic and international conduct."[93] Advocates of EU enlargement have used the cultural position to silence their opposition. If the aspirants present themselves as adhering to European norms, then opponents must either disavow the norms, discredit the aspirants, or define the aspirants as "outside Europe."[94]

Furthermore, we must assume that this European culture is distinct from American culture. Some do argue that the concept of "The West" may have been simply a convenience of the Cold War, as the only part of Europe that Americans identify with culturally is the United Kingdom. Before World War II, Europe and America saw themselves as separate; with the external threat removed, this difference will assert itself in the deepening of the EU.[95] Even during the Cold War, another scholar saw a distinction between the United States and the EC, in which the U.S. approach was "more openly to tolerate a lack of democracy, an absence of the rule of law, and human rights abuses, in the interests of achieving the strategic objective of anti-Communism."[96] Not all agree with this assumption of cultural distinction. Huntington, for example, groups Europe and North America together as "the West," surrounded by the Orthodox, Islamic, and Latin American civilizations.[97] Others argue that the transatlantic community is founded on values as well as on interests and security.[98] The answer to this dilemma, of course, may be that American and European cultures are sub-types of a Western culture, just as national European cultures remain intact within a general European culture. As it turns out, we will find support for this assumption in the many distinctions between American and European laws.

Before beginning to test these hypotheses, let us first discard an alternative cultural explanation that has been set forth as a direct explanation to this puzzle: Europeans embrace multilateralism, and Americans reject it.[99] We will see in this book that this is not consistently true even in recent years. A look at American foreign policy reminds us that multilateralism has often been a necessary factor for the United States to become engaged in the world. While Wilson failed to get the United States into the League of Nations, both the United Nations and NATO were founded on multilateral principles with American support. As a leading scholar of multilateralism has noted, "American advocacy for multilateral world order principles is also well-documented and is broadly accepted as an accurate rendering of U.S. milieu preferences outside the security sphere."[100] If American aversion to multilateralism does not seem to be part of the possible cultural explanation, then we need not argue with Patten and Solana regarding whether or not European culture is tied to multilateralism. In any case, if culture means anything then it must be deeply imbedded—pan-European multilateralism may be rooted in the deepening of the EU, but this is relatively new to Europe. Its influence, if any, would belong to the liberal institutional approach described earlier.

SUMMARY

Each of these three major approaches produces unique sets of hypotheses relevant to U.S.–EU relations. The liberal institutional hypotheses effectively do not apply to the United States since it seems very unlikely that the allies are at odds because the Americans are excessively supportive of multilateral institutions. If American behavior has the effect of constraining others at least as much as it constrains itself, then realism is supported. If the Americans accept limits on their actions without placing similar restrictions on others, then realism is not supported. If the Americans support multilateral policies that extend their own domestic laws, then the epistemic approach is supported. If the Americans either oppose multilateral policies that extend their own domestic laws, or if they support multilateral agreements that contrast with their existing domestic laws, then the epistemic approach is not supported.

For the Europeans, the epistemic approach is evaluated in exactly the same way. If the Europeans act together to support multilateral agreements that constrain American capabilities or freedom of action, or if they act separately to support the American position on a multilateral agreement, then realism is supported. If the Europeans act together to accept constraints on their behavior in the absence of similar limits on the Americans, or if they act separately in opposition to the American position on a multilateral agreement, then realism is not supported. If the Europeans (or Americans) accept the restrictions of a multilateral agreement in the absence of similar constraints on others, or if the Union acts together to promote a more restrictive set of international rules, then liberal institutionalism is supported. If the Europeans do not accept the restrictions of a multilateral agreement in the absence of similar constraints on others, or if the Union acts together to oppose more restrictive sets of international rules, then institutionalism is not supported.

The next four chapters (chapters 3–7) will describe the EU–U.S. relationship in context of four different issue areas: arms control, environment, human rights, and military cooperation. Twenty cases will be presented in all, with each one evaluated in terms of these hypotheses. One must note that the hypotheses are not exclusive: if the United States seeks to require other states to limit a certain action that the United States has already restricted itself from doing—for example, produce certain ozone-depleting chemicals—this would be evidence of both the realist and epistemic approaches. Furthermore, this book adopts a very specific realist expectation for the behavior of individual European states. If a European state seeks to promote a European solution that would isolate the United States, this is seen as evidence of institutionalism, not realism. If a European state acting in the absence of a common European stance takes a self-interested position in opposition to American policy, this is interpreted as evidence of neither institutionalism nor realism. Realism expects weaker states to bandwagon with a unipolar state; this book rejects the slippery view that any state behavior may be seen as self-interested, and thus in support of realism. These points are reexamined in chapter 7.

3

Arms Control

During the Cold War, most arms control initiatives were conducted on a bilateral basis between the United States and Soviet Union, and thus are beyond the scope of this book. The major exceptions to this were efforts to control or ban chemical and biological weapons, which continued into the 1990s, and the Nuclear Non-Proliferation Treaty (NPT) of 1970, which came up for renewal in 1995. Early in the 1990s, the United States and European states compromised over the details of the Chemical Weapons Convention (CWC) and the Comprehensive Nuclear Test Ban Treaty (CTBT). There were few major disagreements between Europeans and Americans with respect to extending the NPT. The Mine Ban Treaty (MBT), negotiated at Oslo and signed in Ottawa in December 1997, was different. Europeans and Americans were unable to agree on the details, and the treaty entered into force without U.S. participation. Similar disagreements persisted in two later cases, the Small Arms Program of Action and a verification protocol for the Biological (Bacteriological) and Toxin Weapons Convention (BWC). In both of these, the United States prevented agreements from being reached. Over this time period, then, we see a sharp decrease in the level of transatlantic cooperation.

Case 3.1: Chemical Weapons Convention

The level of cooperation between the allies was high with respect to the CWC, negotiated in its final form during the George Bush presidency in 1992. The CWC is an odd case to study first, since it exemplifies the opposite of our puzzle by demonstrating that the United States can accept a global, nondiscriminatory multilateral arms control regime. All CWC ratifiers agreed that they could not possess such weapons.[1] Furthermore, a stringent and intrusive verification regime was put in place, which would subject corporations within the United States to the same challenge inspections as the rest of the world.[2] Nevertheless, in distant thunder of the transatlantic storms to come, the U.S. Senate did not consent to the CWC until April 1997, just days before it would have entered into force without it.

International regulation of chemical and biological weapons stretches back into the nineteenth century. American objection to chemical weapons came very early, as it banned the use of poisons as a weapon during the Civil War.[3] At the turn of the century, the two Hague Conventions incorporated restrictions against such weapons due to their indiscriminate effects. Declaration II in 1899 announced that signatories would "abstain from the use of projectiles the object of which is the diffusion of asphyxiating or deleterious gases" in case of war between them. The 1907 convention is a bit more sweeping in its statement that states could not "employ poison or poisoned weapons."[4] Russia and Germany were among those ratifying the ban, while neither the United States nor United Kingdom did so. Notwithstanding, the use of chemical weapons—poisons—was widespread in World War I, circumventing legalistically the delivery means of the First Hague Convention and the definition of poison in the Second.[5]

After World War I, measures were taken to tighten these loopholes. The 1925 Geneva Protocol on Chemical and Bacteriological Means of Warfare clarified the prohibition on "the use in war of asphyxiating, poisonous or other gases, and of all analogous liquids, materials or devices," and extended it to include "bacteriological methods of warfare." In practice, this became a no-first-use rule, as most ratifying states reserved the right to retaliate in kind. The American role in this era was ambiguous. The United States had called for a tougher treaty at Geneva, including the banning of all trade in chemical weapons (rejected by other states as discriminatory against those without their own chemical industry), and had previously proposed a ban at the Washington Disarmament Conference in 1921.[6] In 1932, President Herbert Hoover called for a stricter ban on chemical and biological warfare at the Geneva Disarmament Conference, and President Franklin Roosevelt affirmed the U.S. policy of no-first use in 1937 and again in 1943.[7] Nevertheless, the United States would not ratify this Geneva Protocol until April 1975.

The Western powers maintained their chemical weapons programs during this period. The United Kingdom kept its weapons into the 1950s, France for another ten years after that. The superpowers maintained their own chemical weapons programs up to the very end of the Cold War.[8] Neither chemical nor biological weapons were used against each other by the major states, although they were used in "colonial" wars during the 1930s by Italy and Japan, and within the Third World by Egypt against Yemen in the 1960s (and later by Iraq in the 1980s).[9] In 1969, the United Nations General Assembly (UNGA) voted that American use of defoliants and tear gas in Vietnam violated the Geneva Protocol.[10]

The proliferation of chemical and biological warfare capabilities led the major powers to conclude that they could be used by weaker states to offset the major powers' greater capabilities in conventional arms. In 1968, Sweden put the weapons on the agenda of the UN's Committee on Disarmament (CD), and in the following year President Richard Nixon announced his intention to have the United States ratify the Geneva Protocol. While progress on chemical weapons would take another 20 years, the BWC moved fairly quickly to signature after the United Kingdom proposed separating the two types of weapons in July 1969.[11] The Soviets resisted this division until March 1971; with their objection lifted, the UNGA was able to approve a BWC in December of that same year.[12] The BWC lacked verification or enforcement provisions, a detail that would trouble the U.S.–EU relationship 30 years later, as will be discussed in this chapter's final case.

Various draft CWCs were proposed in the ensuing years, by Europeans, Soviets, and Americans, but serious negotiations on what would become the CWC did not begin until 1983. A 1984 draft proposed by the Americans based chemical restrictions on toxicity alone, which was difficult to support since many highly toxic chemicals have important commercial uses. Sweden's 1985 counter-proposal, to use toxicity as one of several criteria, along with quantity and intended use, led to the eventual three-tiered schedule of chemicals.[13] Some chemicals would be banned entirely, and a second group would have their production and stockpiling strictly limited. The third group of chemicals, dangerous but with many commercial uses, would be regulated based on their quantity and intended usage in areas such as agriculture, medicine, protection, non-weapons military use, or "law enforcement including domestic riot control purposes." Riot control agents could not be used for warfare.[14]

Further progress on developing the CWC would wait until the end of the Cold War, when President George Bush called in May 1991 for its completion within a year.[15] By that time, not only had Lithuania re-declared its independence, but also the Russian Republic, under Boris Yeltsin, was pushing a looser relationship among the Soviet republics. Now a second traditional concern of arms control, avoiding the proliferation of dangerous weapons, could receive more attention. Non-proliferation of weapons of mass destruction had long been a preference of the Soviet Union and the United States, which contributed to the 1975 BWC. By 1990, this meshed with a more general concern about asymmetric warfare. "Asymmetry" in warfare is an old principle based on attacking your adversary where he is weakest, not where he is strongest. Examples include the use of the stand-off longbow against French cavalry at Agincourt and the German submarine campaigns of both world wars. In the modern era, the coalition war against Iraq reinforced what perhaps should have already been clear from the Arab–Israeli conflicts: American weaponry, properly used, could not be directly resisted by any country other than an economic and industrial peer of the United States.

The CWC was submitted to the UNGA in September 1992—reasonably close to Bush's timetable. When it was opened for signature in January 1993, 130 states signed on immediately. Important national issues remained unresolved, however. Prior treaties had bound governments only. The CWC would be limiting the rights of private parties, so further implementing legislation would have to be passed by each signatory.[16] This had not been a major problem with agreements on nuclear weapons, since those were produced in government facilities, or at least under government contract.[17]

Controlled chemicals had many private uses, and many more relevant facilities. Entry into force would wait until 29 April 1997, just five days after the United States ratified it.

Realist approach

Throughout the negotiation of the CWC, American actions conformed to what realists would expect. Initially, the United States tried to retain some chemical weapons capability. Bush told the UNGA in September 1989 that the United States would maintain 2 percent of its current stockpile until all states capable of producing chemical weapons had signed, as it wished to retain the right to retaliate in kind. Furthermore, it would negotiate an 80 percent bilateral reduction with the Soviets before turning back to the multilateral CWC. This bilateral agreement was reached in June 1990, and on 13 May 1991 Bush dropped both the 2 percent retention clause and the right of retaliation.[18] The changing distribution of world power, and the danger of asymmetric attacks, led to a situation where it was in U.S. interests to disarm the poorer states of the world from dangerous weapons that it no longer found valuable.[19]

The primary American concern with completing the CWC surrounded the legal implications of "anytime, anywhere" inspections. "Verification" in arms control is ultimately a political decision, a trade-off between detecting the production of prohibited weapons (and thus deterring such production through the threat of discovery) and imposing an acceptable burden on states and their industries. The 1984 American draft had proposed intrusive on-site inspections, as well as "anytime, anywhere" challenge inspections, which was rejected outright by the Soviets. When the Soviets changed their position in 1987, however, the United States began to back away from its own proposal.[20] In 1988 and 1989, Germany and the United Kingdom proposed that scheduled inspections be conducted on an ad hoc basis at declared facilities. But while the Europeans preferred to have the entire chemical industry declared as potential weapons producers, the United States preferred to include only selected locations. Ultimately the United States agreed that it could only have sufficient confidence in compliance if all industrial chemical facilities were included.[21] Since costs would be imposed on the chemical industries of all states, American manufacturers would be at no disadvantage.[22] The Chemical Manufacturers Association (CMA), which represented about 95 percent of American capacity, supported the CWC since it regarded the odds of inspection at any plant as low enough to be acceptable. Many smaller chemical firms disagreed, as even small facilities would need to maintain copious paperwork on their activities.[23]

Protection of private property within the facility presented a further obstacle to inspections.[24] The United States initially wanted the CWC to incorporate some rights of refusal for challenge inspections, but this would have undermined the whole Convention.[25] Ultimately, and to the dismay of the EU, American implementing legislation for the challenge inspections protected U.S. sovereignty by allowing the president to block an inspection for national security reasons and requiring all samples to be tested within the United States.[26]

European behavior also corresponded to realist expectations. While there were different proposals from different states, on the whole, the Europeans, acting as separate states, supported the U.S. effort to achieve a CWC. Their chemical industry would not be at a disadvantage relative to the U.S. due to the CWC.

Epistemic Approach

European and American policies with respect to inspections conform to epistemic expectations. The Fourth Amendment to the U.S. Constitution prohibits unreasonable searches and seizures. American courts had generally allowed inspections without cause in "closely" regulated industries, but this principle would not apply to facilities possibly subject to "challenge" inspections.[27] This contrasts with Dutch and German law, which allows searches that serve public purposes. U.S. implementing legislation was not passed until 1998, and it required a judge to issue a criminal warrant for challenge inspections. Criminal warrants require evidence, which could only be provided by the Organization for the Prohibition of Chemical Weapons (OPCW), undermining the basic concept of "anytime, anywhere" challenges.[28]

A second legal concern surrounded the question of costs. Once again, the U.S. Constitution came into play, in its Fifth Amendment restriction on government "takings" of private property. Extra paperwork and the disruption of searches imposed costs on industry.[29] More seriously, the CWC gives officials of a non-American agency (which itself poses Constitutional questions) access to one's property, officials who could steal or reveal corporate secrets.[30] The implementing legislation designed a two-step process to get around the sovereign immunity of the inspectors. A damaged party could sue the United States for compensation, which the United States would then recover from the offending state by imposing trade sanctions (which might themselves be questionable under WTO regulations).[31]

In both of these examples, implementation of the CWC mirrors the contrast between American and European values. The epistemic approach is less supported on the question of controlling exports of listed chemicals. The United States had strictly controlled exports prior to the CWC, as had Sweden. EC Council Regulation 428/89 had restricted exports of eight chemicals on 20 February 1989. Austria, Germany, and France moved quickly to comply with the CWC in this area.[32] However, under EU rules, member states could not implement trade restrictions except for national security purposes, and not all items on CWC schedules clearly fit into that category.[33] Thus the Council "harmonised export controls for dual use products" in December 1994.[34] This was not controversial, but it shows that the Europeans were willing to support multilateral restrictions that exceeded those it had previously accepted.

Liberal Institutionalist Approach

The CWC would prove to be one of the few cases in which the United States supported an independent institution. The OPCW would be outside U.S. control—the Conference of States Parties would elect the 41 members of the Executive Committee, which in turn can recommend a director-general and deny challenge inspections. While the United States might expect to be elected as a representative of the "Western and Other" group, this would not be guaranteed; even as a member of the Executive Committee it could be outvoted.[35] The Executive Council could declare a challenge frivolous if 75 percent of its 41 members so voted within 12 hours of the challenge; otherwise, the technical secretariat would conduct the inspection.[36] This inspection would be conducted under a "managed access" system originally proposed by the British, in which inspectors would be allowed in but the facility's operators would have the right to shroud or otherwise conceal secrets unrelated to restricted chemicals. The United States originally opposed this mandatory access, but accepted it in return for having the "managed" perimeter include some area outside the structures themselves.[37]

The EU as a whole played a relatively small role in the CWC, not least because it did not exist during the negotiations. The eventual EU member states did influence the final shape of the treaty, but they acted on their own. The Council considered, but rejected, taking a joint action in July 1994 on ratification of the CWC, leaving that to the member states.[38] Sweden had been the first to do so, on 17 June 1993; Spain, Germany, and Greece would ratify it later in 1994. Other states were slower, with the final ratification (Luxembourg's) coming only ten days prior to the American, but all ratified prior to Entry Into Force (EIF).[39] The EU acted as a group as required, to control exports.

Overall the CWC stands out as a case of strong institutional cooperation between the United States and the European Union. Even in April 2002, after a history developed of disagreements on other multilateral agreements as described in the remainder of this book, the EU supported the removal of José Bustani as head of the OPCW. The United States argued that Bustani was mismanaging the OPCW and exceeding his mandate by moving beyond verification in the direction of counterterrorism. The vote to remove Bustani was 48-7, with 43 states abstaining despite Bustani's plea that abstention amounted to a vote for removal. All the EU members except France voted with the United States against Bustani; France disagreed on the means but not the ends. The United States framed its actions in terms of strengthening the international arms control regime.[40]

CASE 3.2: NUCLEAR NON-PROLIFERATION TREATY EXTENSION

The 1995 NPT extension, as well as the subsequent negotiation of the CTBT, bears some similarity to the CWC process. In all three cases, the

United States and EU member states had agreed on the basic goals of non-proliferation when negotiations began. NPT extension in particular prompted no transatlantic divergence. In contrast to the CWC, which prohibited a class of weapons from all states, American, British, and French nuclear arsenals were protected by the NPT in 1970, which established two classes of state. The five Nuclear Weapons States (NWS) could keep their nuclear arsenals, but would work toward a goal of disarmament. All other states, designated as Non-Nuclear Weapons States (NNWS) could not obtain nuclear weapons; in return they would receive aid with peaceful nuclear energy. In practice, neither of the second clauses held much force, especially the question of disarmament. Many states, led by India, viewed the NPT as discriminatory and declined to sign.

The NPT had European critics as well. France declined to sign until 1992, protesting the bipolar hegemony it sought to enshrine.[41] France also opposed efforts to create international controls on unprocessed uranium, objecting to the European Commission signing on to the International Convention on the Physical Protection of Nuclear Materials.[42] Instead, the Council in 1984 established its own rules on transfers of nuclear materials. France was not alone in Europe. Germany had lobbied to ensure that the NPT would not be permanent, but rather subject to a review 25 years after its 1970 EIF.[43] At the third NPT review conference in 1985, Germany and Belgium objected to the application of full-scope safeguards on nuclear materials; nevertheless, they supported the EC over the next two years in blocking nuclear materials from transfer to Pakistan and South Africa.[44] None of the original six members of the EC ratified the treaty until 1975, pending clarification of the relationship between the International Atomic Energy Agency (IAEA) and the European Atomic Energy Community (EURATOM).[45] This is by no means meant to suggest that Europe was in favor of nuclear proliferation. EU member states supported the goals but not the institutions created to meet those goals, which is the opposite of the puzzle we are investigating in this book.

The end of the Cold War made nuclear proliferation more salient to Europe. Ukraine, Kazakhstan, and Belarus found themselves in possession of parts of the former Soviet arsenal, and other Eastern and Central European states had to reflect on whether the nuclear option was now appropriate.[46] With the major states in agreement, the review and extension conference held during 17 April–11 May 1995 in New York was anticlimactic. All the NWS had agreed on an indefinite, unconditional extension before the meetings began, and their diplomatic preparations had produced a majority. Neither of the two main alternatives, a Mexican plan to place strict timetables for disarmament nor Indonesia's 25-year extension, received much support.[47] The United States and all EU member states cosponsored the Canadian motion to adopt indefinite extension by consensus.[48] The only "condition" imposed was a promise to follow the NPT extension with work toward a CTBT.[49]

Realist Approach

The NPT embodies realism in its differential treatment of states. The general realist arguments for non-proliferation discussed in the CWC case apply with greater intensity here: European states had a greater stake in the nuclear treaties than in the CWC. While both Britain and France had ended their chemical weapons programs before BWC and CWC talks began, they maintain a separate nuclear arsenal. Both Britain and France have nuclear-armed submarines; the French also have nuclear-armed aircraft, based both on land and at sea.[50] In addition, France has periodically advanced the idea of *dissuasion concertée*, a collective deterrent, as a final part of common European defense.[51] Within the EU, only the United Kingdom has expressed much support for this concept.[52] Nevertheless, the two European NWS cooperated with the United States in maintaining an advantage relative to the rest of the world.

Liberal Institutionalist Approach

While the Europeans had not been strong supporters of all aspects of the original NPT, this must be viewed in context of competition between global and European institutions. During the 1990s, the EU strongly supported non-proliferation through its CFSP. Its links to Ukraine, for example, were preconditioned on its disarmament. Once France decided to accede to the NPT, the Council in June 1991 called for universal adherence and acceptance of the Physical Protection Convention. Most dramatically, the Council concluded on 25 June 1994 that they would prepare a joint action calling for the NPT to be extended indefinitely and unconditionally, for wider adherence to the NPT, and for working as a group toward a general consensus in preparation for the 1995 review. This brought the EU into agreement with the U.S. position, and represented limited concessions by member states. Sweden had wanted the extension to emphasize real steps toward disarmament, while Italy, Belgium, Germany, and Ireland were concerned that indefinite extension would end any leverage by the NNWS.[53] In another compromise, Sweden dropped its view that storage of nuclear weapons in NATO NNWS (potentially including Germany, Italy, Turkey, Netherlands, Belgium, and Greece)[54] may violate Article I and II provisions of the NPT. Sweden's view that the NWS needed to work harder on disarmament was shared only by Austria and Ireland in the EU.[55] Without the EU to shape their position, these states would be unlikely to have reached a consensus on NPT extension.

Epistemic Approach

To the extent that the EU institution brought its member states into unity, it undermined support for the epistemic approach. At the most basic level, this approach is supported simply because no one advocated proliferation.

As noted already, however, there were sharp divisions within Europe regarding how to proceed. The nuclear and non-nuclear members view the question differently. Another division has been between NATO and non-NATO members. The Western European Union's (WEU) Hague Platform on European Security Interests of 1987 "reaffirm[ed] both the U.S. and European nuclear role." When it reaffirmed this position at Madrid in 1995, however, Sweden, Finland, and Ireland declined to accept that part of the declaration. Austria also commonly disagrees with NATO EU members. On 9 June 1998, Sweden and Ireland joined six non-EU states as the "New Agenda Coalition" in calling for the "speedy, final, and total elimination of nuclear weapons."[56] This was in response to an International Court of Justice advisory opinion, two years before, that "the threat or use of nuclear weapons would generally be contrary to the rules of international law applicable in armed conflict, and in particular the principles and rules of humanitarian law."[57]

CASE 3.3: COMPREHENSIVE NUCLEAR TEST BAN TREATY

The CTBT would complete the process began with the 1974 Threshold Test Ban Treaty (TTBT) and the 1976 Peaceful Nuclear Explosions Treaty (PNET). This process went no further during the Cold War, although the Soviet Union imposed a testing moratorium on 5 October 1991, and France followed on 8 April 1992. The French position had opponents who said the move endangered the safety of their nuclear arsenal and would not have any meaningful effect on stopping proliferation.[58] The U.S. DoD in 1992 stated, "The United States has not identified any further restrictions on nuclear testing beyond the TTBT that would be consistent with our national security requirements to maintain a safe and credible nuclear deterrent."[59]

The NPT extension created new momentum toward a CTBT, but it was followed by a resumption of nuclear testing. China conducted a test on 15 May 1995, and announced that it would conduct five more before a CTBT would be completed. France resumed testing as well, on 5 September 1995, but the public backlash to the announcement led to a retreat by Chirac. In August, Chirac endorsed a truly comprehensive CTBT after its tests were complete. France conducted its last test on 27 January 1996.[60]

The greatest debate in negotiating a CTBT was over the permitted yield of testing. In the 1994 negotiations in the CD, China had wanted to allow peaceful nuclear explosions, but received no significant support for that concept. The other four NWS, on the other hand, wanted to at least allow "hydronuclear experiments."[61] These had a very low yield, less than 1.8 kg. in the U.S. definition: certainly an immense reduction from the 150 kiloton–yield permitted under the TTBT and PNET. The French, for their part, wanted to allow tests up to 300 tons.[62] After internal agency discussions, the United States endorsed the true zero-yield option on 11 August 1995. This position, which China had already advocated, was rapidly accepted by the other NWS. Further suggestions, by Sweden to prohibit even planning nuclear tests and by Indonesia to prohibit computer simulations, were rejected.[63] The CTBT was signed on 24 September 1996.

The CTBT has not, however, entered into force. The CTBT would not become law until 44 specific states ratified it.[64] As of early 2003, India, Pakistan, and North Korea had not signed; the former two had conducted their own nuclear explosions in May 1998. While all members of the EU had ratified, 10 of the 41 signatories had not ratified by that time, including the United States.[65] The U.S. Senate rejected the treaty on 13 October 1999 by a vote of 51-48 against (67 votes in favor were required for Senate consent). President Clinton responded by stating that the United States would maintain its moratorium on nuclear testing.[66] At the May 2000 review conference for the NPT, the United States continued to officially support the ratification of the CTBT.[67]

Under the Bush administration, the United States moved away from the CTBT. The U.S. position seemed to promote some compromise from signatories, in an effort to get it to ratify. Russia proposed "new negotiations aimed at improving the ability to verify treaty violations." CTBT Conference Chair Wolfgang Hoffmann agreed that the Russian proposal "will obviously be a road down which many delegations will want to go in order to accommodate one very important signatory."[68] Some reports suggest that the United States is interested in pulling even further from the CTBT, even that the Bush administration was recommending making its test sites ready to resume testing in less time than the two years currently estimated.[69] Defense Secretary Donald Rumsfeld answered this report indirectly, saying only that it "certainly doesn't recommend resuming testing."[70]

Epistemic Approach

Both American and European stances on the CTBT are in contrast to what the epistemic approach would expect. Prior to the beginning of serious negotiations, the U.S. Congress imposed its own testing moratorium. Signed by President Bush over objections from Secretary Dick Cheney's Defense Department, the United States would conduct no testing from September 1992 through July 1993. After that, 15 total tests would be allowed through September 1996, followed by a complete ban "unless another state tests after that date."[71] The United States did not exercise its right to test during the window allowed by Congress. The CTBT was signed one week before the U.S. testing moratorium would have expired, as the epistemicists would expect. After the 1992 elections, the new U.S. DoD strongly endorsed a CTBT, which would "strengthen the global norm against the proliferation of nuclear weapons and constrain development of nuclear weapons capability in proliferant states and the nuclear weapons states."[72] U.S. rejection of the agreement stands in contrast to its own position, and its continuing moratorium. France, on the other hand, continued to test after agreeing at the NPT extension to seek a CTBT; it ratified the agreement despite apparently being more willing to test than the United States was. Britain used U.S. test facilities, so had no independent voice to raise on the question, and the other European states did not maintain nuclear arsenals.[73]

Realist Approach

Both the negotiations and later U.S. actions conform better to realist expectations. Besides the meaning of "comprehensive," the other primary dispute concerned the inspection procedures. Europe and the United States pushed for tough inspections, to prevent other states from circumventing the agreement. They agreed that inspections should be based on any intelligence source. Furthermore, they wanted inspections to be mandatory, subject only to a "red light" vote in the CTBT Executive Council, similar to the CWC procedures. China, on the other hand, wanted inspections to be based only on an international monitoring system, not national intelligence services, and wanted inspection to proceed only if a supermajority of the Executive Council endorsed it. In a compromise, the Chinese accepted the use of national technical measures, and the West accepted the Chinese "green light" authorization proposal.[74] The tough ratification requirements also reflect realism, in this case by the United Kingdom. The United States had advocated merely having the five NWS plus a portion of the other states that were considered possible proliferators.

The more recent U.S. position also reflects realism. The Americans have rediscovered concerns about verifiability. Hydronuclear experiments of 4-lb yield or less would be undetectable, but during negotiations the United States had accepted that such experiments also would contribute very little to nuclear proliferation. In a return to other arguments presented in the first Bush administration, the United States argues that the CTBT jeopardizes the safety and surety of the nuclear arsenal. The United States has also used its preferences to weaken NATO statements on the subject. A December 2000 NATO foreign ministers' meeting in Brussels said, "NATO Allies continue to support the ratification, early entry into force, and full implementation of the CTBT."[75] Under Bush, the May 2001 NATO foreign ministers' meeting in Budapest reduced this to "As long as the CTBT has not entered into force, we urge all states to maintain existing moratoria on nuclear testing."[76]

Liberal Institutionalist Approach

While the Europeans did not have a common position on the CTBT, they have developed one since its signing. For example, the Council supported a CTBT conference in Vienna in October 1999 designed to "facilitate the early entry into force of the CTBT."[77] On 19 June 2000, the EU adopted a common strategy to "promote the signature and ratification by Mediterranean Partners of all non-proliferation instruments, including the NPT, CWC, BWC, and CTBT." In support of the Second CTBT review conference, in New York on 11 November 2001, the EU "encourage[d] all States to sign and ratify the CTBT without delay...As a first priority, those States on the list of 44 whose signature and ratification is necessary for the entry into force of the CTBT."[78] As an institutionalist would expect, the EU is a strong advocate for the CTBT—although a realist would note that an EU perceiving itself as double-crossed by the American rejection of the treaty would behave in exactly the same way.

CASE 3.4: MINE BAN TREATY

The campaign to ban antipersonnel land mines drew on prior agreements to outlaw certain weapons. Among the earliest of these was the 1868 Declaration of St. Petersburg, in which 19 states agreed to ban exploding bullets and other lightweight explosive projectiles. The 1899 (First) Hague Convention prohibited in Article 23 the use of "arms, projectiles, or material of a nature to cause superfluous injury";[79] based on the underlying principle that "the right of the parties to a conflict to adopt means of injuring the enemy is not unlimited."[80] Land mine usage could also be seen as conflicting with the provisions of the Fourth Geneva Convention of 1949, which protects "persons taking no active part in the hostilities" from "violence to life and person."[81] This has been interpreted, and enshrined in later conventions, as a positive duty by the parties to a conflict to discriminate between civilians and combatants when using weapons.[82]

Nevertheless, none of these agreements, nor the 1977 Protocol to the Geneva Conventions, specifically spoke to the use of land mines. Protocol II of the 1980 Convention on Conventional Weapons (CCW) would be the first to restrict some use of land mines. The CCW prohibits mines from being directed against civilians, being used indiscriminately, or being used if civilian effects "would be excessive in relation to the concrete and direct military advantage anticipated." Remotely delivered mines must be self-deactivating if their location cannot be mapped, and "effective advance warning shall be given...unless circumstances do not permit." The civilian population must at least be warned of the presence of a minefield, and efforts made to protect civilians from it after the conflict is over. Besides the obvious room for interpretation in the CCW, it had no verification procedures and, like its predecessors, did not apply to internal wars or to non-state actors.[83] Furthermore, as late as 1993 (ten years after its EIF), only 40 states had ratified the CCW. Holdouts included the United States, United Kingdom, and Italy.[84]

Against this background, a transatlantic coalition of NGOs joined forces in the ultimately successful International Campaign to Ban Landmines (ICBL). Even before their first formal meeting in May 1993, the ICBL's members succeeded in drawing attention to their cause and bringing land mines onto the agenda of a CCW review.[85] This review was endorsed by the UNGA that December, but did not begin until September 1995.[86] This review, which lasted until May 1996, did not meet the goals of the ICBL or the states that had accepted the NGOs' positions. Largely this was due to the nature of the CD, which required consensus in its decisions.[87] In the end, the parties only amended Protocol II of the CCW so it would apply to internal warfare and also to limit the use of "dumb" mines to guarded minefields. Since such mines were not prohibited, their transfer would be subject to restraint, not prohibition.[88]

On the sidelines of the CCW review, the number of states favoring an international ban rose from 14 to 41.[89] Germany's decision to ban the use and production of antipersonnel land mines in 22 April 1996 provided momentum for other states to go beyond the CD's decisions.[90] Meeting in Ottawa in October 1996, 50 states including the United States, United Kingdom, and France, rejected a piecemeal approach to ending the stockpiling, production, use and transfer of antipersonnel land mines and made "a commitment to work together to ensure the earliest possible conclusion of a legally binding international agreement to ban anti-personnel mines."[91] With the support of most other European states, Canadian Foreign Minister Lloyd Axworthy called for negotiations to develop a complete ban by the end of 1997. These negotiations would occur outside the CD, so agreement could not be blocked. The treaty would be signed by whatever states were willing to.[92] In Brussels in June 1997, 90 states including all EU member states except Finland and Greece declared their support for a total ban on antipersonnel land mines. The United States opposed this approach, but France and Britain had decided to accept the process after their changes in governments that spring.[93]

Heading into the final negotiations in Oslo in September 1997, the United States found itself isolated as it pushed for five specific changes to the Brussels draft, the first three of which were "non-negotiable." First, it wanted to exempt the demilitarized zone in Korea. Second, it wanted to redefine land mines, so that detached antihandling features associated with its antitank land mines would continue to be legal. Among the attendees, only Japan supported these U.S. positions. A third American condition received no support at all: to place very stringent conditions on entry into force, following the model used for the CTBT in the previous year: 60 ratifications, including all five permanent members of the UNSC and 75 percent of "historic producers and users," followed by a nine-year deferral on compliance. The other U.S. proposals, for stronger verification and the right to withdraw from the Convention on short notice, received a bit more support, but the required two-third majority rejected all such changes, leading to U.S. withdrawal from the conference on 17 September 1997.[94]

The ICBL went on to receive the Nobel Peace Prize in October, and 122 states—including Greece as well as Japan but excluding the United States and Finland—signed the treaty when it was opened for signature in December. The treaty entered into force in March 1999, after 40 states had ratified it.[95] The United States ended up adopting many of the goals of the MBT, but not the treaty itself, and has contributed more than any other country to the elimination campaign (19 percent, although the EU as a group has contributed 48 percent and Norway has sent 15 percent from its much smaller economy).[96]

Liberal Institutionalist Approach

With the MBT, one can clearly see the influence of European institutions in shaping a common position. In May 1995, the Council agreed to "a total ban on exports of nondetectable anti-personnel mines and non-self-destructing anti-personnel mines to all destinations, as well as a ban on exports of all other types of antipersonnel mines to those States which have not yet ratified the [CCW]." Furthermore, the Council called on all member states to ratify the CCW, and to work at the upcoming review on "extending its scope to non-international armed conflicts; substantially strengthening restrictions or bans on anti-personnel mines, including those on transfers of such mines; including an effective verification mechanism; [and] including provisions on technical assistance for mine clearance."[97]

At the conclusion of the CCW review in 1996, the EU "underline[d] that the results of the Review Conference fall short of its expectations and of some of the goals set out in its joint action," in particular verification procedures and quicker compliance. The EU further indicated that the CD's limits on exports were not enough, and said it would "strive towards the goal of their eventual elimination."[98] Just days before the Ottawa meeting, the Union called for "the total elimination of anti-personnel landmines and... the achievement at the earliest possible date of an effective international agreement to ban these weapons worldwide." This Joint Action went on to say, "The European Union shall seek to raise without delay the issue of a total ban... in the most appropriate international forum."[99]

Epistemic Approach

European behavior also conformed to what the epistemic approach would expect. France, following the lead of the European Parliament, passed its own export moratorium on 11 February 1993, and went on to call for the CCW review.[100] In March 1995, Belgium implemented a ban on the use, stockpiling, production, and transfer of land mines, moving ahead of the EU as a whole.[101] Many member states enacted export moratoria that were endorsed by the Council and incorporated into the MBT, although not all had implanted a full ban by the time of treaty signature.[102]

Initially, European policies were not so different from the American. The United States acted first, with Senator Patrick Leahy (D-VT) and Congressman Lane Evans (D-IL) sponsoring a one-year moratorium on the export of antipersonnel land mines. Their bill, signed by President George Bush on 23 October 1992, also called for the President to "actively negotiate under United Nations auspices or other auspices an international agreement, or a modification of the Convention, to prohibit the sale, transfer or export of anti-personnel landmines."[103] The United States extended this export moratorium for three years in 1993. The Clinton administration successfully opposed, however, a June 1994 effort by Leahy and Evans to impose a moratorium on mine production and procurement.[104] Clinton called for "eventual elimination" of antipersonnel land mines in his speech to the UNGA that September, but that was the extent of American action. The United States supported only agreements that conformed to its own current policies, as the epistemic approach would expect.

Realist Approach

The initial stages of the land mine effort, in the CD, agree with realist predictions. The United Kingdom and United States preferred a ban on the use of "dumb" mines while allowing the use of "smart" mines that would deactivate after a fixed time period.[105] Others, including Russia and China, viewed this as an effort by the richer states to lock in an advantage.[106] While the reviews were in progress, Clinton signed into law a moratorium on the use of antipersonnel land mines after 1999 "except along internationally recognized borders or in demilitarized zones."[107] France said it would end production and destroy its stockpiles, but wanted to preserve the right to later use them if necessary.[108] The strongest push in Europe for a mine ban had been from the small (Belgium, Demark, Netherlands, Norway) and the neutral (Austria, Ireland, Switzerland, Sweden). Finland, the one European state with an interest in using land mines, is noteworthy for that stance despite being small and neutral.

After the CCW, Clinton agreed that the United States also would "aggressively pursue an international agreement to ban ... anti-personnel landmines ... as soon as possible," while retaining them in Korea and maintaining the "option" to use self-destructing mines.[109] The question was how to do so. Even after Ottawa, France, the United Kingdom, and the United States preferred to continue to work through the CD, in which they would be able to ensure that any agreement reached would be acceptable to them. All three of these in particular desired to continue to be able to use antipersonnel land mines for force protection.[110] All three were also concerned initially that a voluntary treaty would be weak. Only a "coalition of the angels" would sign, leaving the rest of the world free to ignore the convention.[111] While the United States officially "welcome[d] efforts ... including the freestanding process initiated by Canada," the CD "offer[ed] the most practical and effective forum for achieving our aim of a ban that is global," using the CWC and CTBT as examples.[112]

The final American demands at Oslo also match with realist expectations. The United States did not want to give up weapons that it still found useful. This is in contrast to the CWC, where Americans did not see military utility in retaining chemical weapons. It is particularly noteworthy from a realist perspective that the United States was willing to prohibit "dumb" land mines. The Clinton administration followed military necessity arguments made by its DoD—arguments somewhat undercut by the well-publicized advocacy of a land mine ban by many retired flag officers, including Norman Schwarzkopf, David Jones, and John Galvin.[113]

CASE 3.5: SMALL ARMS PROGRAM OF ACTION

After their success with the MBT, NGO activists sought to extend the precedent to other light weapons, such as grenades, mortars, and all sorts of firearms. As with land mines, these weapons are difficult to control because they are simple to use, easy to conceal, inexpensive, and require very little training to use, even for children. These weapons are distributed around the world through government-to-government sales, commercial sales, and unofficial means such as the raids on Albanian armories in 1997 and sales by Russian soldiers in Chechnya. Due to the profit motive inherent in arms production, the NGO strategy was to both control exports and to limit production.[114] This contrasted with the prior UN focus, which had emphasized only illegal transfers.[115]

An international conference on the subject was held during 9–21 July 2001. At its opening, John R. Bolton, Undersecretary of State for Arms Control and International Security, presented the U.S. position, which included five "red lines." The United States, he said, would not support "measures that would constrain legal trade and legal manufacturing of small arms and light weapons, . . . measures that prohibit civilian possession of small arms, . . . measures limiting trade in small arms and light weapons solely to governments, . . . [or] a mandatory Review Conference."[116] The U.S. position was joined by Russia and China as fellow arms producers and by Arab states wanting to maintain the right to provide arms to Palestinians. The final draft of the voluntary agreement dropped references to prohibitions on private ownership and to limiting arms transfers to states. The United States then agreed to support a follow-up conference in 2006. Nevertheless, Conference Chair Camillo Reyes of Colombia singled out the United States as the state that had done the most to obstruct the conference. While the United States was in a sense trying to maintain the conference's original focus on illegal transfers, the EU was frustrated by the lack of willingness to compromise displayed by the United States.[117]

Epistemic Approach

The American position against this agreement ran counter to what the epistemic approach would expect. The Small Arms Program of Action would call on states to adopt codes of conduct for the transfer of light weapons, just as many already did for heavier weapons. U.S. policy in 1998 already implemented this. It would "restrain arms transfers that may be destabilizing or threatening to regional peace and security." The United States would consider "the human rights, terrorism, and proliferation records" of a potential recipient, along with existing arms control agreements and U.S. interests in regional stability. The United States officially supported "global standards" against "illegal arms trafficking."[118] The EU, for its part, had adopted a similar code on 8 June 1998, which examines how well the buyer meets its international treaty obligations, its human rights record, the presence of internal or external conflict, and the possibility that the weapons would be transferred to other parties.[119]

Liberal Institutionalist Approach

Institutionalist expectations are supported by later EU actions, which restricted small arms exports beyond what the French and Germans had implemented previously.[120] Nevertheless, the Council issued a joint action on the "destabilising accumulation and spread of small arms and light weapons" in December 1998. This sought international agreement on all areas of small arms. States should "import and hold small arms only for their legitimate security needs, to a level commensurate with their legitimate self-defence and security requirements, including their ability to participate in UN peacekeeping operations." Their exports of weapons should be based on a code of conduct similar to the EU's. The EU encouraged "transparency and openness, through regional registers on small arms and regular exchanges of available information, on exports, imports, production and holdings of small arms" and "effective national controls" to "combat illicit trafficking." Articles 3(c) and (d) of the joint action would attract the greatest American attention. The former calls for arms production to be limited to meeting those security needs and legitimate exports—there should be no excess arms production. The latter calls for "the establishment of restrictive national weapons legislation for small arms including penal sanctions and effective administrative control."[121]

Realist Approach

The American position with respect to these proposals conformed to what realists would expect. Bolton aimed to protect U.S. sovereignty, saying, "The United States will not join consensus on a final document that contains measures contrary to our constitutional right to keep and bear arms." The focus should rather be on illegal transfers, not all small arms. Bolton also wanted to protect American freedom of action, as he objected to blanket prohibitions against arms transfers to private individuals or irregular armies, arguing that this "would preclude assistance to an oppressed non-state group defending itself from a genocidal government." All such cases, he said, are better left to the discretion of national authorities than international agreement.[122]

CASE 3.6: BIOLOGICAL WEAPONS CONVENTION VERIFICATION PROTOCOL

For the final arms control case, we return to the BWC, which had entered into force in March 1975. The convention itself did not contain any

provisions to verify compliance, and movement toward a verification protocol was slow. At the first BWC review conference in March 1980, Sweden
proposed setting up a consultative committee to investigate noncompliance
allegations. The United States, United Kingdom, and Soviet Union all
opposed this, even though the United States had accused the Soviets of
using biological agents in Afghanistan and Cambodia.[123] The United States,
despite its position that the BWC was non-verifiable by its very nature,
agreed at a third review conference in 1991, to let a group of "Verification
Experts" (VerEx) work on developing a protocol.[124] In the meantime, the
United States, United Kingdom, and Russia acted outside the BWC to set
up their own trilateral compliance inspections in September 1992; these
lasted only a few years before being suspended.[125]

In the aftermath of the 1990–1 Gulf War, the United Nations set up
another effort to monitor compliance with biological and chemical weapons
through the United Nations Special Commission (UNSCOM) in Iraq. Iraq
quickly began interfering with UNSCOM efforts.[126] By 1997, UNSC unity
was broken as Russia, China, and France abstained from or opposed resolutions aiming at penalizing Iraq further for its resistance.[127] While one can
argue that the UNSCOM strategy had proved so ineffective in motivating
Saddam Hussein to cooperate that it needed to be changed, UN efforts to
make the regime more palatable to Iraq led UNSCOM Chief Richard Butler
to conclude, "The leadership of the United Nations had become a facilitator
of Iraqi concealment."[128] UNSCOM's final departure from Iraq on
15 December 1998 was followed by four days of American and British air
and cruise missile strikes—launched while the UNSC was still discussing
Butler's latest report.[129] UNSCOM was replaced one year later by the UN
Monitoring, Verification, and Inspection Commission (UNMOVIC), which
would be more closely controlled by the UN Secretary General; France
abstained from the resolution (UNSCR 1284) creating UNMOVIC.[130]

Despite these warning signs about the difficulty of BWC compliance, the
United States publicly supported further multilateral steps. On 27 January
1998 Clinton's State of the Union address said that the United States "must
strengthen [the BWC] with a new international inspection system to detect
and deter cheating." VerEx had presented its list of 21 "potential verification
measures" to the BWC States Parties in September 1994. The States Parties
then commissioned an Ad Hoc Group (AHG) with a mandate to "consider
appropriate measures . . . and draft proposals to strengthen the Convention."
These "measures should apply to all relevant facilities and activities, be reliable, cost effective, non-discriminatory and as non-intrusive as possible . . .
and should not lead to abuse."[131]

Through this period, the United States was torn diplomatically between
its technical position that the BWC was essentially unverifiable and its political position that it should maintain the process with the Europeans.[132] The
July 1998 draft compliance protocol proposed that only "relevant" facilities
would need to be declared by BWC ratifiers; these would be subject to rou-
tine and "non-compliance concern investigations."[133] The United States and

Japan in particular objected that this level of inspection could pose a problem for their industries.[134] Furthermore, the steps proposed had already been incorporated into UNSCOM, without confidence in success despite the high level of intrusion imposed on Iraq. In any case, "relevant" facilities could not be determined factually prior to an inspection. Finally, industry representatives noted that the nature of infectious biological agents meant that "the scale of manufacture...may not govern their final impact" in the same way that chemical or nuclear weapons would be limited by small, undetected violations.[135]

The Bush administration concluded that the verification process was futile, and moved to end the negotiations. The EU's representative, along with those from Russia, China, and Iran, endorsed the composite protocol text of the AHG on 23 July 2001.[136] The United States, however, rejected it on 25 July, citing the danger posed to "national security and confidential business information" without a corresponding increase in "confidence in compliance" or deterrence of biological weapons development. Ambassador Don Mahley's statement to the AHG cited the problem of "dual capability" facilities, "damage to innocent declared facilities," including to their public reputation, and the "misdirect[ion] of world attention." Since these problems were inherent in the AHG approach, "no modification of [the mechanisms proposed] would allow them to achieve their objectives."[137] Mahley was instructed, in his words, to tell the AHG that "the United States is not going to sign this protocol or any derivative thereof or agree to its going forward to be signed." Above all, an ineffective inspection would produce a "false positive [that] is actually detrimental to national security" as suggested by the case of UNSCOM.[138] As a more senior state department official described it, "We went to our European allies and said the current text was unacceptable...We saw no possibility of negotiating the text. The Europeans didn't think we were serious."

This position continued after the terrorist attacks of 11 September and the subsequent anthrax mailings. U.S National Security Advisor Condoleeza Rice on 15 October 2001 disputed the notion "that the biological weapons protocol as it is currently drafted would stop the likes of people that we're worried about right now from getting biological weapons."[139] The alternative was "criminalizing the use and import or export of biological weapons, fund[ing] more research into illnesses caused by biological weapons, and shar[ing] information and expertise to minimize the effects if the weapons are used."[140]

At the Fifth Review Conference itself, the United States began by going on the diplomatic offensive. When it opened in Geneva on 19 November 2001, Bolton accused Iraq, Iran, North Korea, Libya, Syria, and Sudan of conducting biological weapons research in violation of the BWC. In this context, Bolton repeated the U.S. concern that no reasonable inspection protocol would be sufficient to detect biowarfare programs and stated as a matter of principle, "We will continue to reject flawed texts like the BWC draft protocol, recommended to us simply because they are the product of lengthy negotiations or arbitrary deadlines, if such texts are not in the best interests of the United States . . . The time for 'better than nothing' protocols is over." In its place, he proposed that states be required to pass legislation making biological warfare activities illegal, which would allow treaty provisions to apply to non-state actors. In addition, he proposed that mandatory inspections of facilities be replaced by investigations of allegations and "suspicious disease outbreaks" authorized by the UN Secretary General.[141]

The conference was suspended on 7 December after the United States called for termination of the AHG mandate. The U.S. proposal for UN-authorized inspections had been countered by the EU's preference for a new international organization, similar to the OPCW. Differences also remained regarding export controls and the treatment of states that are not compliant with the treaty.[142] Rather than have the AHG eliminated, the delegates suspended the conference until November 2002. EU Ambassador Jean Lint said, "We had a kind of agreement with the United States . . . to be informed of their proposals and that one took us totally by surprise and that was totally different from what the European Union wants. So for us this was totally unacceptable." Bolton denied that the U.S. position should have come as a surprise; indeed, the United States on 22 November had said it "would not support the AHG's continuation in any form," and initially, the EU seemed to concur with that view.[143] Other American officials, however, suggest that there was a "gentleman's agreement" not to go through with ending the AHG mandate, an agreement that was overruled within the U.S. government just days before the conference ended. An EU official said they understood the U.S. objections but thought that the AHG would continue to play a role in addressing the new formulation, so they were "shocked" when "Bolton slammed the door."[144]

The November 2002 reconvening of this Fifth Review Conference was less dramatic. The parties agreed by consensus to hold a Sixth Review Conference in Geneva in 2006, and to have annual one-week meetings until then. As the United States preferred, these meetings would focus on the implementation of national measures and safeguards, improving the monitoring of and response to suspicious outbreaks, and developing "codes of conduct for scientists."[145]

Realist Approach

Verification of the BWC is far more complex than the CTBT and CWC, so it raised the realist concerns about these agreements to a higher level. The danger of industrial theft is more significant than with the CWC, since chemical compositions are less secret than pharmaceuticals, and because biological agents are much easier to reproduce, given a sample, than are chemical compounds. The profit margin and investment involved in medical research also makes potential losses much more serious.[146] Furthermore, since many private facilities could theoretically be used to develop and store biological weapons, the impact of verification on Americans would be deeper. Thus

American pharmaceutical interests opposed BWC verification, while the CMA had supported the CWC. The trilateral inspections were viewed very negatively by the American pharmaceutical industry, particularly inspections of Pfizer facilities in Terre Haute, Indiana, and Groton, Connecticut. "The way the Administration handled it really bothered industry because they had to twist the arms of the people to get them to agree to a second visit. The company felt they were being targeted."[147] An industry source bluntly said, "Constitutional rights were thrown out the window. There was no enforcement against Russian violations."

While concerns over theft remained, industry was also concerned about the loss of reputation after being accused of involvement with biological weapons. The industry source said pharmaceutical companies' "relationships with patients are more intimate" than those of chemical companies. This experience decreased American enthusiasm for agreeing to intrusive inspections under the BWC, since it appeared that the difficulty of finding evidence of violations would be compounded by harassment of American corporations. The Pharmaceutical Research and Manufacturers Association (PhRMA) Board issued statements from 1996 to 1998 insisting that challenge inspections be subject to a green light vote of the states, that "site managers control access" to the facility being inspected, and that the facility receive the inspection report prior to its release with a right to respond. In order to defend the companies' reputations, the inspectors would also need to report if "no evidence of a violation [was] found." Similar European and Japanese industry associations later joined PhRMA's position.[148]

Constitutional and corporate issues aside, the smaller infrastructure required to manufacture biological agents would also make verification in other states more difficult than for chemical weapons, so the U.S. position was that only a measure of compliance confidence could be achieved, rather than full verification.[149] While the CWC had banned even possession of certain chemicals, the BWC could not do so—most biological agents have potential legitimate medical or research uses. The BWC also did not set up schedules of agents, simply banning the use of any of them in war.[150]

These realist concerns over signing a treaty that others would violate were intensified in the United States by what officials generally regard as the "failure" of UNSCOM.[151] The effort highlighted an additional problem with BWC verification, beyond the ease of evading inspections and the impact on innocent American (and European) corporations. Ineffective inspections, American diplomats say, lead to a false sense of security. Mahley described the lessons of UNSCOM: "As Iraq demonstrates, we get agreement with Saddam Hussein from some of the Europeans. Why are the French opposing the continuation of sanctions on the Security Council? In part because they argue that we have no proof that he is still pursuing WMD programs." Inspections, he said, "don't complicate [a proliferator's] life enough. He is able to pass through this hoop and once he's done that, and we come up with our own national means and say he has an offensive program, he puts his hand over his heart and says 'But I've done everything you people have asked me to do, and nobody has found anything wrong even once so you can't possibly sanction me and take actions against me.'" Thus inspections can be "detrimental to national security."[152]

Liberal Institutionalist Approach

The EU consistently adopted statements in support of a compliance protocol, but never adopted a common position in support of any particular protocol due to differences in member state preferences. For example, the EU said it would "promote the conclusion of the negotiations, in the BTWC Ad Hoc Group, on a legally binding protocol establishing a verification and compliance regime that will effectively strengthen the BTWC Convention." Furthermore, it called for reaching agreement on the facilities that would be declared and on visits and other "on-site activities."[153] As late as 21 June 2001, the EU–Canada Joint Declaration on Non-Proliferation, Arms Control and Disarmament simply said, "conclusion of a legally-binding Protocol to strengthen confidence in compliance with the BTWC is urgently required," preferably by the Fifth Review Conference. The Council conclusions that followed, on 23 June 2001, re-endorsed the 1999 common position as they

> underlined the need for the early adoption of a legally binding protocol establishing an effective regime of compliance with the BTWC...The essential principles set out in Common Position 1999/346/CFSP...strike the right balance between compliance requirements, national security interests and the economic interests of the States party to the BTWC...The adoption of the protocol would send positive signals demonstrating the international community's commitment to strengthen the multilateral disarmament and non-proliferation regime.

While it seems that EU behavior preparing for the Fifth Review Conference conformed to institutionalist expectations, its behavior in other ways conforms more to realism. Some states briefly considered following the Ottawa model and proceeding without the United States on a verification protocol. This concept was dropped because the inspection agency would then need to be mostly funded by the EU, and most inspections would be of EU facilities since the truly dangerous states would be unlikely to join such an agreement.[154] The EU did not take a position on the role of UNSCOM in Iraq, as France and the United Kingdom were sharply opposed on the issue.

Epistemic Approach

Once again, American behavior does not fully match what the epistemic approach would predict. The United States restricted exports and development of biological agents, as called for in the Verification Protocol, but declined to institutionalize that policy. This evidence is partly balanced by American views on warrantless inspections, which would have been challenged under the Verification Protocol. EU actions also did not fully conform to epistemic expectations. EU unity was blocked by differences in member states' practices. Had a Verification Protocol been implemented, some EU member states would have been required to change their laws.

SUMMARY

In these six agreements, one can see a general pattern over time of increasing American opposition to proposed agreements and increasing EU advocacy of them. On the American side, initial objections were raised to all agreements except the NPT extension, which was also the only treaty that was discriminatory in favor of the United States. The primary American concerns surrounded Constitutional issues, conditions for entry into force, effectiveness of its implementation, and residual military utility. The EU member states were united, and stated so in joint actions or common positions, on the BWC protocol, small arms, and the NPT extension. The EU member states were also in agreement on the CWC, although they could not yet take a common position on it. The Europeans also reached substantial unity on the MBT. After initial resistance from France, the Union was able to overcome internal divisions and promote ratification of the CTBT among its international partners.[155] In sum, we see no divergence between the United States and the European Union on the NPT extension. With the CWC and CTBT, we have some slight initial divergence, which is resolved to mutual satisfaction. On the MBT, BWC Verification Protocol, and Small Arms Program of Action, one finds a clear and unresolved divergence.

This trend of divergence continues if one considers the U.S. announcement on 13 December 2001 that it would unilaterally withdrawal from the Anti Ballistic Missile (ABM) treaty. That U.S. action had long been signaled, so it elicited relatively little official comment at the time.[156] As a bilateral agreement, it lies outside the scope of this book. Coming just days after the BWC Verification Protocol suspension, however, a German official linked ABM withdrawal to "how much the Bush administration respects international obligations."[157] The Europeans had been particularly concerned about Russian reactions, and Chirac had appealed directly to Clinton not to withdraw during his presidency.[158] On the other hand, British, Italian, and German officials publicly accepted the possible need for missile defense.[159] The EU had pointedly not taken a position on the treaty: the Joint Declaration at the Russia–EU Summit on 29 May 2000 said, "The Russian side recalled the need for firmness and the strict obedience of the ABM Treaty which was of basic significance for securing strategic stability." The muted response of Russia, combined with the impact of 11 September 2001 and the long build-up to the decision reduced EU comments at the time. Nevertheless, it is another case in which the United States and the European Union were at odds with respect to arms control.

The realist hypothesis for the United States is that it would accept multi-lateral restrictions on its arms and actions only if they restricted others equally. American behavior conformed to this hypothesis in arms control. The United States accepted the NPT, which restricts others but not itself, and accepted the CWC after concluding that its oversight provisions would adequately enforce the prohibitions on other states. U.S. rejection of the CTBT, a BWC verification protocol and the Small Arms Program of Action conformed to its suspicions that other states might be able to succeed in violating the treaty. The agreements would have limited U.S. power and flexibility without restricting others enough. With land mines, the United States also retained some direct interest in not being restricted even if others were limited; this argument applies to some extent to the CTBT and small arms agreements as well.

The realist approach expects the European states to bandwagon with the United States individually and to advocate multilateral restraints as a Union, but accept these agreements only to the extent that the United States did. European behavior generally conforms to realist expectations, although less consistently than the American. In early agreements, acting as individual states, the Europeans went along with U.S. preferences on the CWC and NPT. The Europeans, acting as a Union, have not been willing to go forward without the United States on BWC verification or small arms. The CTBT is an unusual case, as the French resisted the limits proposed by the United States. With both CTBT and land mines, the Europeans have gone ahead with an agreement opposed by the United States. This evidence against realism is partially mitigated by the fact that the European states ratified the CTBT before the U.S. Senate rejected it. The European Union since then has consistently pressed the United States to reconsider. Land mines present a stronger exception to realism, as the Europeans actively promoted an agreement that left out the United States. Once again, this is somewhat mitigated by the fact that the Europeans, Finland excepted, did not see any need to use land mines themselves, and did not have any expectation that a nonsignatory would use land mines against them. The Europeans restricted their power without the United States restricting its own, but not very much, especially since the United States had imposed its own export moratorium.

The liberal institutional hypotheses both apply to the EU, since there is no reason to believe that the transatlantic differences are caused by excessive American support of multilateralism. One institutional hypothesis is that the EU should support multilateral agreements even if the United States does not, because the agreements inject a measure of law into international anarchy. This hypothesis receives mixed support. Since the United States supported the NPT and CWC, this hypothesis does not apply in those cases. The EU has fully supported both the CTBT and MBT, despite American rejection of them. More recently, however, the Europeans have not gone forward with agreements that do not include the United States. European support for BWC verification and small arms limits seem to be conditioned on American concurrence.

The other institutional hypothesis, that the EU should adopt positions that favor multilateral approaches more than the Americans do, receives more support. EU support for these agreements was consistent, while American support was not. Furthermore, the divergence increased for those agreements where the EU acted as one—small arms, BWC verification, and ultimately the CTBT. This trend is even more notable if one looks back to the pre-Union era, when the member states initially opposed the NPT. The MBT is a mixed case, in that there was transatlantic divergence even though the EU did not adopt a position in support of all its provisions, but it seems that the EU helped create a near-unanimous European position.

The epistemic hypothesis suggests that both the United States and EU should seek to internationalize positions they have already taken. This hypothesis receives mixed support from American behavior. The United States supported international limits on chemical and biological weapons once it had accepted such limits for itself, and the NPT extension conformed to U.S. non-proliferation policy. The United States was willing to support internationalizing its moratorium on land mine exports, and opposed taking the agreement further. On the other hand, the United States declined to internationalize its domestic policy on export controls on small arms and on ending nuclear weapons tests.

The epistemic hypothesis receives even less support from European behavior. The Europeans supported limits on small arms and chemical transfers that they had not yet adopted domestically. Many states had not yet implemented the restrictions imposed by the MBT, either; any likely BWC verification protocol would have also gone beyond some members' domestic policies. European support for the NPT extension required several members to sacrifice prior positions on nuclear weapons. French nuclear tests immediately prior to the CTBT suggest also that France was accepting an international limit that it did not deeply support. Whereas the United States defies epistemic expectations by resisting the internationalization of its own policies, the EU defies them by willing to go beyond its prior positions. On both sides of the Atlantic, the epistemic expectation that states would project their own policies into the international arena is not supported.

As an initial assessment, it seems that both the realist and institutional approaches contribute to our understanding of transatlantic disagreements in the area of arms control. American behavior corresponds much more closely to realist predictions than to the epistemic. European behavior matches both realist and institutional predictions in part. The institutional approach may explain the development of common positions within Europe that go beyond what the epistemic approach would expect. When it comes to implementation, however, in two cases the Europeans proceed without American adherence and in two cases they do not. Given that the realist behavior follows the unexpected American rejection of the CTBT, and given that neither the MBT nor CTBT placed important restrictions on most European states, EU behavior seems to correspond slightly more to realism than to institutionalism in the implementation of agreements.

This is only an interim assessment, however. Epistemic expectations may be met in other issue areas, and American behavior may not be so realist outside the area of arms control, which is near the heart of realist theory. Additional cases will shed light on European actions as well, allowing us to choose between institutionalism and realism. This chapter centered on the MBT of December 1997. The Kyoto agreement on climate change followed hard on Ottawa's heels, so we turn to environmental issues next.

4

ENVIRONMENT

This chapter adopts a somewhat longer view than the others, because agreements on environmental protection have been affected less by the end of the Cold War than the other topics. The Kyoto Protocol of 11 December 1997 represented a rejection of U.S. preferences in environmental policy by an EU-led coalition, similar in effect to the MBT signed a few days before in Ottawa. The overall story here, however, is cloudier than with arms control. A different transatlantic divergence was apparent very early: through the Reagan administration, the United States was clearly more progressive in environmental standards than members of the EC. West Germany was the only large European (Economic) Community (EEC) member state to push for adoption of auto emissions standards similar to those in the United States. Along with Canada and the Nordic states (not then members of the EU), the United States led the way on restricting ozone-depleting chemicals in the Montreal Protocol of 1987. By the 1990s, however, their roles were dramatically reversed. While the United States remained active in protecting stratospheric ozone, the EU matched it in enthusiasm. The Union also promoted action at the 1992 Earth Summit in Rio de Janeiro to prevent climate change, which the United States was against. So while Oslo and Ottawa brought the arms control divergence into focus, Kyoto merely continued a well-known split. In both cases, however, the Clinton administration came away from the negotiations with a treaty containing provisions it had stated were unacceptable. After Kyoto, the United States worked without success to alter the Protocol's provisions; President George W. Bush rejected it altogether and proposed a much less stringent regime in its place.

CASE 4.1: ACID RAIN AND LONG RANGE TRANSBOUNDARY AIR POLLUTION

The June 1972 Stockholm Conference on the Human Environment, one of the earliest official meetings on global environmental issues, led to the creation of the United Nations Environment Programme (UNEP), and put acid rain on the international agenda.[1] Acid rain, or more properly acidic depositions in general, was of great concern in Sweden and Norway. The basic problem of acidic residues from industrial air emissions had been known for over a century. The United Kingdom had applicable laws as early as 1863,[2] and American court cases dated back to 1907.[3] The solution to local air pollution was to disperse it using tall smokestacks—leading to transboundary air pollution.

Action on air pollution would not be initiated at Stockholm, however, but in Helsinki at the Conference for Security and Cooperation in Europe (CSCE) from 1973 to 1975. Norway encouraged adding air pollution to the CSCE agenda, as had originally been proposed by the Warsaw Treaty Organization in 1969. The Final Act of the CSCE extended the Organization for Economic Cooperation and Development (OECD), sulfur dioxide (SO_2) monitoring program to include all of Europe, a task that would fall to the UN Economic Commission for Europe (ECE). The United States and Canada stayed outside this program, although they were beginning to work on their own bilateral issues with acid rain.[4] President Carter's efforts led to the Acid Precipitation Act of 1980.[5] Through the 1980s the United States called for more research before it would consider reductions in SO_2 and nitrogen oxides (NOx) in the Clean Air Act of 1990.[6]

With continued prodding by Norway and Sweden, the North American and European states began meeting in 1978 to discuss a Convention on Long-Range Transboundary Air Pollution (LRTAP). The Nordic draft of July 1978 proposed moving toward a freeze in SO_2 emissions, followed by a reduction. The EEC resisted any such binding targets or timetables. The LRTAP, signed in November 1979, met the EC's conditions, calling only for research and monitoring of pollutants, with the possibility of later protocols that could include measures to reduce pollution.[7] The LRTAP would enter into force on 16 March 1983, with the EC and United States included as ratifiers.

Liberal Institutional Approach

Up to this point, the EC had not played an active role on environmental issues. While the Council of Environment Ministers had been set up in 1973, the Treaty of Rome had not specifically mentioned the environment as within the EC's competency. Much of EC environmental policy addressed trade in hazardous substances.[8] Early examples include directives to member states in 1970 on vehicle noise and exhaust emissions and in 1973 on paint solvents. These directives also addressed concerns over "eco-protectionism": for example, no member state could prohibit vehicles that met the EC standards, even if it preferred a tougher standard. A ruling by the European Court of Justice in 1979 eliminated the need for such directives, by setting forth a principle of "mutual recognition," according to which each member state must accept any product legally produced in another member state.[9]

The first Environmental Action Programme adopted by the Council in 1973 suggested that there might be noneconomic reasons for environmental action. This focused instead on quality of life as a European value. Later

Action Programmes would encourage cooperation within the EC and in other international organizations, as well as set environmental priorities, but progress would be limited by the need for consensus.[10] Among the members at this time, the leaders were the Netherlands and Denmark—joined by Germany in 1981 when the effects of acid rain in the Black Forest suddenly came to public attention, ending German doubts about Swedish allegations of the impact of long-range pollution.[11] The rest of the 1980s would witness an intra-European battle over air pollution. In the 1990s, Austria, Finland, and Sweden would join these three as the strongest advocates for environmental policies.[12]

In the United States, coal power plants were blamed for acid rain. While this was also true initially in Europe—to the extent acid rain was accepted as a problem—German attention quickly turned to auto emissions.[13] In 1983, the Germans proposed that the EC adopt auto emission standards by 1989 equivalent to those already in place in the United States. The EC focus, however, was on maintaining common standards across all members as part of implementing a single market.[14] Individual states were not permitted to enact emissions standards, even ones that allowed three times the pollution that the United States did. France, Italy, and the United Kingdom led the fight against emissions standards, leading to Council rejection of a 1984 Commission proposal to allow American limits to be adopted. After France threatened to take Germany before the European Court of Justice if it unilaterally required catalytic converters, the 1985 "Luxembourg Compromise" suggested allowing stricter emissions limits only on medium and large cars, not on the small cars typical of France and Italy. Under Council unanimity rules, however, Denmark held out for a universal standard and Greece for side-payments in the form of cleaning up Athens' air pollution.[15]

The deadlock broke after the SEA took effect in 1987. The SEA was the first document to bring environmental issues clearly within the competence of the European institutions.[16] It also allowed Qualified Majority Voting (QMV) on issues related to the single market.[17] With QMV, Denmark and Greece could no longer block the Luxembourg Compromise. In June 1988, the Council extended the emissions limits option to all cars.[18] Another relevant institutional change in the SEA gave the EP co-decision authority. As this operated at the time, the EP could amend or reject a council QMV decision; the amendment or rejection could only be overturned by Council consensus. The EP used this provision to make the emissions standards tougher than the Council had initially agreed to.[19] Thus deepening of the European institutions helped to promote a multilateral solution, as the institutional approach would expect. Since the United States advocated this agreement, there was no need for the Europeans to carry it out alone.

Realist Approach

The realist approach expects the Europeans to bandwagon with the American position, which in this case would have been to favor the international agreement. The Americans should be aiming to ensure that the agreement did not reduce their freedom of action. Neither hypothesis fully holds for this case. The United States did work to have agreements to reduce emissions be baselined early enough that it could get credit for early emissions controls. The Americans were not, however particularly aggressive in pushing for an international agreement that would bind others. Thus we lack a clear standard for whether or not the Europeans were bandwagoning.

While we cannot count this as evidence supporting the realist approach, we do see clear signs of national self-interest in the European positions. While the European institutions would eventually make it possible to reach a common standard, early in the negotiations they were used to block regulations that did not serve national self-interests. While the two Scandinavian leaders, along with Finland, Austria, and Switzerland, were all net "importers" of air pollution; EC members were net "exporters" or experienced a balance in trade of this undesired by-product.[20] Once the Germans became more interested in reducing auto emissions, the Dutch, Danes, and Greeks joined them, but none of them were auto manufacturers. Furthermore, Greece held up the agreement to gain rewards for itself.

The period of negotiations over auto emissions coincided with those over the Large Combustion Plant Directive (LCPD). Germany also took the lead on efforts to control these point sources of pollution. It reduced allowable SO_2 emissions from $50\,MW$ or larger power plants to $400\,mg/m^3$. The industry-environmentalist deadlock of the 1970s gave way to a more precautionary approach based on correcting potential problems without requiring conclusive scientific proof—perhaps due to the need to "do something" about the very visible forest damage.[21] German industrial interests, while conceding the environmental argument, pushed for EC-wide standards so they would not be put at a competitive disadvantage. Once again, the Netherlands and Denmark were Germany's main allies, with France this time neutral due to its reliance on nuclear power.

The poorer members of the EC, however, argued that limits would restrict their ability to grow. The United Kingdom also argued against the LCPD since it relied heavily on coal plants and because it said SO_2 cuts were not scientifically warranted.[22] The British position may in part have been due to the relative lack of influence of a Green party in their nonproportional election system or due to a preference for scientific proof before taking potentially disruptive actions. In the end, an economic shift from coal to gas power generation reduced British opposition to the LCPD.[23] When passed in November 1988 as Control of Emissions from Large Stationary Sources, it limited SO_2, NOx, and particulates. It also set forth varying targets: while some states had to reduce emissions by 70 percent, Greece, Ireland, and Portugal were allowed to increase their emissions.[24] This issue of distribution, resolved by forming a sort of "bubble" for the EC as a whole, proved to be the critical negotiating point.[25]

Epistemic Approach

German advocacy of stricter emissions controls also reflects their domestic legislation, while resistance in other states reflected their lack of pollution standards at the time. This fits fairly well the epistemic expectation. This parallels the Germans' realist interest in not being at a disadvantage relative to other European states. The same is true for the Americans, who enacted pollution controls long before the Europeans did. Acceptance of emissions limits by other member states, however, runs counter to the epistemic approach, since those states had to change their policies to reflect the agreement. This case best fits the liberal institutional approach for the Union, and the epistemic approach for the United States.

CASE 4.2: STRATOSPHERIC OZONE: VIENNA AND MONTREAL

Acid precipitation was not the only global environmental concern of the 1970s and 1980s. The danger of increased ultraviolet radiation, due to a depleted layer of stratospheric ozone, suggested serious health hazards. Fears that nitrous oxides (NOx) would damage the ozone layer contributed to American withdrawal from the French–British Supersonic Transport (SST) project. A 1974 study by R. Sherwood Rowland and Mario Molina (whose work would win them the 1995 Nobel Prize in Chemistry) predicted a 7–13 percent loss of stratospheric ozone loss due to synthetic chemicals known as chlorofluorocarbons (CFCs). At the time, aerosol can propellant was one of the largest uses of these chemicals.[26]

The initial industry strategy of resisting calls for limits or bans on aerosol CFCs failed in the United States, but few other countries followed immediately.[27] International efforts to reduce ozone depletion began with the 1977 establishment of a Coordinating Committee on the Ozone Layer within the UNEP.[28] In 1982, the Nordic states proposed the first draft of a Convention for the Protection of the Ozone Layer, which set forth only the general principle without requiring any action. Specific protocols would be negotiated to this flexible convention. Several states, including the Nordics, Canada, and the United States, and eventually Austria, Australia, and Switzerland, pushed for a simultaneous protocol to ban CFCs as aerosol propellants. This so-called Toronto Group was resisted by the EC, Soviet Union, and Japan.[29] They wanted only to limit CFC production. These positions reflected the domestic positions taken already by each side and the excess production capability in the EC. Ultimately, the March 1985 Vienna Convention only required reporting by its members.[30] The U.S. support for global bans on aerosol CFCs might seem surprising, given the Reagan administration's reputation of being anti-environmental and pro-business. The EC was surprised, at least, expecting the United States to share their position rather than join yet another Nordic crusade.[31]

In December 1986, the United States proposed specific movement toward a ban of CFCs and Halons. While the precise timetable was left open, the plan would be for near-term freeze on consumption or emission of ozone depleting chemicals, followed by steps down to 20 percent, 50 percent, and 95 percent of the 1986 levels. This proposal was generally supported by the Nordic states and Canada, although the former wanted to specify a 25 percent cut by 1991. Consumption would be calculated as the amount produced plus the amount imported, minus exports to protocol parties and minus any destroyed or captured chemicals. With exports to non-parties counting as domestic consumption, the EC opposed the U.S. plan. It suggested instead that limits be placed only on production, which would allow it a higher ceiling and the option of reducing exports to ensure a domestic supply.[32]

Moving toward final negotiations in Montreal, the United States and the European Community reached an unscientific compromise of a 50 percent cut in CFCs by 1998. The U.S. 95 percent proposal was based on a need to take significant action; the EC 20 percent was based on a need only for further study.[33] The September 1987 Montreal Protocol also called for Halon consumption to be stabilized at 1986 levels by 1992—the EC had not wanted limits on Halons.[34] The United States had wanted the protocol to not enter into force until 90 percent of all 1986 consumption was accounted for by the ratifying states; the final agreement settled at two-thirds of the 1986 consumption, which occurred by 1 January 1989. The EC was again granted a bubble within which it could apportion national limits.[35]

While the United States cannot be said to have been a pure supporter of Montreal—Interior Secretary Donald Hodel suggested instead wearing hats and sunglasses[36]—its support was more consistent than the Europeans'. Secretary of State George Shultz insisted that Reagan not back away from Montreal, for fear of "damage to the U.S.' international reputation."[37] By the first review meeting, in London in June 1990, the EC had come to match or exceed American enthusiasm for Montreal. The Council quickly ratified the Protocol, allowing it to enter into force very quickly.[38] One of the key changes was in the position of the United Kingdom, which had resisted action on the LRTAP and on ozone protection up to Montreal. In 1988, however, Prime Minister Margaret Thatcher warned the UNGA of the dangers of ozone depletion and climate change.[39]

Diplomatic strategy switched from resistance to acceleration. On 3 March 1989, the Environmental Council agreed to ban CFCs by 2000; the United States followed on the next day. By the London Meeting of the Parties, the Commission had proposed moving the CFC phase-out up to 1997, while Germany and its three enthusiastic neighbors planned on ending CFC use in 1995. Since the United States, Soviet Union, and Japan preferred to end CFCs in 2000, their proposal was adopted at London, but the 50 percent consumption cut was moved up to 1995. Interim targets were also adopted of 20 percent cut by 1993 and 85 percent by 1997—all still from the 1986 baseline.[40] The parties also agreed at London to ban Halon by 2000, and also to add carbon tetrachloride to the list of chemicals to be banned by 2000. Methyl chloroform would be cut 75 percent by 2000 and banned in 2005.[41]

By the time the Parties met in Copenhagen in November 1992, they were ready to further accelerate the chemicals' phase-out. Both the United States and the European Union had decided to eliminate CFCs, carbon tetrachloride and methyl chloroform by the end of 1995. Halons were moved up to 1994, and hydrobromofluorocarbons were added to the list with CFCs. The United States also proposed strict limits on methyl bromide, with elimination in 2000, but EU resistance resulted in only a freeze at 1991 levels by 1995.[42] Once again, the EU position proved temporary. The very next month, the Environmental Council accelerated the schedule on many of the 1996 chemicals. In June 1994, the Council also agreed to cut methyl bromide by 25 percent in 1996.[43]

Epistemic Approach

Policy toward banning CFCs closely reflects what the epistemic approach would anticipate. The United States was an international leader on the subject. Oregon banned CFCs as aerosol propellants in 1975, to take effect in 1977; New York followed Oregon's lead. The federal Environmental Protection Agency proposed a national ban on aerosol CFCs in October 1976.[44] Sweden joined the U.S. ban in 1977, but despite the efforts of President Jimmy Carter to internationalize the policy, only non-EC members Canada, Norway, and Finland joined it in the 1970s.[45] These countries led the way toward the Vienna and Montreal agreements.

Member states of the EC declined to ban aerosol CFCs, although the EP did support doing so.[46] Instead, the EC in 1980 adopted a freeze on CFC-11 and CFC-12 with a 30 percent cut proposed by the end of 1981.[47] The Dutch did call for a voluntary 50 percent reduction in aerosol CFCs, but they did not agree to fully phase them out until 1988, after the Montreal Protocol was signed.[48] Germany also called for voluntary reductions, but the British position was that the 1980 EC reductions should be sufficient.[49] Reaction in other countries was slow perhaps because the decentralized nature of American government made it easier to create local regulations, which then could be nationalized.[50] The Europeans resisted multilateral agreements on CFCs just as they resisted them domestically.

The EC became more flexible in early 1987. Belgium assumed the Presidency; by the end of the year the troika would include pro-Montreal Belgium, Denmark, and Germany. The Germans, influenced by the growing strength of the Green party, announced their own unilateral 50 percent cut in CFCs, giving them the same interest the Americans had in globalizing their domestic choices.[51] This, and the remarkable change of position by Thatcher, led to eventual European support for this environmental agreement.

Realist Approach

These same facts could also be used to support a realist interpretation. Even in the SST controversy, the Europeans accused the United States of trying to gain economic advantage by restricting landing rights. The stark difference between U.S. and European policies on CFCs as aerosol propellants led to a 33 percent drop in sales by DuPont, the dominant U.S. manufacturer, and a matching increase in exports by European manufacturers.[52] Thus the American position reflected business interests as well as those of environmental activists. While DuPont and other manufacturers were not eager to restrict the use of CFCs, they preferred a global ban to unilateral restrictions on American production.[53] The EC, for its part, said a ban was unjustified as it was based on "only American research."[54] The United States argued that the world could not afford to wait for more conclusive research, because then it might be too late to repair the damage.[55] Ultimately, the Europeans bandwagoned with the American position.

The Vienna Convention had established a series of informal technical workshops to help negotiate a protocol.[56] The United States used these to try to persuade the EC to accept stricter limits on CFCs—pointing to its own success in implementing its aerosol ban. At one of these, in Rome in May 1986, the United Kingdom and France took the position that "European consumers preferred the finer mist produced by CFC aerosols."[57] By the time negotiations on a protocol began later in 1986, however, two events shifted the terms of the debate. The first was imagery of the Antarctic "ozone hole," which helped to focus public interest in the problem. The second was DuPont's conclusion that more stringent limits on CFCs would be acceptable. These overcame lingering resistance in the Reagan administration.[58] DuPont's position prompted Europe and Japan to suspect that it simply had developed a lucrative substitute for which it now wanted a market.[59]

The case also reflects the realist approach since provisions were made to include all states in the agreement. Consumption by nonparties in the developing world could defeat the purpose of the agreement, and the negotiators particularly wanted to avoid having CFC manufacturing simply move from parties to nonparties. The Protocol thus provided for an end to imports from nonmembers within six months of EIF, and an end to exports two years after EIF. These trade restrictions applied both to the chemicals themselves and to products made using them. These provisions seemed to succeed in inducing many states from the developing world to join. Montreal offered some carrots to go with the trade stick, in the form of a multilateral assistance fund whose details would be negotiated later.[60] The Protocol further said that developing countries would be granted a ten-year extension on reducing consumption. As this window would be calculated from EIF, not from their accession, developing states would have no incentive to delay joining.[61] The only countries eligible for this delay would be those whose consumption rate was less than one-fourth that of the United States, and they would need to participate once their consumption hit that historic level.[62]

The most contentious issue at the London meeting of parties was the design of this Multilateral Fund. This fund would provide aid to developing states that acceded to Montreal. India and China most strongly pushed for this assistance, but the United States, the Nordic states, and the Netherlands also were early supporters of using the fund to balance equity with the common responsibility for addressing ozone depletion.[63] The developing states were granted their right to develop economically without bearing costs disproportionate to their role in creating the problem, but the developing states in turn acknowledged that they must accept limits on their use of ozone depleting chemicals if the problem is to be solved.[64] The UNEP had in fact wanted this fund to be the seed of a general "earth tax," which could be extended to greenhouse gases, but this was rejected by the developed states. Led by the United Kingdom, these states preferred that the fund be kept in the World Bank, with assessments proportional to Gross National Product; its final design involves joint management by both institutions as well as the United Nations Development Programme (UNDP).[65]

Since decision-making in the fund had been revised to require a majority of both developed and developing states, supplementing the two-thirds overall majority required, the developed states were able to shape the fund mostly in line with their preferences. The fund would be limited to ozone-related activities, such as plant conversion, recycling, and compensation for increased costs. The United States was able to insert language indicating that this fund would not be a precedent for future environmental issues, and that the ozone solutions were the result of scientific proof, not mere precautions. The committee's membership would be split evenly among the two groups of states. The United States had demanded a permanent seat, as a realist might expect; this was finessed by making the United States a region of one state for purposes of electing representatives.[66]

Liberal Institutional Approach

With the United States strongly advocating this agreement, the second institutional hypothesis does not apply: the Europeans did not want to do this at all, especially if the Americans pulled out. We do see some influence of the European institutions, although in the early years these worked against agreement, as they had with LRTAP. The EC disagreed on the ultimate goal, with the United Kingdom (holding the Presidency in late 1986) calling the American 95 percent cut "excessive and nonnegotiable": 30 percent would be the most they claimed they could accept.[67] Germany, joined as usual by Denmark and the Netherlands, and also Belgium, called for deeper cuts, but Council requirements for unanimity prevented the EC from doing more than continue to call for further study.[68]

The EP also provided its weight, calling for an 85 percent cut in CFC emissions.[69] By April, the EC said it would accept freezing CFC-11 and CFC-12 at 1986 levels within two years after the protocol would enter into force, and then cut them 20 percent six years after that. In addition to the internal influences on EC decision-making, the United States was at this point suggesting economic sanctions against those who did not follow its own planned cuts.[70] A reinforcing dynamic developed under Montreal, which incorporated the minimal acceptable effort. Once implemented, however, the parties quickly concluded that they could do more, or act more quickly.[71] Just as this dynamic held for the world as a whole, it held within the EU itself. While the EC was limited to adopting the minimal restrictions acceptable to its membership, this repeatedly led to new baselines for gradually imposing stricter cuts.[72] The United States also discovered that the conversion to newly developed substitutes was less costly than expected; the use of specific targets and market mechanisms such as emissions trading provided an incentive to move more quickly.[73]

CASE 4.3: THE KYOTO PROTOCOL

A much different dynamic applied to the final case in this chapter, the Kyoto Protocol. Kyoto, like the Montreal Protocol, is the implementing measure to a more general agreement, in this case the FCCC. The political similarity ends there, however: the United States and the European Union would adopt diplomatic stances opposite what they had on Montreal. The earlier agreement, like the LRTAP and for that matter the CWC and MBT, addressed an issue that was relatively narrow in its sources or effects. Kyoto is more analogous to the BWC. While earlier agreements had aimed at the prohibition, or least strict limitation, of manufactured products, Kyoto additionally sought to regulate the production of carbon dioxide, a by-product of natural processes as well as of industrial activity that would continue. Thus the same questions about verifiability that applied to the BWC applied to Kyoto, in the American view.

Scientific focus on climate change due to greenhouse gas emissions can be traced to 1979, when both the U.S. National Academy of Scientists and the World Climate Conference warned state leaders that continued increases in atmospheric carbon dioxide would have climate-altering effects. The primary effort began in 1988, when the UNGA declared that climate is a "common concern of mankind" and set up the Intergovernmental Panel on Climate Change (IPCC). As this panel began its work, the divide among the developed countries was apparent: the European countries supported setting fixed targets and timetables for reducing emissions, along the model of Montreal and the LRTAP, while the United States opposed such goals—in particular the idea that the goals should be uniform for all states, as in the precedent agreements. Japan and the Soviet Union agreed with the U.S. position, while Canada, Australia, and New Zealand tended to support the EU.[74]

Formal work on the FCCC was endorsed by the UNGA in December 1990, following the release of the IPCC's first assessment report in August and the second World Climate Conference of scientists in September. In the meantime, several states proposed goals for themselves. In 1988, Canada and Norway called for reducing carbon dioxide emissions by 20 percent by 2005.[75] In June 1990, Germany said it would reduce its emissions by 25 percent, based on a 1987 baseline—a slightly less dramatic step than the 30 percent recommended by a parliamentary commission.[76] Austria, Denmark, Italy, and Luxembourg matched the Canadian–Norwegian target. Other European countries—Norway, Finland, Switzerland, and the

United Kingdom—committed to stabilizing their 1990 emissions in 2000, while France and Japan agreed to stabilize their per capita emissions. Spain, on the other hand, promised only to cap its emissions increase at 25 percent.[77]

The UNGA voted to adopt the FCCC, without any specific targets or timetables, in May 1992. One month later, much of the world met at the Earth Summit in Rio de Janeiro to try for the first time to address truly complex global problems, as opposed to single substances. Rio produced a cluster of statements and agreements, including the Rio Declaration, the Convention on Biological Diversity, and the Statement of Forest Principles. These led to later treaties, such as the 1994 Convention to Combat Desertification, the 1994 International Tropical Timber Agreement, and the 1995 Agreement on Straddling Fish Stocks and Highly Migratory Fish—its spirit contributed as well to the 1997 Agreement on International Humane Trapping Standards.[78]

The FCCC merely established voluntary goals of having the emissions of selected greenhouse gases in industrialized states return to 1990 levels by 2000. Some former communist states were allowed to select an earlier base year, since their emissions had recently dropped involuntarily. The FCCC also required reporting on emissions and carbon sinks, similar to the Helsinki agreement that led to the LRTAP.[79] While it could not be considered a strong agreement, it did signal general consensus that climate change was a concern relevant to the world as a whole, that different states would bear different responsibilities in addressing the problem, and that it was reasonable to take some precautionary measures prior to establishing full proof of the problem.[80] Regarding this final point, significant doubt remained at Rio, at Kyoto, and beyond with respect to the evidence of climate change. Besides the difficulty of modeling the atmosphere, the depletion of stratospheric ozone may mitigate warming trends. Since both CFCs and ozone are greenhouse gases, their simultaneous reduction, prior to probable ozone regeneration, could reduce the effects of other emissions. The impact of aerosols in counteracting atmospheric warming was also unclear. Nevertheless, the EU applied the same argument for the FCCC that the United States had used in Vienna and Montreal: the consequences of delaying action were too great.[81]

The election of Albert Gore to the vice presidency, and the appointment of Timothy Wirth as Undersecretary of State for Global Affairs—both men's support of environmental causes was well documented[82]—suggested that the United States would become more supportive of the FCCC goals. The results were mixed. The United States had ratified the FCCC quickly, on 15 October 1992, while President George H.W. Bush was still in office. Momentum on climate change then cooled. The FCCC did not enter into force until 21 March 1994, after 50 states ratified it, and the first Conference of the Parties (COP) was delayed for yet another year. COP-1, in Berlin, set forth the diplomatic dynamics that would continue through Kyoto. Since the FCCC had not included decision-making procedures, consensus would be used until the parties agreed (by consensus) to change the procedures. This created a strong incentive to accede to the FCCC, but made reaching an acceptable compromise difficult. Berlin's major accomplishments were its Mandate that developing states would be exempt from emissions restrictions, and agreement that an ad-hoc group would draft a Protocol.[83]

The Berlin Mandate only thinly masked fundamental divisions among the parties. The developing states generally favored the Mandate. Among them, the Alliance of Small Island States (AOSIS) worked hard for a Protocol, from fear of climate-induced rises in mean sea level. The AOSIS members would bear little cost from any agreement, and could clearly benefit from it. Most of the other developing states primarily wanted to ensure that they would be able to continue industrializing with inexpensive energy—what they referred to as "survival emissions," in contrast to the much higher per capita "luxury emissions" in the industrialized states. The members of OPEC generally opposed Kyoto, since they had a vested interest in continued oil sales. At times, OPEC opposition to Kyoto would manifest itself in support for a strong Protocol, believing strategically that a tough agreement would never enter into force.[84]

The industrialized world was more divided. On one side was the EU, which consistently favored significant across-the-board reductions in greenhouse gas emissions. This suited its economic interests as a fossil-fuel importer, and reflected concern about the impact of dramatic events such as a shift in the Gulf Stream. Almost everyone else disagreed. The United States, Canada, and Australia were more dependent on fossil fuels for transportation due to the size of their territory and dispersion of their population. Japan and Iceland already had low levels of greenhouse gas emissions, due to their exploitation of other forms of power and early imposition of conservation. Norway shared their position, and also shared the OPEC interest in exporting fossil fuels. Russia and other members of the former Soviet Union in a sense fit the OPEC interest group even more closely: they also wanted to export fuels, needed to redevelop their industry, and did not see climate change (especially in the form of global warming) as necessarily a bad thing. Switzerland, New Zealand, and South Korea also tended to oppose the EU position.[85]

When COP-3 began on 8 December 1997 in Kyoto, the United States was in a more restricted negotiating position than it had been at Oslo, when the MBT was agreed upon. In Norway, American instructions were merely derived from the official position of the DoD, which did not represent a monopoly opinion within the security community. In Japan, American instructions were derived from a resolution of the U.S. Senate. On 12 June 1997, the Senate had voted 95-0 against the United States signing any Protocol that restricted U.S. emissions unless it also included "specific scheduled commitments to limit or reduce greenhouse gas emissions for Developing Country Parties within the same compliance period." This resolution, cosponsored by Senators Robert Byrd (D-WV) and Chuck Hagel (R-NE), directly contradicted the Berlin Mandate.[86] The United States was unable to change the Berlin Mandate at Kyoto, and so it opposed the Protocol there.

The final agreement at Kyoto nevertheless included many provisions that favored U.S. preferences over European. One of these was implementation. The EU favored "common and coordinated policies and measures," such as common energy taxes throughout the developed states that were members of the OECD.[87] The United States also won concessions on the means of calculating targets and timetables for emissions reductions. Wirth had, at COP-2 in Geneva in July 1996, accepted the principle of negotiating "realistic verifiable and binding medium-term emission targets." The United States did not, however, agree on what they should be, nor that they should be equal for all states. At this time, Germany was calling for a 10 percent reduction in emissions by 2005 and a further 5–10 percent cut by 2010. Australia, Russia, and OPEC countries were among those who resisted any such targets, so the COP, in a parliamentary maneuver, merely "recognized" the Geneva Ministerial Declaration on targets and timetables, as opposed to adopting it by consensus.[88]

As the parties moved toward Kyoto, the EU proposed a 15 percent reduction by 2010 with an interim 7.5 percent cut by 2005. Japan was willing to support only a 5 percent cut by 2010. The developing states endorsed the EU position and added a requirement for the industrialized states to cut carbon dioxide by 35 percent by 2020. The U.S. position in October 1997 was simply to return to the emissions levels of 1990, as applied to a weighted basket of greenhouse gases: carbon dioxide, methane, nitrous oxide, sulfur hexafluoride, hydorfluorocarbons, and perfluorocarbons.[89] While the EU and Japan opposed including the latter three gasses, the basket approach was adopted with a baseline of 1995 rather than 1990.[90] The final agreement at Kyoto required an 8 percent cut for the EU from the 1990 baseline, 7 percent for the United States, and 6 percent for Japan. It should be noted, however, that these targets were essentially arbitrary, like those at Montreal. Prior to Kyoto, the scientific opinion on climate change was that greenhouse gas emissions needed to be cut by at least 50 percent immediately if climate change from prior emissions was to be avoided.[91]

Other economic factors apply to Kyoto beyond the direct impact of reducing energy consumption or changing energy sources. One asserted impact of climate change is an increased probability of severe weather, including more severe hurricanes and deeper droughts. More long-lasting climate risks could be an increase in mean sea level or a shift in the ocean currents that give northwestern Europe a much warmer climate than similar latitudes in North America. Assessing the risk of such hazards, however, requires that one has a reasonable idea of the economic impact of the changes and also a probability of occurrence, neither of which is easy to determine. Another risk may be a wider range for vector-borne diseases and agricultural pests. These may also be controllable—"tropical" diseases like yellow fever and malaria were once common in the United States and have been eradicated through public health measures, not a cooling in global climate. The question, once again, is how to balance the cost in additional health efforts against the cost of reducing greenhouse gases—now with the added imponderable of the value of human life.[92]

Given the question of equity, the economic uncertainties and the problems of free riding by developing industrial states like India and China, Kyoto and climate change may have the most complex ramifications of all the multilateral issues discussed in this book. It is too simple to say that "green" environmental interests are stronger in the EU and "brown" industrial interests are stronger in the United States. The EU was hardly united on the side of "green" until a compromise was reached that gave certain states the right to increase emissions, or to not be required to reduce emissions as much as others. The pattern of energy use in Europe and the benefits of communist collapse also contribute to reducing the relative cost of Kyoto in Europe—as recognized in the greater reduction target assigned to the EU. As the largest single state, and one that perceives its costs to be higher and benefits lower than other states, the United States succeeded in forcing many compromises at Kyoto from those more interested in reaching an agreement. These included a lower emissions target than others had proposed and the incorporation of a variety of economic mechanisms. The Senate's stand regarding the obligations of developing states also added to American leverage at Kyoto, since American negotiators could emphasize that any Protocol must meet Senate conditions.[93]

The informal and formal negotiations for Kyoto were marathon sessions over the nights of 9–10 December, concluding at nine in the morning on 11 December. Chairman Raul Estrada of Argentina's style was to announce a consensus position and require a two-thirds vote to overturn it.[94] To overcome exhaustion, the United States rotated its team of negotiators, which may partly explain why the United States was successful in shaping many areas of the Protocol.[95] The United States followed Gore's mandate, delivered in person in Kyoto, to be flexible: the United States accepted higher emissions cuts than it wanted, and also gave in on the question of borrowing emissions. The EU was less flexible at Kyoto. Led by British Deputy Prime Minister John Prescott acting for the troika (given the limited capacity of Luxembourg in the Presidency), the member states had not given the Commission authority to negotiate for them and so were forced to try to renegotiate a common position if they wished to compromise. While the EU succeeded in establishing firm targets and timetables—although not as high as they had wanted—they failed to establish common implementation policies, had to accept the budget concept and banking into it, allowed the use of sinks, adopted the basket approach rather than their preferred single-gas limits, and were unable to implement regulations on the various market mechanisms incorporated into Kyoto.[96]

Despite American success in many areas, the Kyoto Protocol did not meet the Senate's preconditions for developing state participation, so it was not greeted warmly. Senator John Kerry (D-MA) warned Clinton that he would need to move "very slowly as to ratification." Republican Frank Murkowski of Alaska more bluntly stated that the treaty was "fundamentally flawed and dead on arrival." Byrd, the West Virginia Democrat, said that if the provisions were not changed, he would join in "stabbing it in the heart" if signed and submitted to the Senate.[97] The Senators continued to regard the Protocol's provisions as unfair, and cited the danger of limits being placed on American economic growth.[98] While the United States signed a year later, it never was submitted for Senate consent, despite continued efforts by the Clinton administration to make it more acceptable.

The next COP was held in Buenos Aires in November 1998, at which point the United States signed the Protocol. The Umbrella Group of Kyoto opponents refused to allow any limits on trading, as some of its members wanted unlimited purchasing while others wanted an unlimited ability to sell their "hot air."[99] Argentina and Kazakhstan broke with the Berlin Mandate and agreed to accept voluntary emissions limits, thereby becoming eligible for joint implementation projects. The parties agreed at Buenos Aires to resolve all differences with respect to economic measures, defining sinks, and review and enforcement within two years.[100]

Those two years passed without result. At the Bonn COP in 1999, the United States recommended extending the deadline and moving the next meeting to spring 2001 from October 2000, when it would be at the height of the upcoming presidential campaign in which expected nominees George W. Bush and Vice President Al Gore had adopted sharply different opinions.[101] This suggestion was rejected at the time, although COP-6 was eventually moved to mid-November 2000. In the meantime, few states had ratified. Romania in March 2001 was the first Annex 1 industrialized state to ratify it. By February 2002 only the Czech Republic had joined it.[102] The convoluted requirements for EIF gave leverage to the Umbrella Group members: 55 states must ratify, accounting for 55 percent of all 1990 emissions. With the United States alone accounting for 36.1 percent, almost all other states would need to ratify before it would take effect. The Russian 17.4 percent of global emissions would be critical if the United States did not ratify; even Japan's 8.5 percent added to the United States would form a virtual block on implementation. Oddly, the United States had proposed one of the mildest EIF conditions: only 50 percent of all emissions (along with 65 states), while Japan and Canada had pushed for 65 percent and 60 percent respectively.[103]

With the inauguration of George W. Bush, American policy shifted away from attempts to make Kyoto comply with Senate wishes. Bush announced in March 2001 that the United States would not ratify Kyoto, to which the Stockholm European Council noted "its deep concern at the fact that this Protocol is being called into question" given the EU's "strong commitment to the Kyoto Protocol."[104] Bush's thorough explanation of his opposition waited until his trip to the Goteborg Council meeting in June 2001. Prior to leaving Washington, Bush said the agreement was "fatally flawed in fundamental ways." He based the new U.S. position on uncertainty as to the extent and cause of climate change, on the emissions limits that were "arbitrary and not based upon science," on its exemption of China, India, and other countries, and on concern over the economic impact of reducing emissions. Bush said work on climate change must be global, measurable, flexible, and market-based, and it must allow for economic growth. His goal, returning to U.S. positions prior to Rio, was to "stabilize" emissions.[105]

Leading up to the July 2001 COP, again in Bonn, entry into force appeared unlikely. Japanese Prime Minister Junichiro Koizumi had announced after a 30 June meeting with Bush, "Presently I do not have the intention of proceeding without the cooperation of the United States."[106] With its participation critical, international attention focused on Japan. Delegations from the United Kingdom, EU, and United States all visited Tokyo in the early part of July.[107] As the meeting opened, the Europeans also were displeased that Undersecretary of State Paula Dobriansky failed to propose any alternatives to Kyoto, as had been promised in exchange for delaying the meeting from May.[108]

Contrary to expectations, the Bonn meeting did reach agreement on most of the issues that had plagued the protocol since Buenos Aires. This achievement primarily resulted from the EU accepting most of the terms posed by the Umbrella Group, with the exception of the American requirement for developing country participation. Liberal credit was given for carbon sinks, which benefited Japan, Russia, Canada, and Australia. The EU also dropped its insistence on limits to emissions trading, which had contributed to the breakdown of the Hague COP the previous November. Finally, in a key concession to Japan, binding penalties for noncompliance by 2012 were dropped in favor of an agreement that states which did not meet the 2012 targets would face tougher limits as the treaty was extended beyond that year. While all of these compromises also met U.S. demands, National Security Adviser Condoleezza Rice quickly said that the American position on ratification was unchanged because "developing countries will have to be a part of [the] solution." The net effect would be to reduce the required global reduction in greenhouse gases from 5.3 percent to an estimated 1.8 percent, if states lived up to their commitments.[109]

The Parties met again at Marrakech, Morocco, from 29 October to the early morning of 10 November 2001, to further refine the details. Given the leverage each Party now had, the EU made further concessions to ensure that ratification would remain a possibility. Russia insisted that its carbon sink credit had been incorrectly measured, and was rewarded by having its total "sink" allowance doubled to 33 million tons from 17.6 million tons of carbon dioxide. Japan was granted a delay in determining whether emissions targets would be legally binding, or merely politically binding. Emissions trading would be liberal, with non-Annex I countries being granted sellable credits for voluntarily reducing their emissions. The United States attended this meeting, but did not actively participate, nor did it present any alternatives, citing the ongoing war in Afghanistan. Referring to that conflict, Dutch Environment Minister Jan Pronk said, "After the events of September 11th, if there is any reason for the United States to call for international, global approaches, [it should also] join a global approach to the existing global problem of climate change."[110]

On 14 February 2002, Bush announced his own plan for controlling greenhouse gas emissions. He proposed providing incentives to reduce the "intensity" of such emissions so that they would increase at one-third the rate of overall economic growth. These incentives included tax breaks for consumers who use solar power or more fuel-efficient cars, and tax credits for constructing power plants that did not use fossil fuels. No mandatory targets would be set unless a review in 2012 showed that the plan had not been successful in reducing greenhouse gas intensity by 18 percent. In the meantime, businesses were encouraged to report their greenhouse gas emissions so they could receive credit if a stricter policy were imposed later.[111]

The EU and its 15 member states presented their ratification to the United Nations on 31 May 2002. By the end of that year both Japan and Canada had ratified, leaving only Russia to bring Kyoto into force. Russian Prime Minister Mikhail Kasyanov announced on 3 September 2002 his country's plans to ratify the Protocol "in the very near future."[112] One year later, Russia still had not done so. Ultimate compliance remained in doubt, as both the United Kingdom and Germany, two of the states that were expected to lead the EU's reductions, reported that their emissions in 2001 had increased 3 percent and 1.5 percent, respectively, over 2000.[113] In May 2003, the European Environment Agency's abstract to its 2001 greenhouse gas inventory said bluntly, "Greenhouse gas (GHG) emissions from the European Union have increased for the second consecutive year, moving the EU further away from meeting its commitment to achieve a substantial emissions cut by the 2008–2012 period."[114] More specifically, while the linear path to the 8 percent reduction would require a 4.4 percent cut in the GHG basket for this reporting period, the Union had only cut them by 2.3 percent—and carbon dioxide emissions had actually increased 1.6 percent from the 1990 baseline.[115]

Liberal Institutional Approach

Evidence supporting the first institutional hypothesis is very strong in this case. European institutions provided the means for developing a common position, and the Environmental Council exerted leadership on the member states. The history above has noted the divergent proposals from the European states regarding the extent of emissions cuts. In March 1997, the Environmental Council, led by the Netherlands, proposed that the EU would cut greenhouse gases 15 percent from 1990 levels by 2010. This would be accomplished, however, via "internal burden sharing." Portugal, Spain, Greece, and Ireland were given room to increase emissions primarily due to their economic underdevelopment, while Sweden would be allowed its small increase and France and Finland to implement no change, primarily as a nod to their pre-1990 reliance on energy conservation and nonfossil fuels. Taken as a group, the EU proposal added up to only 9.2 percent, well short of the declared 15 percent but deeper than any other proposals set forth.[116]

The EU also worked hard to make Kyoto acceptable to others. The EU's regional "bubble" was criticized as counter to the spirit of national reductions. The Union argued that its regional "bubble" represented the unique nature of the organization, and that other states should not be allowed to take advantage of ad-hoc bubbles. By the end of Kyoto, however, the bubble option had been made available to others. Once the EU signed the Kyoto Protocol on 29 April 1998, the members renegotiated their individual requirements. Since the EU as a whole was not required to cut emissions as deeply, most states received lighter allocations at the June Council meeting (the United Kingdom being the exception, offering to cut by 12.5 percent). Kyoto's industrialized opponents, now calling themselves the Umbrella Group, began discussions with Russia and Ukraine on forming their own bubble, although this idea was never consummated.[117] Reacting to this, the Environmental Council accused the United States of trying to buy its way out of the Kyoto Protocol and proposed that at least 50 percent of each signatory's cuts must be achieved through domestic reductions.[118]

We have also seen the concessions on emissions trading and the calculations of carbon sinks, all designed to ensure ratification of the Protocol. The Union even tried to revise the Berlin Mandate. The United States accepted the principle that developing states should not face the same burden as the developed states.[119] On the other hand, unlimited emissions by developing states would ultimately overwhelm reductions made in the states covered by Kyoto. One option was that developing states would maintain a constant share of global emissions, leading to proportional cuts by all states. This, however, had the appearance of locking in the developed states' economic advantage. Another was that individual developing states would assume limits when their per capita emissions matched that of the Annex 1 states, similar to the provisions in the Montreal Protocol.[120] In the months leading up to Kyoto, the EU did propose that Mexico and South Korea should be required to adopt limits, and that the Protocol should include evolutionary provisions to eventually include all states. Chairman Estrada rejected these ideas, however, as being contrary to the terms of the Berlin Mandate, which was the basis for a protocol.[121]

On the surface, the second institutional hypothesis is also supported. Clearly the EU has worked to implement an agreement that it knows will not include the United States. Nevertheless, one must consider whether or not this agreement is parallel to the MBT, in that its impact on the EU is less dramatic than one might think—and recalling that the Protocol calls for greenhouse gas cuts far below what advocates argue is required. Most significantly, the EU was benefiting from what came to be known as "hot air." By 1995, German emissions had indeed dropped by 12 percent since the 1990 baseline year, but this was due to the closure of former East German factories—greenhouse gas emissions in the former West Germany increased over the same period.[122]

As it has noted itself, the EU is not on schedule to comply with Kyoto. Projections in 1999 were that the EU would increase its emissions by 6 percent by 2010 rather than cut by 8 percent.[123] Only five states at that point had implemented a form of tax on fossil fuels: Denmark, Finland, Norway, the Netherlands, and Sweden.[124] Even this represents a change, as the Dutch government much earlier had proposed reducing tax credits for energy consumers. The unpopularity of this indirect tax increase contributed to the fall of its coalition government in 1989.[125] The U.S. ambassador to the EU, Richard Morningstar, noted in May 2001: "Europe, too, needs to recognize that it has a credibility problem about its ability to truly implement its own environmental commitments. The majority of member states are far away from their target paths toward Kyoto...The gulf between the EU's rhetoric on climate change and the reality on the ground gets wider."[126] This pattern has continued in the 2003 Greenhouse Gas Inventory, in which the trend from 1999 to 2001 was to increase the gap between actual emissions and the linear reduction line.[127] As Russian ratification came to be seen as less likely in 2004, doubts were expressed within the Commission over the wisdom of implementing Kyoto without Russian and American adherence.

Realist Approach

Clearly, the realist expectation that the EU would bandwagon with the United States on this agreement is not supported. Regardless of how much significance one places on the extent of European emission cuts, the Union is proceeding without American adherence. Early in the process, there were hints of another approach. In October 1990, the EC proposed that it would have its 2000 CO_2 emissions equal those of 1990, on condition that it could use a bubble to allow for increases in some member states.[128] This Council goal, however, was conditioned on Japan and the United States adopting similar measures, which they did not.[129] This latter point was insisted upon by the United Kingdom, which also blocked adoption of any EU-wide taxes on energy.[130] In May 1992, the Commission had proposed (but the Council never implemented) a common tax on energy, which would protect European industry by taking effect only if the United States and Japan enacted the same tax.[131]

American behavior, on the other hand, strongly conformed to realist expectations. It did not implement any internal taxes, for fear of harming its own economy—any compensatory measures could violate the provisions of the WTO.[132] As George Bush had campaigned against tax increases, he did not propose any. Paul Tsongas did promote a carbon tax in his unsuccessful 1992 presidential campaign, but both this and the BTU tax eventually proposed by Bill Clinton were aimed as much at energy conservation as climate change. In any case, the BTU tax failed.[133] Generally speaking, the United States preferred nontax economic measures, like emissions trading among industries, to meet air standards as set domestically or through international agreement as at Montreal.[134] This pattern would persist after Kyoto was signed—Clinton proposed meeting 75 percent of the Kyoto targets by trading emissions with Russia and other former communist states.[135]

The American position had been for a return to the 1990 levels, rather than actual reductions. The United States also wanted compliance measured against a "budget" of years, 2008–12. This would allow flexibility due to economic or weather conditions that might affect annual energy use, although it would also make it difficult to assess compliance until 2012.[136] Against EU opposition, Kyoto allows emissions reductions from earlier years to be "banked," saved as credit to allow higher emissions in later years. The U.S. proposal for "borrowing" emissions was not accepted, however. Borrowing would allow a state to maintain higher emissions for a time, then make deeper cuts when advances in technology make it more costeffective.[137] The risk in this proposal is that states could simply credit their high emissions, build up an insurmountable emissions "debt," and then withdraw from the agreement.[138]

Both clustering greenhouse gases, so states could decide which to cut first, and the budget mechanism, so states could decide when to make cuts, are economically efficient ways to reach the ultimate goal of reducing the gases in the atmosphere. A third set of efficiencies involves allowing states higher emissions if they helped to reduce emissions elsewhere.[139] One such trade-off was "carbon sinks." Carbon dioxide emissions could be offset by increases in forest cover, which would absorb carbon dioxide as they grow. The effectiveness of such sinks would be very difficult to measure, and may only be temporary solutions. A more direct market mechanism was emissions trading—states emitting greenhouse gasses at a lower rate than permitted could sell their "excess" to other states. This produces a financial incentive to reduce emissions more quickly—but it also allows states to sell their "hot air." Joint implementation projects allow members to pay for reducing emissions in other members, which may be less expensive than doing so at home. Finally, clean development mechanisms credit states for emissions-reducing projects in nonmembers, including the development of carbon sinks. A significant problem with joint implementation and clean development projects is the establishment of a baseline. Even if one can roughly calculate the carbon sink represented by growing a forest, it is not clear whether the point of comparison should be barren land, the natural regrowth that would occur on the land, or reforestation that might have been done even without aid from the industrialized state. Thus the EU wanted emissions trading and other market mechanisms to be supplemental to domestic measures.[140] All of these market mechanisms were advocated by the United States as a way of reducing its own costs, and also as more acceptable (or invisible) to the general public than taxation or regulation.[141]

Despite these concessions to U.S. preferences, the Kyoto Protocol did not mandate any action by the developing states. This was the primary condition laid down by the Senate, and the U.S. negotiating team worked to at least cap the growth of their emissions. On 6 October, President Clinton called for "meaningful, but equitable commitments" from the developing states—accepting the FCCC's premise that the industrialized states should face tougher restrictions. The latter had contributed the most to the greenhouse gas buildup in the atmosphere to date, and also had higher emissions per capita. Nevertheless, as Wirth pointed out on 17 October, not all developing states were alike. Some, such as Israel, Singapore, South Korea, Argentina, and Mexico, were relatively rich and could afford to take some steps to reduce emissions. India and China were poor, but their aggregate emissions were large and growing. Ultimately, any global climate change solution must incorporate global emissions.[142] Besides the impact of developing-state industrialization, the promise of unlimited emissions could encourage some factories to relocate rather than cut back on greenhouse gases.[143]

Kyoto also faced difficulty in devising a plausible enforcement method. The benefits of a stable climate cannot be denied to those who do not participate, so each state has an interest in having others pay the costs while still enjoying the benefits. This in turn reduces each state's interest in participating, especially if it regards its own costs to be higher than others—or regards the benefits it would gain as lower than others. The Montreal Protocol had placed trade restrictions against products made with or containing ozone-depleting chemicals. This solution was impractical for climate change, since greenhouse gas emissions will not be prohibited entirely. While Kyoto imposes strict targets and timetables, it leaves enforcement to be negotiated in the future. Furthermore, since Kyoto does not specify what emissions levels will be allowed after 2012—again, unlike the permanent nature of the provisions in Montreal—states that exceed Kyoto's emissions limits can imagine that a Kyoto II would backpedal to accept higher limits.[144]

Epistemic Approach

Evidence for and against the epistemic approach can be derived from the discussion already presented. American legislation did not call for mandatory emission cuts, and there was no national policy at all until Bush's incentives proposal in 2002. As the epistemic approach would expect, the United States opposed an international agreement that did not conform to its domestic policy. The Europeans, on the other hand, signed on to a Protocol that would direct significant changes in its industrial policy. The bubble approach somewhat conforms to epistemicism (and realism), as each state tried to minimize the impact on its own economy. Ultimately, however, one must see EU support for the Kyoto Protocol as evidence against the epistemic approach.

SUMMARY

The most striking observation in regard to these 30 years of environmental negotiations is the complete reversal of position between the United States and the European Union. Through Montreal, the EC was extremely reluctant to take steps on transboundary air pollution that led to acid rain or on preserving stratospheric ozone, despite the encouragement of Germany, Denmark, and the Netherlands. By 1990, the EC is accelerating ozone protection and calling for global measures to combat climate change. This shift in position corresponds to the enactment of the SEA, which allowed for QMV and legitimized action on environmental issues. The United States, for its part, enacted measures to protect ozone very early, although its record on acid rain was less active. Later, the United States used the same arguments

that some EC members had: there is no need to disrupt our economy by
acting quickly; we can wait until there is more scientific proof; and current
measures will be enough.

Unlike on arms control, the United States and the European Union
diverged initially on each of these agreements. Also unlike arms control,
non-EU members tended to link up with the United States. Japan, Canada,
Australia, New Zealand, Switzerland, and the former Soviet states all tended
to agree with the U.S. position on ozone and climate change. Even more
striking is the position of the Nordic states and Austria. They all supported
the U.S. position on ozone and opposed the EC's reluctance to act on
LRTAP. Norway continued this stance through Kyoto, while the others
entered the EU. While in arms control the United States tended to stand
alone against the other industrialized states, on the environment it was the
EU standing as a group for a time against the other industrialized states.

The cases in this chapter support the realist approach for the United States,
which expects the Americans to reject any agreement unless it affects others
as much as itself. The United States preemptively rejected Kyoto unless it
were to apply globally, and raised questions about its enforceability overall.
This suggests concerns that the Protocol would limit American power more
than it would others. On the other hand, the United States supported
Montreal, with its robust global application. There was less concern there
about cheating, and furthermore American industry had developed products
that would take advantage of a ban on ozone-depleting chemicals. Unlike at
Montreal, American industry did not see any benefits from Kyoto; this could
help explain why the Reagan administration accomplished more on such
global issues than did the Clinton.[145] With the LRTAP, the Americans
focused on getting credit under the agreement for prior antipollution efforts.

Evidence for realism on the part of the Europeans is not as strong in these
cases. The Europeans did not bandwagon with the United States on any of
these agreements, and they did not have the option of proceeding without
the Americans on the first two. The Europeans did exhibit suspicions that
Montreal was designed to American advantage, and there was also substantial intra-European bargaining over the distribution of limits under Kyoto.
These observations are not central, however, to applying the realist approach
in this case. More significant is the question of whether or not the EU follows through with the Kyoto Protocol. It was not on target to meet its commitments as of 2004, but a more intense effort may allow the Union to be
in compliance with Kyoto by 2012. A realist would expect that it will not
bear such costs without the United States.

Very clear evidence can be found in these cases supporting the first institutional hypothesis, that deepening the European institutions will lead them to
advocate more multilateral approaches. With weak European decision-making,
the EC could not set limits on air pollution—indeed, the institutional vetoes
were used to block such limits. European institutional reform led directly to
the air pollution breakthroughs, and European integration in general seems to
correspond to the greater support for environmental agreements in the 1990s.

The second institutional hypothesis is generally supported as well, although with the same caution that applied to the realist approach. The EU has worked diligently to have the Kyoto Protocol enter into force, knowing during its most intense efforts that the United States led by George W. Bush would not be joining the agreement. Such support for building a web of international regulation is precisely what the institutional approach expects. One remaining question is whether or not the Kyoto Protocol was so weakened by the concessions made in 2002 that it no longer represents a serious effort to address climate change. The more significant question is whether or not the Union will live up to its agreements. If it does not, then one sees a limit to the institutional approach—because under that approach, Russian abstention should not stop Europeans from implementing a program that is in the general good.

In the environmental cases, we also see support for the epistemic hypothesis in American behavior. U.S. support for Vienna and Montreal may be seen as a way of globalizing its own environmental restrictions. It also supported the LRTAP, which brought the rest of the world into compliance with its existing clean air provisions. The United States was not willing to change its laws to comply with Kyoto, which is also what the epistemic approach predicts. In this case, realist and epistemic behavior line up closely, so we would have to say that both are supported.

There is also some evidence for the epistemic approach among the Europeans, particularly in the early years. EC members were reluctant to adopt measures, like energy taxes, that might make their products uncompetitive with other members, and they did not want an international ban on ozone-depleting chemicals that they found acceptable. The EU as an organization also discouraged member state environmental policies that might have the effect of creating internal trade barriers.[146] Moving toward Kyoto, the Union agreed to take steps its members had not yet been implemented by the members. This is counter to the epistemic expectation, although once again it remains to be seen how well the member states honor this commitment. The epistemic approach would expect that they would not do so.

The pattern on environmental issues is less clear than on arms control. Kyoto may be an anomaly for the EU, or Montreal may be an anomaly for the United States. In this issue area, we have fewer issues being negotiated over a longer time period. The disagreement over Kyoto does seem to have prompted a more intense, and bitter, divergence than arms control, perhaps because it touches more closely on topics that the general public can sense. Indeed, up until the aftermath of 11 September 2001, it was probably the most publicized of these divergences in the United States. While there was a moral dimension to arms control, environmental protection may have added a layer of deeper moral imperative by touching on the deadly sins of greed, sloth, and gluttony (and perhaps just a little envy as well). Disputes over human rights involve issues that generally would touch Americans less deeply—capital punishment being the exception—but these even more intensely include a moral dimension. We turn next to these issues, in particular the ICC.

5

HUMAN RIGHTS

American policy on human rights has long been paradoxical. Few concepts are as central to American founding documents, and to the relationship of American citizens to their government, than "inalienable rights" which "Congress shall make no law" to diminish. Almost as central, however, are an intense sense of national sovereignty and suspicion of foreign powers. While the United States helped design the United Nations Human Rights Commission (UNHRC) and the Universal Declaration on Human Rights (UDHR), the United States has been reluctant to ratify treaties respecting these rights. It took 40 years for the Senate to ratify and implement the Genocide Convention, and the United States is the only country not to have ratified the 1990 Convention on the Rights of the Child (CRC), given Somalia's declaration of intent in May 2002. Perhaps then it is not surprising that when Ambassador David Scheffer returned to Washington in July 1998, having represented the United States as one of seven states to vote against the Rome Statute on an International Criminal Court (ICC), his efforts were hailed by Republicans Jesse Helms and Rod Grams and Democrats Joseph Biden and Diane Feinstein alike.[1] The Rome negotiations developed much like those in Kyoto: the United States forced many changes into a multilateral agreement, distorting it from what most European states preferred, then walked away with a single nonnegotiable demand remaining. As with Kyoto, President Clinton signed the Rome Statute (in this case on 31 December 2000, the final day on which it could be signed) and President Bush renounced any attempt to implement it. With the ICC, the United States took the extraordinary step of formally withdrawing its signature on 6 May 2002, less than a month after the required sixtieth state ratified the Statute on 11 April. Unlike with environmental issues, however, there is no Montreal Protocol to contrast with these stances. American use of the death penalty contrasts with the policies of the Council of Europe (CoE), and the International Court of Justice (ICJ) has sanctioned the United States for failing to honor foreign citizens' rights to consular aid in some such cases. In the rare cases when the United States does ratify a human rights instrument, it does so with reservations that have been rejected by several EU member states.

CASE 5.1: THE GENOCIDE CONVENTION

The ICC was not the first attempt at developing a judicial process for international crimes. Among the earliest examples was the trial of Peter von Hagenbach by the Court of the Holy Roman Empire in 1474 for "Crimes Against God and Humanity": excessive torturing of civilians. The 1815 Congress of Vienna considered establishing a court for prosecuting slave traders, but did not do so. The ICC's lineage can more directly be traced to the 1919 Paris Peace Conference, which set up a Commission on the Responsibility of the Authors of the War. No international trial was conducted, however. One objection came from the United States, which did not want to set a precedent for trying government officials internationally for acts done as part of their duties.[2] U.S. Secretary of State Robert Lansing said this properly was the job of the national military or civilian courts, and did not want to force Germany to surrender suspects.[3] The Dutch, having given asylum to Kaiser Wilhelm II, concurred; other concerns raised included the general erosion of national sovereignty over individuals, the lack of a pre-existing law that had been violated, and the detrimental effect a trial could have on post-war reconciliation.[4] In the end, the Germans tried 901 suspected war criminals in Leipzig after World War I. Of these, 888 were acquitted and the other 13 soon escaped from prison.[5]

In the absence of a preexisting criminal code, the only possible basis for international prosecution would have been a clause inserted in the 1907 Hague Convention by Feodor Martens of Russia. This stated that even if states do not adhere to the Convention, "the inhabitants and the belligerents remain under the protection and the rule of the principles of the law of nations, as they result from the usages established among civilized peoples, from the laws of humanity, and the dictates of the public conscience." While the United States did not want to invoke this after World War I, it was the basis for what otherwise would have been *ex post facto* prosecutions of Germans and Japanese after World War II. As Justice Robert Jackson noted at Nuremberg, the principle that murder is unacceptable dates back to Cain in the Western tradition.[6] Nuremberg overturned the precedent set in Paris: individuals could be held accountable, even for acts committed in an official capacity, and international law could be superior to national law in some cases. It also set a precedent for conducting a full judicial process, as opposed to the summary executions favored by the British.[7] Even so, the International Military Tribunals remained political: Emperor Hirohito was not prosecuted as Japanese leader, and trials were not held for Italian fascists.[8]

Under the mantle of "never again," the UNGA adopted the Convention on the Prevention and Punishment of the Crime of Genocide, better known as the Genocide Convention, on 9 December 1948. The United States was the first to sign it.[9] First to sign, but not one of the first to ratify. The convention entered into force in January 1951—a very rapid ratification process—but the U.S. Senate did not consent until 1986. Formal ratification waited until 1988, after implementing acts were passed by Congress. The final result, with two reservations and five understandings applied to the Convention, produced reciprocal objections by several European states. The combination of these reservations was rejected by nine European states, six EU members plus Norway, Sweden, and Finland; the Netherlands went so far as to state that it did not consider the United States to properly be a party to the Convention since its reservations so deeply contradicted its "object and purpose."[10]

Realist Approach

The long delay in ratifying the Genocide Convention fit a pattern of U.S. behavior with respect to UN criminal procedures. In the Vandenburg Amendment, the United States reserved the right to exclude itself from all cases brought before the ICJ, unless it is part of a multilateral grouping being tried as a class. The United States invoked this principle most notably on the question of clandestine mining of Nicaraguan harbors in the 1980s. The United States also asserted its unilateral right to intervene militarily to protect its interests as a Senate amendment to the 1977 Panama Canal Treaties.[11] This fits the realist expectation that the United States would resist multilateral limits on its freedom of action.

This preference was reflected in one of the American reservations, or limits to the application of the Convention, approved by the Senate. Article IX of the Genocide Convention states that disputes would be referred to the ICJ for resolution. The Senate, taking note of the ICJ's ruling in the Nicaraguan case, said this would only be permitted if the U.S. government specifically consented to it.[12] The Senate also asserted that the Genocide Convention was not self-executing; in other words, it would apply in the United States only as separately implemented by Congress after its ratification. The Proxmire Implementation Act of 1988 granted the United States jurisdiction over any crimes of genocide committed in the United States or by Americans anywhere.[13]

In addition to the reservations, the Lugar–Helms–Hatch Sovereignty Package of 1986 included five understandings, or interpretations of treaty wording that protected American sovereignty. In general these reflected an unwillingness to subject Americans to an independent, non-American court. The American Bar Association led the opposition to ratification—which had been supported by every American President—until 1976. The United States had, during the negotiation of the Convention, advocated the creation of a court to try cases of genocide. The Senate now specified that such a court would require a separate treaty establishing it. The President could not simply agree to such a court as an outgrowth of the Convention.[14] In addition, if such a Court were created, the United States would not waive its right to try its own citizens as opposed to extraditing them.[15]

The European States generally ratified the treaty by 1960. The Netherlands, Spain, and the United Kingdom followed by 1970 and Luxembourg in 1981, still ahead of the U.S. standard. Only Portugal took longer than the United States, as it did not accede to the Genocide Convention until 1999.[16] This is contrary to realist expectations for the Europeans, as they were not bandwagoning with the American position, nor were they requiring the United States to be bound by the agreement.

Epistemic Approach

Genocide of course is not permissible under either European or American law, so the epistemic approach would expect rapid ratification on both sides of the Atlantic. This generally held on the European side, but not on the American. On the other hand, the American position on the Convention took care to place in context with American law. The other reservation placed by the Senate asserted that the U.S. Constitution would have primacy over the treaty, restating a position taken by the U.S. Supreme Court in *Reid v. Covert* (1957).[17] The other understandings reflected anxiety that the Genocide Convention could be applied to American race relations, treatment of American Indians, or the conduct of the Vietnam War.[18] The Senate understood that the genocidal act of "mental harm" would mean "permanent impairment of mental faculties through drugs, torture, or similar techniques": the mental harm inflicted by experiencing segregation or other forms of discrimination would not constitute genocide.[19] With respect to Vietnam, the United States had already been "convicted" of genocide by an unofficial private tribunal. Since "killing" was an act of genocide, and since (as Senator Christopher Dodd pointed out) all war involved politically motivated killing, one could construe all war as genocide. The Senate addressed this by understanding "intent to destroy, in whole or in part" to mean "specific intent to destroy, in whole or in substantial part," and furthermore that wartime killing was not genocide unless linked to such an intent.[20]

Liberal Institutional Approach

Since the European institutions were weak when EU members ratified the Genocide Convention, the first institutional hypothesis could not operate in this case. As noted, however, one could argue that the Europeans demonstrated a willingness to accept this international restriction even without American adherence. As with the MBT, this evidence in favor on institutionalism is slightly attenuated if one notes that the Europeans had no wish to retain genocide as a foreign policy option: they were not giving something up in this case.

CASE 5.2: THE INTERNATIONAL CRIMINAL COURT

The International Law Commission (ILC) of the United Nations first drafted a statute for an ICC in 1951. The issue was dropped, however, until 1988, when Trinidad and Tobago, following up on the UN Narcotics Convention, asked the UNGA to develop a court that would prosecute the new international crime of drug trafficking.[21] Other regional states concurred, and the ILC was recommissioned to draft an ICC in 1990.[22] The United States agreed with this focus, and also wanted the court to address terrorism, given the difficulty faced in bringing the Lockerbie hijackers to justice.[23]

By the time the UNGA endorsed the ILC's work, and set up an ICC Preparatory Committee (PrepCom) in December 1995, two events had turned its focus toward genocide, war crimes, and crimes against humanity. The first of these was the Rwandan genocide of April–July 1994. The United Nations had not defended the Tutsis against their attackers—instead, the French and Belgians focused on extracting their nationals and peacekeepers from harm's way after ten Belgian soldiers were killed. Around 800,000 people were killed in about 100 days. The second was the growing awareness of the Bosnian genocide, which lasted from 1992 to 1995. 200,000 people died there, with victims and killers among all three major ethnic groups, with the UN's failure at Srebrenica in July 1995 particularly salient. Serbs led by Ratko Mladic executed some 7,000 Muslims.[24] In April 2002, the Dutch government resigned in response to its own report assigning it partial responsibility for the massacre.[25]

Prior to Srebrenica, prior even to Rwanda, the UNSC had set up International Criminal Tribunals—the first since Nuremberg. The United States proposed the first, for the Former Yugoslavia, in fall 1992. This Tribunal created the precedent that crimes against humanity under the Geneva Convention are not limited to international conflict—they could occur even in peacetime or during internal conflicts. The first trial, of Dusko Tadic, did not begin in The Hague until May 1996, nearly a year after Srebrenica and even after the Dayton peace accords had been signed. The Rwandan Tribunal in Arusha, Tanzania, was created by the UNSC in November 1994, after the genocide ended.[26] The Rwandan Tribunal's jurisdiction included only genocide, since war crimes could only occur in an international conflict. These Tribunals, under UN direction, were international in a way that Nuremberg had not been, and they included the right to appeal.[27] Ironically, Rwanda had a seat on the UNSC in 1994. Its Hutu government naturally opposed action during the genocide, but its new Tutsi government then opposed the tribunal on the grounds that it was too weak: it excluded the genocide's planning prior to 1994 and did not allow the death penalty. Rwanda was free to execute lesser criminals for their participation, but the leaders would live under international jurisdiction.[28]

Lessons from these two Tribunals helped to shape the ICC. They set a precedent for ensuring procedural legitimacy for courts. They also demonstrated the value of using court proceedings to create an official public record of the truth. On the other hand, the Yugoslav tribunal suffered for a long time from the noncooperation of the Serbian (Yugoslav) government. A future ICC thus would need to try to overcome such defiance. The ad hoc nature of the Tribunals slowed down justice—Tadic was finally sentenced in 2000—and also reduced any deterrent value. A permanent court could act more quickly, and would dispel any hope that a UNSC patron would protect a genocidal government.[29]

For a long time, the United States and EU member states generally agreed on the future shape of the Court. A 1994 draft statute required cases to be initiated by states or by the UNSC. It provided for the principle of complementarity, meaning that states would have the right to conduct their own investigation and trial prior to the ICC's involvement. It also provided for state consent over criminal jurisdiction.[30] As the PrepCom met through April 1998, however, differences of opinion arose between the United States and most EU member states in several areas: the crimes and penalties that would be included in the statute, the court's jurisdiction, the court's rules and procedures, the ability of the prosecutor to initiate cases, the role of the UNSC, and most critically, specific protections for American military personnel.

The Rome Statute includes four types of crime: genocide, war crimes, crimes against humanity, and aggression. Neither drug trafficking nor terrorism, the original focus of the UNGA, is included, although many acts committed by terrorists could fall under one of the other crimes.[31] The Convention adopted a supplemental resolution regretting that these could not yet be agreed upon.[32] India led a group seeking to criminalize the use (or even the threat) of nuclear weapons, but its motion to so amend the final statute was tabled—rejected—by a vote of 114–16.[33] The nuclear issue was finessed by including the war crime of "employing...weapons, projectiles and material and methods of warfare [which] are the subject of a comprehensive prohibition."[34] If a nuclear weapons convention is ever reached, then their use would be an international crime. "Aggression" was so controversial that it was left for the states parties to establish a definition later by a 7/8 vote (Article 121). Pending that definition, "aggression" would be defined by a vote of the UNSC in accordance with the UN Charter.[35]

The Rome Statute lists over 30 different war crimes. Among the more controversial is the prohibition of "the transfer, directly or indirectly, by the Occupying Power of parts of its own civilian population into the territory it occupies."[36] This was a main reason Israel voted against the ICC.[37] The United States did not shape the war crimes definition to entirely fit its preference. The United States had wanted war crimes to be prosecutable only if part of a plan or policy. The final draft allows jurisdiction "in particular when committed as part of a plan or policy or as part of a large-scale commission of such crimes," which leaves more room for interpretation.[38] France also pushed for such scope limits on war crimes, and was more satisfied than the United States with the final wording.[39] The United States was successful in shaping the scope of crimes against humanity. Such crimes must be "part of a widespread or systematic attack directed against any civilian population, with knowledge of the attack"; the United States advocated both the widespread threshold and the inclusion of any civilians. The United States also led the specification of various crimes against women.[40]

The extent of ICC jurisdiction became a serious issue between the United States and much of the rest of the world. Some, including Germany, pushed during the PrepComs for universal jurisdiction over all listed crimes, but there was little support for this.[41] South Korea offered four criteria for jurisdiction: the ICC could prosecute if the crime occurred on the territory of a state party, if the accused was a national of a state party, if the victim was a national of a state party, or if a state party had custody of the accused. Germany supported this provision, which was strongly endorsed by many Latin American and African states—such as Sierra Leone—for whom the concept of international crime was most vivid.[42]

The United States raised two alternatives to this proposal. One was that ratifying states should be able to opt out of ICC jurisdiction over crimes other than genocide. Russia, France, Israel, and Japan offered some support to the United States on this, but France also expressed concern about developing a "supermarket court." Ultimately, the Conference compromised in a way acceptable to France (as the strongest hold-out remaining), but not the United States—states could opt out of war crimes jurisdiction for seven years after the Court entered into force.[43]

Moving into the final negotiations in Rome, from 15 June to 17 July 1998, the participants were divided into three major groupings. The "like-minded states," about 42 in all and including most EU members as well as Norway and Canada, favored universal jurisdiction and an independent prosecutor unfettered by the UNSC. States like Mexico, India, Israel, and Nigeria were primarily concerned that the UNSC not be unduly empowered to interfere with their sovereignty. The UNSC members, on the other hand, wanted "a court controlled by the Security Council." By the time Rome began, the United Kingdom had moved into the like-minded grouping, and France and Russia chose to accept the results of negotiations. In the end, the United States would be one of seven states to vote against the Rome Statute.[44] While the vote was not officially recorded, the six others are generally accepted to be China, Iraq, Israel, Libya, Qatar, and Yemen.[45]

Scheffer returned from Rome to bipartisan thanks and congratulations from the Senate Foreign Relations committee.[46] Helms asserted that an ICC would have prosecuted U.S. actions in Libya, Panama, Grenada, and even World War II.[47] He vowed to offer no support to the ICC and to revise the U.S. relationship with its allies to ensure that Americans would be exempt from it.[48] Helms's position echoed Bolton's: "no financial support..., no collaboration..., and no further negotiations...[in order to] maximize the chances that the ICC will wither and collapse."[49] The Clinton administration did not wholly follow that advice, as it continued over the next two years to try to change provisions relating to official acts and the rights of non-ratifiers, with little success.[50] On the last day possible, 31 December 2000, Clinton signed the Rome Statute so the United States would be able to continue to "influence the evolution of the court." Given "significant flaws in the Treaty," however, he did "not recommend that my successor submit the Treaty to the Senate for advice and consent until our fundamental concerns are satisfied."[51] The ICC came into being—with that American signature "removed"—on 1 July 2002. The "un-signing" would remove the obligation under the 1969 Vienna Convention on the Law of Treaties that an unratified signatory not act in ways that undermine the "object and purpose" of the agreement. U.S. requests for exemption from ICC jurisdiction then immediately collided with renewal of the UN mission in Bosnia, and overall patterns of U.S. military aid, as discussed in chapter 1.

Realist Approach

Since the states of the EU joined the ICC without American participation, their policies do not support the realist approach—but American actions certainly do. The key issues for the United States were the related questions of jurisdiction and the vulnerability of Americans to prosecution. The United States took a hard line against the four South Korean criteria for jurisdiction. Secretary of Defense William Cohen suggested to his German counterparts that the United States would need to reconsider its role in NATO if jurisdiction were so broad, while other defense officials were rumored to be pressuring Latin American militaries to lobby their home governments. France was the closest to the U.S. position, being particularly resistant to the idea of including the "custodial" state. Not only would this increase a suspect's vulnerability to prosecution if he or she traveled to a treaty party from his own nonparty state, it would also imply a positive duty to pursue accused criminals one is hosting in exile. The victim's state was also quietly dropped, leaving jurisdiction only with the state where the crime occurred or the state of the accused's nationality. The final amendment proposed before adoption of the Statute was by Scheffer, who wanted to require *both* the crime scene and the accused's state to be parties. This was soundly tabled (113–17).[52]

At the end of these negotiations, the United States was in many ways further from its desired goals than if it had accepted the German proposal for universal jurisdiction or South Korea's four jurisdiction options.[53] For example, crimes against humanity committed by a non-party against its own people would now be off-limits to the ICC—even if nationals of a state party were included among the victims. Scheffer pointed out that in such a case, U.S. forces sent to intervene under a UN mandate, even if the United States is not a party, would be vulnerable to charges of war crimes, while the original offenders would remain immune—because the non-party could offer to accept ICC jurisdiction in a particular case. To add insult to injury, other coalition partners—treaty members—could be immune from prosecution for the same crimes if they chose the seven-year opt-out provision, as France did.[54]

The United States argued that this definition of jurisdiction imposes illegal duties on nonparties. This claim seems hard to substantiate legally or by U.S. precedent. A nonparty need not cooperate in any way with the ICC; only its nationals are vulnerable to the court if they leave the protection of their home state (or are captured initially at the scene of the alleged crime). Furthermore, the United States was willing to accept universal jurisdiction over genocide, had its Supreme Court accept universal jurisdiction over piracy in 1820 (130 years before it had an international definition), prose-cuted nationals of non-parties under the Hostage Taking Convention of 1979, and had approved an International Criminal Tribunal without Yugoslav consent.[55]

Besides the issue of exemption, which arguably was never a reasonable demand for any state, the United States also was defeated on the question of how cases could be brought before the ICC. The draft statute had said cases could be initiated by petition of a party (with case-by-case consent of the states affected) or at the referral of the UNSC. This would have essentially created a standing facility for the UNSC along the model used for Rwanda and Yugoslavia. It also would have left the balance of power in the hands of the permanent members of the UNSC, who could veto referral to an ICC. Other states preferred giving the right of initiative also to the ICC's prosecutor.[56]

In August 1997, Singapore proposed that the UNSC could vote to block an independent prosecution for periods of one year. This persuaded the United Kingdom to join other members of the EU in the like-minded group, while the other four permanent members opposed the provision.[57] U.S. executive opposition to the independent prosecutor, rooted perhaps in the vivid example of Kenneth Starr, was bolstered by Senate Foreign Relations Committee Chair Jesse Helms (R-NC) who said such a provision would make that Statute "dead on arrival" in his committee.[58] The United States was not entirely opposed to prosecutorial discretion: it had proposed that the UNSC would merely refer a situation to the ICC, leaving the pros-ecutor free to select individual cases for prosecution.[59] In this case, the inves-tigations might well turn out as in Rwanda: the leading criminals would be brought before the international court where they would receive fair treat-ment and protection from the death penalty. Lesser criminals, on the other hand, might receive harsher punishment from local courts—and the inno-cent would receive less protection.[60]

An independent prosecutor could pursue cases even if many states—including those directly involved—believe that peace and reconciliation would better be served by an amnesty.[61] This rationale applied to not indict-ing Slobodan Milosevic over Bosnia, because he was seen as needed to bring peace at Dayton.[62] On the other hand, gentle treatment of Milosevic—"trading justice for peace"—may have helped encourage him to repeat his strategy in Kosovo. Sierra Leone's Foday Sankoh provides another example of national reconciliation gone wrong.[63]

Perhaps the heart of the U.S. objection to the ICC's right of initiative is that the Court stood isolated from a political framework. Thus Scheffer told the Sixth Committee of the United Nations on 21 October 1998 that the treaty "contains flaws that render it unacceptable" despite "many provisions that the United States supports." For example, complementarity does not guar-antee that Americans would not be brought before the ICC. Even if a multilateral organization approved American action, two-thirds of the judges would suffice to bring a case into action—and any member of the UNSC could veto a resolution to defer the case.[64] Even if the judges were well intentioned, they might believe that they should appear even-handed, or at least not one-sided, in their indictments.[65] Serbia would try to bring such cases to the ICJ in May 1999 based on unlawful use of force in Kosovo, but the ICJ rejected this since Yugoslavia had not accepted jurisdiction in the past and since "the threat or use of force against a State cannot in itself constitute an act of genocide."[66]

Such attempts could continue since there would be neither constitution nor legislative language to restrict the ICC's ability to create or interpret law.[67] With the elements of crimes unspecified in the treaty, the ICC member states and judges—judges who could be from any party, including non-democratic states hostile to Western values—could define and redefine the crimes and elements to suit their own preferences. This is a departure from traditional international lawmaking by consensus.[68] Louise Arbour, the head prosecutor of the Yugoslav Tribunal criticized these fears in a speech at Harvard on 6 October 98: "An institution should not be constructed on the assumption that it will be run by incompetent people, acting in bad faith from improper purposes."[69] Perhaps one should not assume incompetence, but the assumption of bad faith and improper purpose is essentially the basis of *Federalist 51*, which argues that only checks and balances can ensure freedom:

> Ambition must be made to counteract ambition... It may be a reflection on human nature, that such devices should be necessary to control the abuses of government. But what is government itself, but the greatest of all reflections on human nature? If men were angels, no government would be necessary. If angels were to govern men, neither external nor internal controls on government would be necessary.

This basic belief illuminates Bolton's statement to the Senate, "Europeans may feel comfortable with the ICC structure, no political accountability and no separation of powers, but that is a major reason why they are Europeans and we are not."[70]

Protecting American soldiers would become a large part of the rallying cry against the ICC in the United States, culminating eventually in the July 2002 brinkmanship over renewing the UN mission in Bosnia described in chapter 1. Prosecution of individual soldiers seems unlikely, although possible. When the United States stations troops abroad, it negotiates a Status of Forces Agreement (SOFA) with the host. This typically states that the United States would have criminal jurisdiction over crimes committed by soldiers. The host country would only have jurisdiction over local crimes that were not part of the Uniform Code of Military Justice (UCMJ). This model could easily be extended to UN operations, in which the United States told Rome it is indispensable. Indeed, a SOFA is built into the ICC by the principle of complementarity—a state party has the right to investigate and try its own people before the ICC can step in. Since it is difficult to find an international crime that would not be covered under the UCMJ, American soldiers would be nearly invulnerable to the Court.[71] Furthermore, Americans arrested overseas for local crimes, including soldiers outside the SOFA protection, already are subject to local rules, and the United States even extradites to countries with somewhat different legal systems. Double jeopardy based on overruling complementarity is not a factor, since it is similar to federal cases being pursued after a local acquittal.[72]

This is not a perfect check on prosecution, however, because as a check against sham trials, the ICC could review the party's effort and deem it to have been "unwilling or unable genuinely to carry out the investigation or prosecution."[73] Even as the Rome Conference was underway, the Italian government dropped investigation of the Marines involved in the death of 20 people when their aircraft severed cable car wires at Cavalese, since the United States was pursuing the case.[74] In the Cavalese case, his court martial acquitted the pilot in March 1999.[75] Although the pilot was later dismissed from the Marines for obstructing justice by erasing a cockpit videotape; the Italian press was outraged.[76] Officially, this was accepted as a proper trial, but even two years later some informed Europeans regarded this as an example of a situation in which an ICC should assert jurisdiction.[77] With this difficulty even for low-ranking "suspects," one can see that this problem would be even more likely for political decision-makers. It would be very difficult for a state to convince the ICC that it has sincerely investigated its own leaders.[78]

The only way to provide a guarantee against prosecution for Americans is to make Americans explicitly exempt in the course of their official duties. Such an exemption does not now exist for Americans stationed overseas accused of non-UCMJ crimes.[79] This proposal was poorly received at the Conference. Botswana called it "breathtakingly arrogant," while Fiji pointed out that many states contribute soldiers to peacekeeping operations without demanding their people be exempt. Others brought up past American demands for special privilege, such as on land mines, or cited the large debt owed the United Nations by the United States. Canada reminded the Conference that it took 40 years for the United States to ratify the Genocide Convention and that the United States was the only functioning country to be holding out on the CRC.[80]

Beyond resentment of the U.S. position, such exemption would open the door to any country seeking to be exempt—this essentially was opt-out under another name. As Canadian Foreign Minister Lloyd Axworthy commented, "There are so many safeguards built into the treaty that the chances of a U.S. solider being hauled before the court are minute."[81] Bolton made it clear that was not his primary focus: "Our main concern from the U.S. perspective is not that the prosecutor will indict the occasional U.S. soldier... Our main concern should be for the President...and other senior leaders responsible for our defense and foreign policy. They are the real potential targets..."[82] U.S. officials could be investigated for their choice of strategy, as some international lawyers suggested could have been done over U.S. use of depleted uranium and targeting of water supplies during the 1999 Kosovo campaign—which did not have UN authorization.[83] Bolton pointed to the definition of aggression as a problem for both the United States and Israel, and Scheffer also called this a "major problem" since the United States must be able to "enforce international law [without being] subjected to spurious claims of violations of international law for having done so."[84] The crime of aggression could, in principle, criminalize American national leaders for deciding to use force.[85]

Such worries were by no means spurious. Amnesty International charged that "NATO forces did commit serious violations of the laws of war leading in a number of cases to the unlawful killings of civilians" during the conduct of the 1999 war in Serbia and Kosovo. These included the attack on state radio in Belgrade, and maintaining attacks on bridges despite the presence of civilians. Amnesty argued that both cluster bombs and depleted uranium shells were used without proper care, but the core issue was NATO rules of engagement. Airstrikes were conducted from high altitude, to minimize the risk of allied casualties, and the result was an inability to properly distinguish among targets. Amnesty thus called for an International Criminal Tribunal for the former Yugoslavia (ICTY) investigation of NATO behavior.[86] Helms told the UNSC during this investigation, "Any attempt to indict NATO commanders would be the death knell for the ICC...No UN institution is competent to judge the foreign policy and national security decisions of the United States."[87] ICTY prosecutor Carla Del Ponte reported back on 2 June 2000 that the evidence did not support such charges.[88]

Epistemic Approach

There are many aspects of the Rome Statute that support epistemic expectations for the United States, and not for the EU. American influence can be clearly seen in many aspects of the Court. For example, the Americans wanted to have elements of war crimes included in the Statute. Europeans, who found the concept alien to their continental law system, nevertheless accepted this in principle, as Article 9. The elements themselves, however, are left to be defined later, by two-thirds vote, and would only "assist" the court, not bind it.[89] With respect to actual court procedures, the United States succeeded in designing due process criteria similar to those found at times in the United States. Trial would be before a panel of judges, with a 2-1 vote needed to convict. U.S. courts martial are before a six-member panel, also requiring a two-thirds vote to convict. The Americans and Europeans agreed that all parties would be required to "cooperate fully" with the ICC and "surrender" persons to the court promptly. The term "surrender" was used in this context because of European national laws on extradition that might prevent the transfer of suspects.[90]

The United States did not prevail on all such issues. One significant difference from American practice is that both the defense and the prosecution would have the right to appeal.[91] Another U.S. defeat with respect to court design was in the selection of judges. The United States wanted a Nominating Committee that could select judges from anywhere in the world, but the British proposal that only parties to the ICC could nominate judges prevailed.[92]

The United States also played a constructive role in resolving a dispute over punishments. Many states, especially in the Islamic world and in the Caribbean, wanted the death penalty to be an option for international crimes; many others, including European states, insisted that it could not be an option. Scheffer helped to smooth over this problem by focusing on complementarity. Since the ICC must defer to national courts acting in good faith, any country would be free to try and execute those guilty of genocide. The single international court, however, could include only penalties accepted by all—in this case life imprisonment.[93]

There was precedent on all sides for the prosecution of foreigners for severe crimes, including foreign leaders. Shortly after the Rome Statute was signed, Augusto Pinochet Ugarte, former ruler of Chile, checked into a British hospital. His fate would speak to all sides with respect to the ICC—the danger it posed to national leaders, the difficulty in bringing such leaders to trial, and the power of a dedicated prosecutor. On 16 October 1998, a warrant for his arrest was served at the request of Spain's Balthasar Garzón, who asked the United Kingdom to extradite him for crimes against Spaniards and for violations of the 1984 Convention Against Torture (CAT). While the British Chief Justice said Pinochet had immunity for his acts as leader of a sovereign state, the House of Lords overruled him. Immunity, they said, only applied to official state functions, and customary law against torture trumped that. While Pinochet was ordered extradited on 8 October 1999, he suffered a stroke and was returned to Chile as no longer fit to stand trial.[94]

Pinochet's case was not entirely unique: the United States had denied sovereign immunity to Ferdinand Marcos in 1992, although he died during his trial for torture and murder—and unlike Pinochet, his home country did not object.[95] Panama's Manuel Noriega had been convicted by the United States, although his case differs in that he was never the *de jure* leader of his country. The United States also recognized the universal jurisdiction of the CAT in its 1994 ratification.

One more element of American opposition to the ICC also fits the epistemic approach. Since the Statute prohibits any reservations from being filed to it, the Senate would have to drop the reservations it had applied to the Genocide Convention.[96] As future Undersecretary of State John Bolton pointed out to the Senate, "the statute's definition of genocide could not be accepted by the U.S. Senate in its present form."[97] Kirsch, the Chair at Rome, responded directly to Bolton's charge that the no-reservations clause was aimed at the United States, saying that while "the contribution of the United States was uniformly useful and constructive," by the end of the Convention, "the strength of the statute had been diluted through a long series of concessions," and could not survive any more.[98] Brown was less diplomatic, writing, "The U.S. delegation...failed to show flexibility or to accept compromise on key issues...Some delegates began to wonder if the United States were really 'negotiating' at all."[99] Having prohibited amendments for seven years after EIF, the like-minded states found themselves left with all the concessions, and no U.S. ratification to show for it.[100]

Liberal Institutional Approach

These concerns about a weak court provide evidence for the institutional approach from the Europeans. They, and others, viewed the Rome Statute as weakened in order to accommodate the United States, who then still didn't join it—much like Kyoto. The entire strategy of requiring the ICC have no jurisdiction over nationals of nonparties only makes sense if the United States did not intend to ratify it. As Hans-Peter Kaul of the German Ministry of Foreign Affairs put it,

> Article 12 [jurisdiction] is relatively weak and is further weakened by the many other safeguard provisions that our American partners so successfully disturbed practically all over the Statute. It is therefore an irony that the American delegation—in my view probably the most successful delegation in Rome—was not able to vote for the Statute...In Rome a very high number of important concessions were made to the United States.[101]

The members of the EU unanimously supported the creation of the ICC, as the institutional approach would expect. Austria, speaking for the Union at Rome, noted that 13 of the 15 members signed immediately at the conclusion of the Rome Convention, and said "The European Union was extremely satisfied with the outcome." Furthermore, the EU "hoped that all states, whether or not they voted for the adoption of the Statute, would recognize the benefits of a universal criminal court."[102] The Council did not adopt a Common Position, however, until June 2001, following up on EP resolutions dating back to November 1998. In its Common Position, the Council called for "early entry into force" and vowed to raise the issue in "political dialogues with third States...whenever appropriate," in order to bring about "the widest possible ratification."[103]

All members of the Union ratified the ICC before it entered into force in 2002. As discussed in the introduction, the Europeans were shocked at the U.S. "unsigning" of the Statute in May of that year, and further outraged by the American attempt to block renewal of the UN peacekeeping missions if it was not granted immunity. The EU was willing to accept this international court without the United States, in the clearest major support for the institutional approach. While the Council made concessions to the American position on immunity and on Article 98 agreements, these can best be seen as compromises—and not very large ones—in the name of preserving the ICC and other international goals. The only caveat to the institutional approach is in the Belgian retreat—under pressure from other Europeans—from its law of universal jurisdiction, and also the French use of the seven-year exemption from war crimes. Even the Belgian case, however, can be seen as rejection of a unilateral approach to war crimes.

CASE 5.3: CONVENTIONS ON THE RIGHTS
OF WOMEN AND CHILDREN

The Genocide Convention was not the only international human rights convention that the United States was slow to ratify—indeed, it is one of the few that the United States has ratified at all. The United Nations adopted the Convention on the Elimination of All Forms of Discrimination Against Women (CEDAW) in December 1979. In the initial stages, both the United States and Western European states favored the measure.[104] After work began on the Convention in 1974, however, it quickly became tied to other issues. During the 1975 conference in Mexico City, the CEDAW was linked to the New International Economic Order (NIEO), the Charter of Economic Rights and Duties of States, the Panama Canal Zone, tribal war, and apartheid; and an additional declaration was proposed to equate Zionism with racism. The United States, Denmark, and Israel voted against the final Declaration of Mexico City, while other Western countries abstained.[105] When the CEDAW got to the UNGA in 1979, most Western states abstained from the preamble, which linked women's rights to "apartheid, colonialism, and nuclear disarmament."[106]

While the CEDAW does not seem to be high on the long list of transatlantic disagreements, it symbolizes how additional issues at times have sidled onto the UN human rights agenda. At a 1985 follow-up conference in Nairobi, for example, the United States fought nearly alone (and unsuccessfully) to decouple the convention from apartheid and the NIEO, and against special recognition for Palestinian women. The United States did avoid a vote once again to link Zionism with racism by getting the chair to rule it out preemptively.[107] A full history of the Zionism-racism equation lies beyond the scope of this book, but the issue reappeared at the 31 August–8 September 2001 United Nations Conference Against Racism, Racial Discrimination, Xenophobia and Related Intolerance, better known by its location in Durban, South Africa.

After the CEDAW, the next major group human rights convention was the CRC, which was adopted by the UNGA in November 1989 and entered into force less than a year later. The CRC developed from the 1959 Declaration of the Rights of the Child and a similar Declaration by the League of Nations in 1924. The CRC is as close to a universal convention as one can find: with Somalia's 10 May 2002 signature and declaration of intent to ratify, only the United States has not ratified it (it signed in 1995).[108]

The provision of the CRC that most directly affects transatlantic relations concerns the status of children as soldiers—protecting them from the horrors of war as opposed to allowing them to seek self-fulfillment in battle.[109] In general, the CRC establishes 18 as the age of adulthood, but Article 38 sets the minimum age for soldiers at 15—leaving intact, however, Article 32's barring children from "any work that is likely to be hazardous . . . or to be harmful to the child's health . . ."[110] Sweden led the fight for a higher limit, joined by Belgium, Austria, and Germany, while the United Kingdom, United States, and Canada joined the Soviet Union in the successful effort to leave the age at 15.[111]

Those states wanting a higher age developed an Optional Protocol on Child Soldiers, beginning in 1994. While the goal was to set an absolute minimum age of 18, negotiations focused on setting a minimum age for recruitment, the status of schools and training programs, and applicability of the Protocol to non-state actors.[112] The compromise reached in January 2000, suiting the demands of the United States and United Kingdom, was to allow voluntary recruitment at age 16 but no "direct part in hostilities" or "compulsory recruitment" under the age of 18. Non-state actors are forbidden even from recruiting soldiers under the age of 18. Adopted by the UNGA in May 2000, the Optional Protocol entered into force on 12 February 2002.

Epistemic Approach

For the most part, state positions on both the CEDAW and CRC reflect their own national standards. For example, while the European states had tended to criticize the United States for the reservations it placed against other human rights agreements, European monarchies tended to place reservations against the CEDAW regarding the rules for succession. All members of the EU ratified the CEDAW by 1991.[113] On 30 July 2002, the Senate Foreign Relations Committee voted to send CEDAW to the Senate, despite opponents' concerns about the status of women in combat, income based on a comparable worth standard, and rights such as paid maternity leave and free family planning services.[114]

Epistemic principles are also reflected in the framing of the CRC. Abortion was one very contentious issue, resolved ambiguously by noting that children have needs both before and after birth. Germany and Italy favored that, while Denmark, the Netherlands, Norway, and Sweden were among many countries advocating for a clear statement that the CRC only applied after birth. Both the United Kingdom and France made declarations upon ratification that they read the CRC as placing no restrictions on abortion.[115] In recent years, this topic has tended to more strictly divide the United States from Europe. At the Child Summit in May 2002, the United States argued against the European desire to include the term "reproductive health services," which could include abortion and contraceptives. Among those supporting the U.S. position were some Islamic and African countries, including Libya, Syria, and Sudan.[116] Along with access to abortion or contraception, the CRC is silent on issues relating to gender, such as sex-selection abortions and female infanticide, child prostitution, and female genital mutilation (clitoridectomy).[117]

Debate also arose over rights to government services. The Netherlands, United States, and United Kingdom all opposed including a right to free education, while the United States particularly opposed a right to free health care. The United States promoted children's civil rights, while Norway, Sweden and the United Kingdom preferred that these rights be limited according to the "evolving capacities of the child," like many other rights.[118] The United Kingdom is among those who disagree that the CRC prohibits corporal punishment, and this would no doubt be an additional issue for the United States.[119] This issue may remain active in Europe, since the European Court of Human Rights has used the CRC to elaborate on areas not clearly addressed in the European Convention on Human Rights.[120]

While the United States has not ratified the CRC, the Child Soldiers Protocol was ruled open even to mere signatories. The U.S. rationale for its position against a 15-year-old age limit went against its own practice, which is to allow enlistment at age 17 only with parental consent. The United States also avoids deploying 17-year-olds to combat. The United States raised a point of legal principle. The age 15 limit is found in the 1977 Additional Protocol to the Geneva Convention, and the United States preferred not using human rights law to amend international humanitarian law.[121] The protocol fit American preferences, and on 19 June 2002 the Senate consented (unanimously) to the Child Soldiers Protocol and the less controversial Optional Protocol on the sale of children, child prostitution and child pornography, without reservations. The Senate did set forth understandings that this would not bind the United States to the CRC or the ICC. Not all EU members had completed their ratifications at that point, although it is too soon to suggest that any of them are reluctant to do so.

Liberal Institutional Approach

With the European states divided in their interpretations of the CEDAW and CRC, the institutional hypothesis that the Union would encourage unity on this point are not borne out. One institutional effect may be seen, however, in that many European states have prohibited corporal punishment of children since the CRC took effect. The other institutional hypothesis does receive support, since the Europeans have accepted these conventions even though the United States has not.

We do see support for the first institutional hypothesis in a related area. The 2001 Durban Conference ended up becoming dominated by two topics: reparations for the transatlantic slave trade and whether Israel should be condemned as being inherently racist. Both the United States and Israel walked out of the conference on 3 September, but the EU delegation worked to delete language that condemned Israel—leaving in statements acknowledging the "plight of the Palestinian people under foreign occupation."[122] The EU delegation even threatened to follow the United States out of the conference if condemnations of Israel were not eliminated.[123] On the question of reparations, the EU again worked to deflect the matter. While both slavery and colonialism were condemned, the recommended solution to the damage caused was development assistance in the form of "debt relief, poverty eradication, building or strengthening democratic institutions,

promotion of foreign direct investment and market access."[124] The EU
added, "The declaration and the program of action are political, not legal
documents. These documents cannot impose obligations or liability or a
right to compensation on anyone. Nor are they intended to do so."[125] In
short, the EU succeeded in rewording the Durban conference declaration
into conformance with U.S. preferences.[126] While it is understandable that
this EU victory on 8 September 2001 quickly was overshadowed by other
events, Durban represents a significant victory both for the EU and for the
EU's preferred style of bargaining.

Realist Approach

The realist hypothesis for the Europeans, that they would bandwagon with
the American position, is not supported in these conventions. All the
Europeans ratified them, even if they occasionally raised questions about
them. As realists would expect, however, the United States opposed these
multilateral agreements on the grounds of maintaining its own internal
sovereignty.

CASE 5.4: DEATH PENALTY

If the ICC is the most complex and most public transatlantic disagreement
on human rights, American use of the death penalty is the most visceral. Few
responsible commentators would argue that the United States opposed the
ICC because it favors war crimes or failed to ratify the Genocide Convention
for many years because it supports genocide. The death penalty, however, is
more like Kyoto or the Small Arms Program of Action in allowing an argument to be made that Europeans and Americans differ on fundamental values. All EU member states have abolished the death penalty, which is also a
membership criterion for the CoE. On 4 October 1994, the CoE adopted
Resolution 1044, which stated "the death penalty has no legitimate place in
the penal systems of modern civilized societies."[127] In the United States,
according to Amnesty International, over 3,700 prisoners were on death row
at the beginning of 2002, with 749 executions since 1977—66 of them in
2001, including Oklahoma City bomber Timothy McVeigh.[128] Of
McVeigh's execution, Lord Russel-Johnston, president of the Council of
Europe's Parliamentary Assembly, said it was "sad, pathetic, and wrong."[129]
    Initially, the death penalty might not seem to most Americans as fitting
within this book's framework of multilateral agreements. It is a difference
between European and American practice, but this book does not claim to
address every such difference. Yet this difference is embedded in international agreements. Besides appearing in the punishment debates over the
ICC and the Yugoslav and Rwandan Tribunals, references to the death
penalty can be traced back to the UDHR and are implemented in an
Optional Protocol to the International Covenant on Civil and Political
Rights (ICCPR). Besides the general opposition to the death penalty,

Europeans (and others) protest violations of Article 36 of the Vienna Convention on Consular Relations, which gives prisoners the right to consular assistance in preparing for their case, with an associated state responsibility to inform the prisoner of that right.

The UDHR, passed in 1948, does not explicitly address the death penalty. The first rights it lists are "life, liberty, and security of person."[130] Some see this as implicitly arguing against the death penalty; its silence is a compromise between those who wanted to call for a ban, which many states would have rejected, and allowing for the death penalty, which would have undercut eventual abolition.[131] Article 29 makes it clear that none of these rights were absolute—else prisons would violate the right to "liberty"—but that the rights "shall be subject only to such limitations as are determined by law solely for the purpose of securing due recognition and respect for the rights and freedoms of others and of meeting the just requirements of morality, public order and the general welfare in a democratic society."

The agreements that followed this nonbinding declaration, such as the 1953 ECHR and the 1966 ICCPR, accepted the death penalty as long as it was imposed in a nonarbitrary manner. They imposed limits, however, on its use. As a common standard, the ICCPR prohibits the execution of pregnant women or anyone convicted of a crime committed before they turned 18 years old. It allows the death penalty only for "the most serious crimes." It also prohibits inhuman or degrading punishment in its Article 7. In the UNGA, Colombia, Uruguay, Italy, and Finland were among those who wanted an outright ban on executions, but France led the pragmatic argument that such a ban would lead to fewer states ratifying the Convention. Instead, Article 6 on the death penalty begins its list of limits with "in countries which have not abolished the death penalty..." and concludes with "nothing in this article shall be invoked to delay or to prevent the abolition of capital punishment."[132]

This abolition movement grew in strength during the 25 years after World War II throughout the West. Norway, Sweden, and the Netherlands had prohibited peacetime executions even before World War II. By 1972 they had been joined by Denmark, Italy, and Portugal; the sentence had been unconditionally ended also in Austria, Finland, and (West) Germany. These figures hid a deeper trend: legal or not, the only future EU members to have carried out an execution after 1964 were Franco's Spain, the colonels' Greece, and democratic France.[133] Belgium was one of the last to formally ban it, in 1998, but its prior use of the death penalty were for World War II and Holocaust collaborators. The last ordinary Belgian criminal executed was in 1917, under the principle that mere prison was too light a punishment during wartime.[134] While the United Kingdom would not fully end the death penalty until 1998, it had in 1965 limited its application to cases such as "treason, piracy, and committing adultery with the wife of the monarch's eldest son."[135] Even if legally allowed, such cases were not penalized by death. In addition to moral opposition to executions, the European position also reflected nervousness about giving such power over life and death to the government. In that context, it seems a bit ironic that this concern is not shared by the Americans who worry about genocide investigations and runaway ICC prosecutors.

The trend in the United States had been similar. By 1972, 12 states had ended the death penalty, beginning with Michigan in 1846.[136] As in Europe, legality did not equal practice. Luis Monge, in Colorado on 2 June 1967, was the last execution up to that time, and was the only execution in the United States that year. Popular sentiment in 1966 was 42 percent in favor, 47 percent opposed.[137] As early as 1963, Supreme Court Justice Arthur Goldberg had said that the Eighth Amendment criteria for "cruel and unusual punishment" must meet "evolving standards," including international views.[138] This set the stage for *Furman v. Georgia*, 30 June 1972, in which the U.S. Supreme Court found the application of the death penalty from state to state and case to case to be "arbitrary and capricious." The Court ruled that mandatory death penalties were unconstitutional, that the death penalty could only be imposed for murder, and mandated an appeals process. With that, over 600 sentences were commuted nationwide.[139]

France was the slowest to move on the death penalty through the early 1970s. While sentiment toward abolition grew through the 1960s, the public demanded the death penalty for two prisoners who executed prison guards they had taken hostage. The sentence was imposed on the same day as *Furman v. Georgia*, and carried out five months later. A few other executions were carried out through 10 September 1977, the last executions in Western Europe, but the turning point in France came in January of that year. A jury convicted a man of kidnapping and murdering a child, which provoked a public outcry similar to other cases, demanding death. Even though the suspect had himself suggested that someone guilty of such a crime deserved execution, the jury gave Patrick Henri neither liberty nor death, but rather life in prison. France abolished the death penalty in 1981.[140]

Reaction in the United States to *Furman*, however, defied this pattern. Within four years, 35 states and the federal government had rewritten their death penalty statutes to try to address the Court's concerns. In *Gregg v. Georgia*, 1976, the Court ruled that death penalties imposed on the basis of specified aggravating and mitigating circumstances met its standards, and were not inherently "cruel and unusual."[141] Gary Mark Gilmore was the first to be executed under the new rules, on 17 January 1977 by a Utah firing squad—four days before Henri's sentence in France. While three more states and the District of Columbia would go on to end the death penalty, four states restored it, maintaining the pre-*Furman* balance.[142] While the Court did say that the insane could not be executed in 1986, the mentally retarded could be. There have been 35 such executions since the death penalty was restored, including Ricky Ray Tucker, whose death warrant Governor Bill Clinton left the campaign trail in 1992 to sign. By that time, support for the death penalty in America had risen to 70 percent.[143]

Opposition in Europe, on the other hand, became even deeper. On 7 July 1989, the ECHR identified "Death Row phenomenon" in *Soering v. UK*.

Jens Soering was a German national who fled to the United Kingdom after committing murder in the United States. The United Kingdom was willing to extradite him, since at the time the death penalty remained legal there. The ECHR overruled the British position, stating that simply being on death row—awaiting death for an indeterminate amount of time—itself amounted to inhuman and degrading punishment, which would violate Soering's rights. Ultimately, the Commonwealth of Virginia agreed not to charge Soering with capital murder, so he was extradited, convicted, and sentenced to 99 years in prison. A later case, *Joy Aylor-Davis v. France*, 20 January 94, addressed the issue of extradition more directly. Since France had abolished the death penalty, it resisted extradiction to the United States. The ECHR ruled that a Texas prosecutor's promise not to seek the death penalty for Aylor-Davis would be sufficient to allow his return to the United States.[144] This policy, of not extraditing suspects if they could receive a death penalty, has become general among the EU members, and has also begun to include resisting mutual legal assistance with criminal investigations such as that of suspected al-Qaeda terrorist Zacarias Moussaoui if the accused could face death if convicted using European-provided evidence.[145]

Realist Approach

Initially, both European states and the United States resisted multilateral restrictions on the death penalty. As early as 1959, Austria and Sweden sponsored a UN study of the death penalty, but France and the United Kingdom opposed the 1962 results as interference in sovereign affairs.[146] In 1980, debate began on a Second Optional Protocol to the ICCPR, which would abolish the death penalty. The United States and United Kingdom were opposed, although the American position, consistent with realism, was that "it would have no reason to object if other countries wished to adopt and accede to the draft Protocol." By the time this Protocol was adopted, in December 1989, the remaining opposition came from Japan, China, many Islamic and Caribbean states, and the United States. All then and future EU members voted in favor.[147]

The abolition movement then moved back to the UNHRC. In 1994, Italy sponsored a resolution calling for a moratorium on the death penalty, which was supported by Germany, speaking for the EU. The resolution failed that year, as Singapore inserted an amendment affirming that states had the right to punish criminals as they deemed appropriate—which undercut the spirit of the resolution.[148] Italy was more successful in 1997, fending off amendments and then U.S. opposition to the resolution itself. The United States argued that in the past, UNHRC resolutions had been based on universally accepted standards, which did not exist for the death penalty. Furthermore, Italy was ignoring states' sovereign rights—but this would not be the first time the UNHRC had done so.[149] The resolutions became annual, and were accompanied by similar EU calls for a moratorium and also by a 1998 UNHRC report that criticized the United States for executing children and the mentally disabled, for racial disparities in executions, and for not following its obligations under the ICCPR. Helms called the report "an absurd UN charade," and U.S. Ambassador to the United Nations Bill Richardson said it would simply "collect a lot of dust."[150]

Epistemic Approach

The ICCPR is the only broad human rights agreement that has been ratified by the United States. When it consented on 8 September 1992, however, the Senate placed reservations against both Articles 6 and 7, which included statements limiting the death penalty to severe crimes, prohibiting its arbitrary imposition, and prohibiting torture (the United States did later, in 1994, ratify the Convention against Torture and Other Cruel, Inhuman or Degrading Treatment or Punishment). As a practical matter, the U.S. Constitution already prohibits cruel and unusual punishment, conviction without due process of law, and the U.S. Supreme Court had by then prohibited the death penalty for all but the most severe crimes—so this reservation amounted only to maintaining the ability to execute people for crimes committed when juveniles.[151] As in the other human rights cases, the American position reflects an unwillingness to accept multilateral treaties that largely conform to pre-existing American standards. European states objected to the American reservations against the ICCPR. Eleven, primarily members of the EU, argued the reservations were "essentially incompatible with the spirit of ratification of the Convention."[152] The UNHRC concurred that the U.S. reservations were invalid in March 1995, leading Congress to threaten to cut off the Commission's funds.[153]

The juvenile standard is significant, however, because American practice was very different from the European. In *Thompson v. Oklahoma* (1988), the Court recognized "the lesser culpability of the juvenile offender, the teenager's capacity for growth, and society's fiduciary obligations to its children" in overturning the sentence of a 15-year-old, but the following year in *Stanford v. Kentucky* said sentences for crimes committed by 16-year-olds were acceptable in a national context. This directly contradicted the CRC, which exempted children under 18 from executions, or even from a sentence of life without parole.[154] Two hundred such death sentences have been imposed, with the United States accounting for half of the world's 18 executions for juvenile crimes from 1990 to 1998.[155] The U.S. standard was joined only by Iran, Nigeria, Pakistan, and Saudi Arabia.[156]

Two judicial rulings in summer 2002 began to push the United States closer to European practices. The more conclusive of the two came on 20 June 2002, when the U.S. Supreme Court ruled that execution of the mentally retarded was "cruel and unusual," and thus violated the Eighth Amendment to the Constitution. *Atkins v. Virginia* overturned *Penry v. Lynaugh* (1989) on the grounds that a national consensus had grown against it: while only 2 states prohibited such executions in 1989, 18 did in 2002 (along with the 12 states that prohibit executions altogether). Justice John

Paul Stevens wrote, "It is not so much the number of these states that is significant, but the consistency of the direction of the change." Dissenters argued that the persistence of the punishment in the remaining 20 states suggested that their publics did not find it cruel or unusual; as for international standards, Chief Justice William Rhenquist wrote, "The viewpoints of other countries simply are not relevant."[157] This viewpoint had been stated by Oliver Nette of the European Commission's delegation to the United States, who noted, "The European Union has a longstanding policy against the death penalty. We also have a more specific policy of intervening in cases of people facing the death penalty if they were a minor, if they are mentally deficient, and third, if they were a foreign national unable to contact their home nation."[158]

It would be inaccurate, however, to say that views on the death penalty are radically different at the grassroots level. When France abolished it in 1981, 62 percent of the public favored its retention.[159] One year after the United Kingdom ended most common applications of the death penalty in 1964, 76 percent wanted it restored—and the number went up to 82 percent by 1975.[160] While these numbers have dropped somewhat since then, public support has remained near 50 percent in Italy, France, and Sweden, and over 65 percent in the United Kingdom. The ending of the death penalty in Europe would seem then to be an elite-driven enterprise, as opposed to a deeply held cultural difference—although their positions nevertheless support the epistemic approach, since the Europeans are internationalizing domestic positions.[161] In the meantime, support for the death penalty in the United States was also down to 65 percent in mid-2002, with a majority favoring a moratorium on executions.[162] Such a moratorium was imposed on 31 January 2000 by Republican Governor George Ryan of Illinois after 13 people on death row were found to be innocent out of a total population of 159 (12 convicts had been executed since 1977); Maryland followed suit in May 2002.[163] On 11 January 2003, Ryan took this a step further, as he commuted the sentences of the remaining death row inmates.[164]

The more dramatic U.S. judicial ruling came on 1 July 2002, when a U.S. district court ruled that the entire federal death penalty was unconstitutional. While the ruling would only apply to federal cases brought in Connecticut, Vermont, and New York, it suggested a potential change in judicial thought that mirrored the Illinois and Maryland moratoria. Rather than arguing from an Eighth Amendment standpoint of cruel or unusual punishment, the case suggests an inherent violation of due process that had not been anticipated by prior rulings. People had assumed that convictions of innocent people were rare, but with 100 or so such exonerations in recent years, it is "fully foreseeable that in enforcing the death penalty, a meaningful number of innocent people will be executed who otherwise would eventually be able to prove their innocence." Because this ruling is not based on anything specific to the federal death penalty, the argument could be applied to the state death penalties that dominate the landscape: only 27 of the 3,700 or so convicts on death row are in the federal version, and only two of them had been executed as of June 2001.[165]

Liberal Institutional Approach

Actions by the Europeans support both aspects of the institutional approach. While the death penalty had fallen into disuse, except in France, European initiatives led to its formal prohibition. The CoE adopted Protocol 6 to the ECHR in 1983, which prohibited executions or death sentences except in wartime.[166] All EU members have ratified Protocol 6, although some did not do so until 1998 or 1999. Turkey, as part of its quest to join the EU, has also limited the peacetime death penalty to acts of terrorism or acts against the state, and in 2002 began steps to eliminate those cases as well. Only Kurd leader Abdullah Ocalan was on the Turkish death row, which has not seen an execution since 1984.[167]

Since prohibition of the death penalty is now a criterion for membership in the CoE, all 41 European members have at least a moratorium on the death penalty.[168] The United States and Japan, observers in the CoE, were anomalies to that standard—as pointed out by Ukraine and Russia as they changed their laws to comply with CoE rules. On 25 June 2001, the Parliamentary Assembly of the CoE passed Resolution 1253, which "requires Japan and the United States of America: i) to institute without delay a moratorium on executions, and take the necessary steps to abolish the death penalty; and ii) to improve conditions on 'Death Row' immediately, with a view to alleviating 'Death Row phenomenon:'" Without such progress by 1 January 2003, the CoE was to reevaluate their observer status. They did not, and in April 2003 Renate Wohlwend, leader of the effort, was saying that the issue of revoking American observer status would now wait until September. She applauded Ryan's steps in Illinois, but said that progress in Congress was slow: "There hasn't been any notable progress along the lines we advocated in the resolution we adopted in summer 2001—which Washington totally ignored. If we want the Council to stay credible, we need to think very seriously about the next step."[169]

Another area where the Union strongly defends international law as it relates to the death penalty is the right to consular access. Under Article 36 of the Vienna Convention on Consular Relations, prisoners have the right to consular access when detained by law enforcement, and the custodial state has the duty to inform the prisoner of that right. Amnesty International has tracked 10 cases of Europeans subject to the death penalty who were not so informed. Two such were Karl and Walter LaGrand, who did not realize the relevance of their German birth until well after their murder convictions. Germany's late intervention into the appeals process did not prevent Karl's 24 February 1999 execution in Arizona. On 2 March, Germany asked for, and the next day received, an injunction from the ICJ "that the United States should take all measures at its disposal to ensure that Walter LaGrand was not executed pending a final decision of the Court." On that same day, Walter LaGrand was executed. Germany persisted with its case, and the ICJ ruled on 27 June 2001 that "the United States has breached its obligations to Germany and to the LaGrand brothers under the Vienna Convention."[170]

A similar fate had befallen Paraguayan Ángel Breard, executed 14 April 1998 in Virginia after the U.S. Supreme Court disregarded another ICJ ruling that his Vienna Convention rights had been violated.[171] As a result, the EP asked the Commission to assess U.S. procedures and their compliance with international law.[172] On 31 March 2004, the ICJ issued a similar ruling, this time involving 51 Mexicans on American death rows.

SUMMARY

If there is a global norm for human rights, it is a European norm more than an American one. The U.S. position on the death penalty most closely corresponds to that of countries whose policies it otherwise routinely condemns. The U.S. official position on women's rights is again joined not by its European allies but primarily by Islamic states, including ones that it accuses of promoting terrorism. With regard to children's rights, the United States simply stands alone. This is not to say that the United States in any way should be singled out as an abuser of women's and children's rights—many of the states parties to the CEDAW and CRC fail to honor their commitments. That, however, makes the American abstention from these agreements that much harder to understand. In arms control, the United States changed its preferences on chemical weapons and nuclear testing in moving toward international agreements. With environmental treaties, the United States has tended to try to codify its own practices but not change in the face of international positions. With human rights, the United States tends to decline even from enacting its own practice—as seen in its reservations to the ICCPR on cruel and unusual punishment. The result, in general, has been that the EU's preferences have been enacted and American ones have not—except for the Child Soldiers Protocol to the CRC, one of the few agreements the United States favored.

In human rights, as in the other areas studied so far, American behavior corresponds to what a realist would expect. Rather than being a limit on pure power, most human rights agreements suggest a limit to sovereignty. The United States resists restrictions on its internal autonomy, under the apparent belief that other states—even if they signed the agreements—would not be equally bound. American support for the International Criminal Tribunals demonstrates that the United States is not opposed to punishing human rights violators. American opposition to the ICC and the Senate debates over the Genocide Convention and the conventions on women's and children's rights suggest that the United States is hesitant to subject itself to outside scrutiny. The death penalty is also shielded from external review.

EU behavior, on the other hand, does not correspond very well to realism in the area of human rights. The one major exception to this is on the lower age limit set for child soldiers, for which some European states joined the United States in carving out exemptions for their own current recruiting and training policies. In other cases, European states accepted human rights conventions even though the United States declined to be bound by these. In particular, the EU and its members have strongly supported the ICC, which places external constraints on their own militaries without constraining the United States to the same degree.

Thus we see that the second institutional hypothesis is strongly supported in this issue area. This is clearest of course for the ICC, which the EU has ratified despite the American refusal to do so. While some European states have been receptive to the Article 98 exemptions for the United States, in some ways that can be seen as further support for institutional explanations. One can argue that exempting Americans weakens the ICC, but as a practical matter the Europeans had no choice but bow to the reality of American noncooperation. Instead, the Europeans have chosen to bind themselves with an international court that now even less closely restricts the United States. The Europeans also led the way to ratifying the other human rights agreements, knowing or at least assuming that the United States would not do so nearly as rapidly.

The first institutional hypothesis, that the European institutions should lead the way to multilateral solutions, is also supported. The Europeans have strongly supported the ICC, as well as the movement for national abolition of the death penalty and the rights of children. In some cases, the institutions have not been the EU itself, but that should not penalize the hypothesis. European states have adopted international agreements and altered their domestic policy to conform to them. This is most clear in the death penalty extradition cases, where the ECHR took precedence over national sovereignty. In addition, the Europeans remained at Durban after the United States walked out, ensuring that an agreement could be reached.

For these reasons, however, the epistemic approach is not supported by either American or European behavior. This is not meant to suggest that changing ideas and values have no role to play in human rights. Changing beliefs about proper ways to punish criminals have affected policy both in Europe and the United States. We are not trying to explain, however, why death penalty rules have changed. We are trying to explain transatlantic divergence, and in this case we do not see the internationalization of domestic policy. The United States has resisted international agreements even where its own domestic record is far superior to those of other signatories. The reservations to the Genocide Convention stand out in particular, but the United States also withheld approval of international restrictions on cruel and unusual punishments that would be prohibited under its Constitution already. Even with the ICC, most of the criminal code adopts American standards for military justice. In Europe, on the other hand, the multilateral agreements often went beyond national policy. Domestic changes were made to meet international standards on the death penalty and the rights of children. The ICC presented Europeans with new requirements for extraditing—surrendering—their citizens to an external court, which they accepted.

The mid-2002 ratification of the CRC's Optional Protocols and the *Atkins* decision suggest some movement by the United States in the direction of international human rights agreements. On the other hand, the

United States continues to be apathetic with respect to the CoE's position on the death penalty and to the CEDAW and CRC in general. Its position on the ICC goes well beyond apathy, as it has worked to ensure that it does not apply to Americans. The United States may eventually decide to ratify the conventions, but it seems unlikely to change its position on the ICC or even on the death penalty in general—further restrictions, if any, on the death penalty will be drawn from domestic sources rather than international law. There is far more cooperation on military matters, as described in the next chapter. The death penalty, however, has begun to interfere with U.S. efforts against terrorism, while opposition to the ICC has called into question U.S. commitment to international peacekeeping—providing, perhaps, greater impetus for the EU to develop its own military capability.

6

MILITARY COOPERATION

Each of the three previous chapters featured a large multilateral conference held in a major world city: Oslo, Kyoto, Rome. At each of these conferences, the United States failed to bring a treaty text into full compliance with its preferences, and each time opposition to the U.S. position was led by the EU and its member states. The closest analogy in the area of military cooperation, in contrast, is the French–British joint declaration at the French town of St. Malo on 4 December 1998. At St. Malo, almost one year to the day after the signing of the MBT and the Kyoto Protocol, the United Kingdom dropped its long-standing opposition to creating an EU defense capability. Over the next several years, this capability would be enthusiastically endorsed by the EU. St. Malo is not a defeat for the United States in the same way as the other agreements, since the United States had no formal voice in this internal EU decision and the evolution of the force held fairly closely to American preferences. Nevertheless, it signifies a shift toward European solidarity in security cooperation, an area in which American dominance has been most manifest.

These cases on military cooperation are presented last because they are in many ways different from those of the other three chapters. The earlier cases focused on negotiating a specific multilateral agreement to address a problem of global relevance. This chapter describes the process of conducting a military action or of transforming an international organization. Multilateralism appears either in seeking authorization for military action or achieving consensus within an organization. The problems are also more tied to a specific location than in the other chapters, although they are seen as local manifestations of a general global concern with arms control, human rights, or international peace and security. These cases are also more difficult to separate from one another. NATO transformation and the development of a European Security and Defence Policy (ESDP) overlap in time with the specific conflicts. Despite these contrasts, these cases must be included in this book because in the final analysis NATO is the one major institution that is specifically transatlantic. NATO and military cooperation are why the United States and much of Europe are labeled as "allies."

We will begin and end in Iraq. Iraq's invasion and annexation of Kuwait in August 1990 made salient the changes in the international system that had begun with the Eastern European revolutions of the previous year. The acquiescence of the Soviet Union to UN collective action against its client symbolizes the end of the Cold War as much as any other event. The need for collective defense against the Soviet Union had helped to create the transatlantic alliance, and that sense of a common threat helped sustain it throughout the Cold War. Yet that 40-year "war" was in many ways actually a long peace for Europe.[1] Now for the first time since Korea the allies fought together. The crises in Croatia and in Bosnia-Herzegovina[2] brought post–Cold War security cooperation into focus. The diverging role of the European Union and United States in the Balkans through mid-1995 showed Europeans the risks of conducting diplomacy without the military power to back it up, confirming Frederick the Great's warning, "Diplomacy without armaments is like music without instruments."[3] In the meantime, NATO's structure and purpose were being reassessed. The alliance was adding new members to the East and creating a capability for members to act in coalitions of the willing under NATO supervision even if the United States declined to participate. Through this period, the United States maintained its authoritative role. Even after St. Malo, the Kosovo intervention reconfirmed U.S. leadership. As U.S. attention shifted in 2001 to Afghanistan, and then back to Iraq, the nature of military cooperation between it and European states began to change significantly. As noted at the beginning of this book, disagreement over the 2003 war in Iraq brought transatlantic differences to everyone's attention.

CASE 6.1: THE AFTERMATH OF
ÐESERT STORM

This case focuses on the long aftermath of the 1991 Gulf War, rather on the war itself, which is a poor fit for this book. The UN-authorized response addressed a local case of simple aggression. Its aftermath invoked more general values of non-proliferation, protection of minorities, and sustained enforcement of UN resolutions. During the war, the Europeans followed the American lead, and the EC as such did not influence the war. France, the United Kingdom, and the United States all agreed that Iraq had been weakened enough that sanctions could finish the job without continuing the war in 1991.

Saddam Hussein did not fall from power then, however, and he used his surviving military and helicopter forces to quickly put down a Kurdish rebellion in the north. In response, the UNSC passed Resolution 688 on 5 April 1991, calling for an end to internal oppression in Iraq. This resolution would become the basis for the no-fly zones later set up in both northern and southern Iraq by the United States, United Kingdom, and France without further consultation with the UNSC. More immediately, the resolution led to humanitarian relief for Kurds along the Turkey-Iraq border. UNSC 687 set conditions for lifting comprehensive sanctions on Iraq, including acceptance of the Kuwaiti border and demonstration of disarmament to UNSCOM. The IAEA would inspect Iraqi facilities for compliance with the NPT. Finally, Iraq was required to set up a compensation fund to make reparations for damages to its neighbors and the environment. Iraq accepted these provisions under duress, noting bitterly that Israel had never complied with UNSCR 487 in 1981, which called for similar safeguards and compensation after it destroyed Iraq's nuclear facility at Osirak.[4]

The United States and Europe remained united with respect to Iraq for quite some time, as Saddam's poor behavior and intransigence were evident. France and the United Kingdom joined the United States in air raids against Iraq in January 1992 after surface-to-air missile (SAM) batteries were moved into southern Iraq. The United States supplemented this with a Tomahawk cruise missile strike against a suspected nuclear parts plant. A second, unilateral, cruise missile strike was ordered by President Bill Clinton in June 1993, on the heels of an assassination plot against former President George Bush and a second attempt to place air defenses within the no-fly zone south of the thirty-second parallel, which had been set up in August 1992. An October 1994 crisis, in which Iraq massed 60,000 soldiers and 1,000 tanks near the Kuwaiti border, ended after the United States built up forces in response. UNSCR 949 instituted a "no-drive zone" to prevent a repeat. Another crisis was averted in August 1995. Iraq had given UNSCOM an ultimatum to leave the country by the end of that month if it would not certify its compliance with biological weapons disarmament. Lt. Gen. Hussein Kamel's revelations of ongoing violations ended that possibility and justified maintaining the sanctions. Through this period, up until Saddam's attack on Kurds at Irbil at the end of August 1996, the United States, France, and United Kingdom remained united in their patrols of Iraqi airspace.[5]

Irbil shattered that unity. France did not join the retaliatory airstrikes, which had no effect on Saddam's operation, and joined Russia and China in condemning the use of cruise missiles as part of the response. The United Kingdom and United States moved the southern no-fly zone up to the thirty-third parallel, the suburbs of Baghdad, but France declined to recognize that step. Later that year, France pulled its air force out of the mission entirely.[6] This was followed by the events discussed in chapter 3: escalating harassment of UNSCOM and French and Russian opposition to the use of force in response.[7] British Prime Minister Tony Blair described UNSCOM leader Richard Butler's 15 December 1998 report as "damning. It is a catalogue of obstruction. It shows quite clearly, one more time, that Saddam has no intention whatever of keeping his word." Thus "the threat is now, and it is a threat to his neighbours, to his people, and to the security of the world." Clinton described the report as "stark, sobering, and profoundly disturbing." Thus Saddam "presents a clear and present danger to the stability of the Persian Gulf and the safety of people everywhere."[8] Four days of the ensuing Operation Desert Fox included 300 strike sorties and 400 missile attacks on both suspected weapons sites and infrastructure. Russia and China openly opposed this operation, which effectively ended the enforcement of UNSCR 687, and France "deplored" it both in itself and for its result: the end of weapons inspections for the next four years.[9] The resumption of weapons inspections, and the subsequent overthrow of Saddam Hussein, will be taken up in the final case in this chapter.

Liberal Institutional Approach

The humanitarian crisis that followed the 1991 war brought the EC together in a way Kuwait had not, suggesting that an institutional pull toward multilateral remedies operated even before the Union existed. On 3 April 1991, the EC condemned Saddam and encouraged the UNSC to call for an "end to repression of the Kurds." Once UN agreement was achieved, the United Kingdom led the EC to agree to set up safe havens in Iraq, an operation the United States agreed to join on 12 April. This operation, Provide Comfort, set up camps that would ultimately be turned over to the United Nations. EC member states—acting on their own, having rejecting the French preference that this become a mission for the Western European Union (WEU)—contributed about half of the force, including contingents from the United Kingdom, France, the Netherlands; Italy, Spain, Germany, and Belgium. American and European forces would remain until September, despite the American preference to pull out earlier.[10] The EC then became silent, except for European Commission President Jacques Santer's advocacy of "a diplomatic solution" to the Irbil crisis.[11]

Interpreting the Iraqi case in terms of a European preference for multilateral solutions is more difficult. At one level, the British could argue that they were helping the Americans uphold properly enacted UNSC Resolutions, with military force if necessary. This view was supported by Butler, who wrote, "During 1997–1998, Iraq's stance and interests were increasingly supported by Russia, France, and China even though it was defying the law they had made in the Security Council."[12] American Secretary of State Madeleine Albright said continued Iraqi provocations demonstrated that Saddam could not be trusted ever to comply. At the least, she said, limits on oil sales should continue until full compliance with UNSCR 687 has been achieved.[13] An official American assessment at the time was that France "opposes [the] use of force, except possibly as a last resort, and says it will not join any military operations against Iraq in this crisis."[14]

One could also interpret French actions as favoring multilateral solutions. The same American report noted that France "believes the United States has not given Iraq incentives to comply with applicable UN resolutions."[15] France argued that it was trying to develop a more productive solution, given that the old method was accomplishing little. Saddam might comply if he were given some hope for the future—if he believed that the United States will never trust him, then he may as well resist. The French preference was to lift sanctions and monitor Iraq's compliance with disarmament, as opposed to maintaining sanctions without monitoring. France thus joined Russia and China in abstaining from UNSCR 1284 in December 1999, which promised a suspension of sanctions after 120 days of good behavior from Iraq with UNSCOM's replacement, the UNMOVIC.[16] While evidence in support of institutionalism is weak, one can at least conclude that all Europeans, as well as the Americans, couched their policy in terms of multilateralism. The EC and EU were not able to develop a common institutional position, except on Kurdish relief.

Realist Approach

The evidence for realism in this case is somewhat stronger. The United States did act to maintain its freedom of action, which was easy to accomplish since the UN's Iraqi policy could not be changed without its approval. Realists would expect the EU member states, in the absence of a unified policy, to bandwagon with the United States. Many, but not all, did. The United Kingdom joined U.S. policy, and was generally supported by Germany and the Netherlands. In spring 1998, the United States had 35,000 soldiers, 40 ships and 275 aircraft in the Gulf region. The United Kingdom had 2,500 soldiers, 5 ships, and 45 aircraft. Belgium and the Netherlands each had sent a frigate while the Danes contributed a C-130 and 33 men.[17] The French position, opposing military action, was generally supported by Spain and Italy, the latter being concerned about "unintended adverse consequences for Middle East stability."[18]

Epistemic Approach

While there is no precise match in domestic law to the Iraqi operations, one may usefully compare them to sanctions levied against other states for similar reasons. One thus finds evidence in support of epistemic expectations from the United States and France, and at least a slight contradiction from countries like the United Kingdom. The United States passed the Iran-Libya Sanctions Act (ILSA) in August 1996, just prior to Irdil. ILSA applied economic penalties against any company that did more than $40 million of business in either country (later dropped to $20 million). The Europeans argued instead for a "critical dialogue," with those states, and would continue to do so especially after the election of Mohammed Khatami in Iran in May 1997.[19] John Bolton, a private citizen during the Clinton administration, interpreted opposition to ILSA and to the Helms-Burton Act as evidence that "some Europeans have never lost faith in appeasement as a way of life."[20] One can say with more certainty that the French were being consistent after Irbil with their policy on other sanctions, as the epistemic approach would expect. The British and other supporters of the Iraqi sanctions regime were being somewhat inconsistent with their position toward other states, but the match is imperfect since Iraqi sanctions could cite UN authority and ILSA could not.

CASE 6.2: WARS OF YUGOSLAV SECESSION: CROATIA AND BOSNIA

Military cooperation in the former Yugoslavia operated in a very different diplomatic environment than it did in Iraq. The EC and EU never formed a united position on Iraq, and matters were handled through the UNSC. In the Balkans, Europe led the policy, and it was the United States filling the role France would later take in Iraq, consistently advocating a different policy. When the Yugoslav National Army (JNA) moved into Slovenia on 26 June 1991, Luxembourg Foreign Minister Jacques Poos announced for the Presidency that "this is the hour of Europe," and Commission President Jacques Delors said, "We do not interfere in American affairs. We hope they will have enough respect not to interfere in ours." The Europeans negotiated a cease-fire at Brioni on 7 July, and the Community sent observers to monitor the cease-fire in that smallest of the wars—65 dead on both sides.[21]

The ensuing lull ended with general fighting breaking out in Croatia in September and the JNA attacking both Dubrovnik and Vukovar in October. This was met with arms and trade sanctions from both the EC and UNSC, and ended with a UN-brokered cease-fire on 23 November. In March 1992, 14,000 UN peacekeepers began monitoring the agreement.[22] During this period, the primary debate within Europe was whether or not to recognize Slovenia and Croatia as independent states. Germany took the lead on recognition, but Belgium, Italy, and Denmark joined its position. The United Kingdom, France, the Netherlands—and the United States—all opposed recognition, but agreed to set up a commission to assess which republics deserved it. Without waiting for the report—which would advise a referendum first in Bosnia—Germany announced on 23 December that it would recognize Croatia and Slovenia on 15 January in any case. The rest of the EC acquiesced.[23] Bosnia held its referendum on 29 February 1992, and the EC and United States both recognized Bosnia on 7 April, one day after the siege of Sarajevo began.[24] Given that these recognitions occurred after war broke out—in the Croatian and Slovenian cases, even after the initial phase of the war ended—it is difficult to accept the common accusation that Europe (or Germany specifically) thereby caused the wars to occur. As Holbrooke has written, "Germany was scapegoated for what happened in Bosnia by people seeking to deflect attention from their own failures."[25]

As the Bosnian war grew more intense, the United Nations imposed an embargo on all of the former Yugoslavia in May 1992. UNSCR 776 followed in September, allowing the use of NATO airpower to supplement the UN Protection Force's (UNPROFOR) protection of aid shipments. UNSCR 781 in October imposed a no-fly zone over Bosnia. Both the EC and the United States supported these steps at the time. French President François Mitterrand led the way toward an international negotiating process, which would be conducted by David Owen for the EC and Cyrus Vance for the United Nations.[26] The outcome of this peace process, and the validity of continuing the arms embargo against Bosnia, would be two of the main factors separating the European Union and the United States once Clinton took office.

NATO took no action until February 1994, although it had been authorized to enforce the no-fly zones and protect aid shipments in a dual-key arrangement with the UN commander. The 5 February 1994 Sarajevo marketplace massacre led to a NATO ultimatum to the Serbs to pull their heavy weapons 20 km. from Sarajevo. The Serbs complied, but responded to NATO actions against its forces attacking the safe haven of Gorazde by seizing 200 peacekeepers as hostages. Their deterrence worked, as the United Nations for several months declined to authorize further airstrikes to enforce a pull-back from the six safe havens.[27] Another round of hostage-taking followed NATO attacks on an airfield in Serb-controlled Croatia that had been used to attack the safe haven of Bihac in November 1994.[28] By that time, the United States had withdrawn its forces from the embargo-monitoring mission in the Adriatic.[29] With frustration growing as every peace plan was rejected, the Europeans began discussing pulling their forces out. The United States agreed on 7 December 1994 that it would send 25,000 troops as part of a NATO mission to either monitor a peace agreement or to withdraw forces under fire.[30]

The Bosnian situation remained relatively stable until May 1995, when Croatia's successful three-day campaign to liberate Western Slavonia demonstrated the vulnerability of Serb positions.[31] Serbs in Bosnia retaliated with sustained attacks on all six safe areas. NATO airstrikes led to another 350 peacekeepers being taken hostage and chained to ammunition bunkers. After further NATO counterattacks, Serbs overran the Srebrenica safe haven on 9 July, massacring 7,000 people by Red Cross estimates and taking Dutch peacekeepers hostage.[32] As Serb forces turned to the nearby safe haven of Zepa, the United Nations ordered the peacekeepers out and advised the Bosnians to defend Gorazde on their own. French President Jacques Chirac proposed a ground offensive to liberate the safe areas, but was overruled by the Dutch and British—whom Chirac then compared to Neville Chamberlain at Munich while threatening to support the U.S. lift and strike option.[33] On 21 July, the allies met in London and agreed to use air power in case of an imminent attack on Gorazde, a promise later extended to all the safe areas.[34]

Conditions changed suddenly when Croatia launched Operation Storm on 4 August, recapturing the Krajina, relieving Bihac, and creating 150,000 Serb refugees. The offensive in northwest Bosnia would continue to the end of the war, with Serb forces pushed out of the land they had not wanted to give up peacefully.[35] After another marketplace mortar in Sarajevo killed 38 Bosnians on 28 August, American, British, French and Dutch aircraft and artillery attacked ammunition depots, gun and tank positions around Sarajevo. Spain and Germany joined the effort in the air after a four-day bombing pause, as NATO extended its attacks to bridges and communication links as far as the Drina River.[36] On 14 September Bosnia Serb commander Ratko Mladic agreed to end the siege of Sarajevo.[37]

In many ways, the methods used to achieve peace in Bosnia—sustained strategic and tactical airstrikes combined with a ground offensive by local forces—were a validation of the position that the United States had been advocating since Clinton took office. One must recognize, however, that after Srebrenica, the European states engaged in the region had come to endorse such action as well. Furthermore, the outcome has been a *de facto* ethnic partition similar to what the EU had proposed three years prior. Nevertheless, the public impression has been that after three years of European ineffectiveness, culminating in a Dutch surrender in July, it took only two months of the American plan to end the war. While the airstrikes were multinational, about two-thirds of the sorties were American. The United States insisted, over French objections, that the peace talks be held at Wright-Patterson Air Force Base near Dayton, Ohio.[38] The lead American negotiator, Richard Holbrooke, wrote later, "We did not want the United Nations at Dayton, they did not deserve to be there, they would have mucked it up."[39]

Under Dayton's terms, Bosnia's future was split among four organizations. The Organization for Security and Cooperation in Europe (OSCE) would manage elections, the United Nations would handle aid, the EU would offer funds for reconstruction, and NATO would send 50,000 troops keep the peace. The United States, United Kingdom, and France would each command a zone in Bosnia, all under NATO command, for one year as the Implementation Force (IFOR). This was then turned into the Stabilization Force (SFOR).[40] This division of labor irritated the Europeans, as they felt they had little input into the terms of Dayton, and were now left with the expensive but invisible task of rebuilding.[41]

Liberal Institutional Approach

The evidence in this case supports both of the institutionalist hypotheses. European proposals led others to support multilateral approaches. EC negotiators helped to end the Slovenian war and took early steps to try to prevent the war in Bosnia. Their Cutileiro plan would have created three autonomous regions within a unitary republic. This plan was accepted in principle by the leaders of Croatia, Bosnia, and Serbia, but rejected in its details (as would many later plans) by both the Bosnian (Muslim) government and the leaders of the Bosnian Serbs. Accusations at the time that the United States helped sabotage this plan in the name of Bosnian unity appear unfounded, although it seems clear that the United States stepped aside from promoting the proposal.[42] Further peace proposals followed along the same lines and with the same results. When peace was finally achieved at Dayton in November 1995, French Prime Minister Alain Juppé said, "Of course, it resembles like a twin the European plan we presented eighteen months ago."[43] The EC also took the lead in extending 1991's UN arms embargo on the entire former Yugoslavia to cover all trade with Serbia and Montenegro.[44]

The Europeans were also willing to take action independently of the United States and to support the UN approach. They took strong action together after the Serbs took hostages in May 1995. The French counterattacked at the Vrbranja Bridge in Sarajevo, freeing their hostages, and fought to maintain control of weapons collection points. British forces took an active role in holding off Serbs around Gorazde while the Bosnian army moved into position itself. Concluding that stronger action was needed, the British and French led the formation of a 10,000-man NATO (European) Rapid Reaction Force to support UNPROFOR.[45] They worked to maintain the use of these forces within a UN or NATO mandate. France, Spain, and Greece all protested the American cruise missile attack on 10 September 1995 near Banja Luka as an "unauthorized escalation."[46]

Realist Approach

American actions, on the other hand, correspond to the realist expectations that they would seek to maintain a free hand. The main goal during the Bush administration seemed to be to avoid involvement as much as possible, tempered only by needing to avoid having the war spread. Among the causes of this were a fear of a Vietnam-like quagmire and belief that the war was a manifestation of ethnic hatreds.[47] Secretary of State Lawrence Eagleburger (James Baker having left to lead Bush's reelection campaign) said in September 1992, "Until the Bosnians, Serbs, and Croats decide to stop killing each other, there is nothing the outside world can do about it."[48] George Kenney, who worked on Yugoslav issues in the State Department, wrote in the November 1992 *Washington Monthly* that U.S. policy was to make the United States "appear active and worried about what was going on there, and at the same time not give the impression that the United States were actually ready to do anything about it... The aim was... good relations with the public."[49] This continued under Clinton. In April 1993, new American Secretary of State Warren Christopher said this was "a problem from hell for which one cannot expect a solution from anyone." A final element of U.S. policy has been described by Baker: "an undercurrent in Washington, often felt but seldom spoken, that it was time to make the Europeans step up to the plate and show they could act as a unified power."[50]

During the first two years of the Clinton administration, U.S. policy toward Bosnia had two major elements, which the Europeans saw as going beyond Bush's benign neglect to an attempt to undermine European policy. The first element was a negative approach to every peace proposal, on the grounds that they rewarded Serb aggression and threatened the unity of the Bosnian state. Following this lead, the Bosnian government often rejected the plans, and the Bosnian Serbs were even more reliable on that score. This pattern had begun with the Cutileiro Plan, and continued with four more major peace efforts.[51] French Foreign Minister Hervé de Charette said of Dayton, "One cannot call it an American peace... The fact is that the

Americans looked at this affair in ex-Yugoslavia from a great distance for nearly four years and basically blocked the progression of things."[52] This perspective continues to be held in the EU.[53]

European leaders were even more displeased with American advocacy of "lift and strike." This policy was driven in the United States by the perceived inequity of the arms embargo, which was locking in place a severe material disadvantage against Bosnia, a recognized member of the United Nations.[54] The United States recommended lifting this embargo and using air power to strike Serb forces until the government had built up its strength. In May 1993, Christopher toured European capitals to promote this plan, but was rebuffed. Clinton then promoted a policy of protecting the six safe havens in Bosnia, but the threat of unilateral lift and strike would continue to be raised by Congress.[55] Europeans raised two objections to this proposal, one moral and one practical. British Foreign Secretary Douglas Hurd described the policy as "leveling the killing field."[56] More arms would only undermine chances for a negotiated peace by giving the government forces an incentive to continue fighting—and encourage the Serbs to fight harder before their advantage slipped away. The practical objection was that European forces were on the ground as part of UNPROFOR. These troops were vulnerable to Serb retaliation if Serb forces were attacked, as was later demonstrated.

When the Europeans adopted a more aggressive policy in May 1995, it created a dilemma for the United States. Chirac was publicly calling for either stronger action or withdrawal of the force. If the United States did not now support action, it would undermine NATO unity—and undermine its own two years of advocacy for stronger action—and even if it did not support action, it was nevertheless committed through NATO to aid the withdrawal. Faced with a military commitment either way, the United States opted to support military action, and then proceeded to dominate the decision-making within NATO.[57]

After the war's end, the U.S. Congress and Secretary of Defense William Cohen both wanted U.S. troops to leave in June 1998, but the United Kingdom and France made it clear that they would not return to a model where they have forces on the ground and the United States is free to undermine their efforts. Here, as well as in Chirac's May position, one can see the element of realism also in European behavior. Institutionalism had its limits. As a realist would expect, the Europeans were no longer willing to absorb the cost of peacekeeping alone, and wanted the Americans inextricably tied to the problem.[58] In July 2002, the United States was contributing 2,500 of the 16,600 troops in SFOR.[59]

Epistemic Approach

The epistemic approach does not have a perfect match in the Bosnian case to domestic policy. One can compare the actions to public opinion to get a rough estimate. Public opinion in the United States and throughout Europe supported a more active role in ending the war.[60] On 1 August 1995, the U.S. House of Representatives passed (by a bipartisan veto-proof margin) a long-threatened resolution to lift sanctions on Bosnia, as the Senate had done a week before.[61] In the end, Americans and Europeans followed their publics' preference, but it took a long time for the idea to be implemented, which counters the epistemic expectation.

CASE 6.3: NATO RESTRUCTURING AND ENLARGEMENT

One outcome of the Bosnian experience was to bring France closer into cooperation with the NATO military command.[62] France had drifted from NATO after it did not receive American support in Suez, Algeria, Lebanon, and Vietnam. In March 1959, France withdrew its Mediterranean fleet from the NATO command structure. Over the next seven years, France pulled more and more of its forces out of NATO missions until President Charles de Gaulle announced in March 1966 that it would "cease its participation in the integrated command and no longer put its forces at the disposal of NATO."[63] Besides distrust of the American commitment and a desire to be fully independent in its military policy, the French also wanted to avoid risking NATO oversight over its nuclear forces.[64]

Bosnia demonstrated to all, the French included, that Europe remained dependent on U.S. forces. Bitter though it might be to accept, Bosnia had shown that Europe lacked the "will ... credibility ... or efficacy" to act even in adjacent areas.[65] If they wanted to act in the absence of American participation, they needed to have a way to act on their own.[66] The only viable options would be to develop an EU force or reform NATO so the European members could act without the United States. Despite the institutionalization of a CFSP as the Second Pillar of the EU at Maastricht, as of Dayton in 1995 there was little interest outside France in a purely EU solution.[67] Until St. Malo, the debate would center on how the Europeans could act within NATO. The next case discusses the other option, centered on the WEU, a security institution that did not include the United States.

The fundamental questions for NATO after the Cold War were its purpose and identity. NATO was founded to defend its members; now its key opponent had imploded. From the first weeks after the Berlin Wall fell, the United States pressed to maintain NATO, arguing that NATO was needed to keep Europe at peace, to defend against any lingering military threat, and to manage the relationship with Russia.[68] The United Kingdom strongly supported this vision of a strong NATO with a strong U.S. role—it saw little in French performance in the Gulf War to suggest that an alternative existed. The French withdrawal from NATO military structures would hobble their efforts to promote a different European model. In May 1991, a Rapid Reaction Corps was set up under British command to address non-Article 5 (nondefense) NATO contingencies. France at the time disliked this expansion of mission, and at first opposed using such a force in the former

Yugoslavia. Nevertheless, France supported having the United States retain a role in Europe; it only wanted the United States to be less dominant.[69]

The compromise reached at NATO's Rome summit in November 1991 was to advocate a "European security identity and defense role," which became known as the European Security and Defense Initiative (ESDI), within NATO. This served French interest in the possibility of independent action as well as U.S. interest in burden-sharing. The French and Germans had expanded their Cold War brigade-level cooperation into a Eurocorps in October. This would grow to include forces from Belgium, Spain, and Luxembourg, and was integrated into the NATO command structure in January 1993, just after France agreed to let NATO play an official role in Bosnia. As we have seen, France played an active role in that operation, including enforcing the no-fly zone, from the beginning. In January 1994, at Brussels, ESDI was given shape in the form of Combined Joint Task Forces (CJTFs), which would be "coalitions of the willing" operating under European command.[70] The Rome Summit also inaugurated the North Atlantic Cooperation Council, the first of many versions of structured cooperation between NATO and the states to its east.[71] In reaction, French Foreign Minister Pierre Joxe worried, "if we are not careful, I shall soon be the only defence minister in all Europe who doesn't participate in NATO meetings."[72]

Over the next few years, France increased its participation with NATO committees, holding out the possibility of fully re-integrating at some point. Jacques Chirac's election as president in May 1995 provided more impetus for this. His foreign minister, Hervé de Charette, rejoined the NATO military committee on 5 December 1995, announcing that France could return fully to NATO if it was "renovated."[73] In the end, however, French demands for NATO restructuring would not be met, other than appointing a European as Deputy Supreme Allied Commander in Europe (SACEUR). At the Madrid Summit of July 1997, Chirac announced that France could not fully reintegrate into NATO after all.[74]

Madrid also would see the climax of the other great debate within NATO: enlargement. In February 1991, Hungary, Czechoslovakia, and Poland met at Visegrad and called for integration into "Western security structures." In October they upgraded this into a call for joining NATO.[75] Concern over the Russian reaction to enlargement and the Central European reaction to non-enlargement would remain present through both the 1997 and 2002 enlargement decisions.[76] The United States and Germany were the quickest to support NATO enlargement. The United States began pushing for enlargement shortly after the EU announced in June 1993 at Copenhagen that it was open to new members. Clinton suggested during visits to Prague and Warsaw in 1994 that accession was "no longer a question of 'whether,' but of 'how' and 'when.'" The Republicans called in 1994 for the four Visegrad states (Slovakia and the Czech Republic having split) to accede. Slovakia effectively dropped out of the competition in 1995 under the controversial leadership of Vladimir Meciar, but Clinton formally endorsed the remaining three during the 1996 elections.[77]

While anywhere from 8 to 12 European states supported a bigger enlargement, the smallest preference won out as it must under consensus rules. Hungary, Poland, and the Czech Republic officially joined NATO on 12 March 1999, two weeks before the NATO action over Kosovo began.[78] The next set of members would be chosen in November 2002. At Prague, Bulgaria, Estonia, Latvia, Lithuania, Romania, Slovakia, and Slovenia were all invited to begin formal accession talks.[79] No significant dissent from this decision was evident. As in the previous round, those not invited—Albania and Croatia—were encouraged to try again soon.[80]

Realist Approach

Overall, the NATO case supports the realist prediction that the United States would seek to maintain maximum power and flexibility. The United States was not entirely happy with the outcome at Berlin, but it did succeed in containing ESDI within NATO and requiring American approval for any European use of NATO assets. In exchange, France had dropped its opposition to NATO enlargement, which it had wanted to delay pending NATO restructuring.[81] Over the next year, the United States would block most French suggestions, beginning with the July 1996 suggestion that a European could serve as SACEUR. The United States rejected this suggestion outright, with concurrence from the Europeans. France followed this in August with a proposal that Allied Forces South (AFSOUTH) be converted from an American headquarters to European, to be rotated among French, Spanish, and Italian officers. While this suggestion seemed more plausible than the SACEUR proposal, it also received very little support and was rejected out of hand by the United States. Both the number of NATO headquarters and the proportion held by Americans had already been starkly reduced, and AFSOUTH was closely linked to the U.S. Sixth Fleet.[82]

While France obviously was not bandwagoning with U.S. preferences, other members followed the U.S. lead on restructuring. The United Kingdom and Germany were also happy with the Berlin outcome, which seemed to signal a resolution of intra-alliance disagreements.[83] Italy preferred the existing arrangement where it held the Deputy AFSOUTH under the United States, and the perception among other NATO members was that France was demanding too much for itself. Among its unilateral actions during this time were the resumption of nuclear testing and its decision to develop its own Rafale fighter rather than join the European Fighter Aircraft program. Furthermore, Germany and Italy felt that France was seeking too many rewards just for returning as the prodigaul son, without having already paid its dues on the NATO committees and with force contributions.[84]

Germany also supported enlargement on American terms. Defence Minister Volker Rühe was promoting enlargement as early as March 1993, based on both the legitimate needs of the Visegrad states and Germany's own interests in stable neighbors. Foreign Minister Klaus Kinkel, however, was more concerned about Russian reaction, and Chancellor Helmut Kohl declined to take a position in favor until fall 1994.[85] While some German politicians considered Slovenia, or Romania, or even Denmark's advocacy of a Baltic state, in the end Germany preferred the Visegrad accessions. The British took the same stance, although they were concerned that enlargement might weaken NATO, and thus loosen the transatlantic bonds.[86]

Liberal Institutional Approach

Far from fitting realist expectations, the French strongly and consistently advocated maximizing the European role. Part of de Charette's proposal at Berlin was to have the WEU act as the European pillar within NATO, helping to resolve the command and access difficulties inherent in the CJTF concept. NATO adopted this proposal in June 1996. NATO officials would be "double-hatted" as WEU officers for CJTF missions, including having a European Deputy SACEUR serve as commander for European missions. Consensus of the North Atlantic Council (NAC) would be required before a CJTF would begin, thus retaining a U.S. role, but afterward NATO would only have oversight, not control, of the mission.[87]

The French were also concerned about the impact of NATO enlargement on EU enlargement. On the other hand, France wanted Germany to remain locked into the European institutions, and the Visegrad accessions would help with that. France did not want to stand alone against enlargement, so by fall 1996, Chirac also agreed to support it.[88] On other issues, the Europeans were more united. While the United States initially suggested that NATO could stretch its action into Asia and Africa, the Europeans opposed this.[89]

Epistemic Approaches

The closest thing to an epistemic impact in the NATO cases would be in states' preferences for enlargement. On the whole, states either preferred nearby states (Denmark wanting a Baltic state, Germany Visegrad, and Italy Slovenia) or states with which they had historic or cultural ties. France thus pushed for Romanian accession, while the American position was seen as popular for the large immigrant communities from the Central European states.[90]

CASE 6.4: ST. MALO AND THE RRF

Having failed at Madrid to reform NATO to its liking or to bring its preferred members into the alliance, France returned to advocating alternatives to NATO. It had done so since the March 1947 Dunkirk Treaty, in which the French and British agreed to take joint action against renewed German aggression. The French had wanted a more proactive arrangement against even the threat of a hostile Germany, but the British did not want to exclude the United States from such deep security arrangements.[91] One year later, this arrangement was transformed into the WEU via the Treaty of Brussels to include the Netherlands, Belgium, and Luxembourg. The April 1949 Treaty of Washington, founding NATO, mostly superceded the WEU as an effective organization—the other European NATO members were invited to join the WEU.[92]

With the WEU becoming entangled into NATO, France in October 1950 proposed a European Defense Community (EDC). Under the EDC, all forces larger than a brigade would be multinational—with the West Germans reined in by having no independent military forces at all.[93] After the other five states approved a treaty to that effect, the French Assembly rejected it in August 1954 primarily due to its supranational characteristics. Its legislative opponents preferred a more confederal, intergovernmental approach to defense cooperation.[94] For the duration of the Cold War, France did not get another good opportunity to promote its vision of a strong Europe within an alliance of equals as opposed to one dominated by the United States. Increasingly, its ideas were rejected by those who feared undermining transatlantic ties, in particular West Germany and the United Kingdom.[95] As with EDC, however, the French also found themselves rejecting their own plans if not implemented precisely as they wanted. For example, in 1962 they terminated de Gaulle's Fouchet Plan for European political cooperation, after the Netherlands insisted that the United Kingdom be included in it.[96]

Thus when the EEC was created in Rome on 25 March 1957, it did not formally incorporate foreign and security policy.[97] Nevertheless, the EC members found that they could not fully ignore foreign policy. In the 1970s they began a process of European Political Cooperation, which was made formal in the SEA of February 1986. This provided a basis for revitalizing the WEU. Its Hague Platform of October 1987 called for an additional EU defense identity, represented by a more active WEU working with NATO.[98] This was already taking shape, as the WEU carried out a minesweeping mission outside the NATO area in the Persian Gulf in 1987–8, during the Iran–Iraq war.[99] During the 1990–1 Gulf War, the WEU provided three-fourths of the naval forces used to monitor the arms embargo against Iraq.[100]

The WEU more closely refined its role in June 1992 at its summit near Bonn. The "Petersberg tasks" included "humanitarian and rescue tasks; peacekeeping tasks; [and] tasks of combat forces in crisis management, including peacemaking." The WEU also instituted a military planning cell, but not a situation center or other operational command facilities. Subsequent WEU actions included operations in the Adriatic Sea and the Danube River to monitor the arms embargo against the Former Yugoslavia in 1992–3 (after which the operation was merged into NATO), a policing operation in Mostar, Bosnia-Herzegovina, from 1994 to 1996, and mine-clearing in Croatia. Larger missions on the ground in Bosnia were blocked by the United Kingdom, as were a 1994 French proposal for intervention in Rwanda and a 1997 Italian proposal for intervention in Albania.[101]

The Gulf and Balkan activity masked a lingering incongruity in the WEU's role: what was its relationship to NATO and the EU—and by extension, what was the direct relationship between NATO and the EU? As early as September 1990, Italy proposed having the EC absorb the WEU. France and Germany endorsed the idea, but the United Kingdom and the Netherlands led European opposition. The United States shared this opposition, unless the WEU would act merely as a European "pillar" within NATO. By the following year, the Italians had joined the United Kingdom in suggesting that the WEU would be merely "a bridge between NATO and the European Community."[102] While the French and Germans proposed "an EC army operating outside the existing NATO alliance," the British and Italians proposed that the WEU act as "the means to strengthen the European pillar of the alliance." By the end of 1991, the disputes had been resolved with the usual ambiguity: the WEU, meeting in parallel to the Maastricht Summit, suggested that it be both "the defence component of the European Union and . . . a means to strengthen the European pillar of the Atlantic Alliance." NATO's November 1991 Rome Summit endorsed the idea of "interlocking institutions,"[103] and its call for a "European security identity and defense role" met both U.S. and French preferences.[104] Some questions nevertheless remained unresolved: under what conditions would the WEU be able to use NATO planning resources?[105] What was the role of non-EU members of NATO, especially Turkey?[106] To what extent was NATO assuming a commitment to protect non-members who were now in the WEU?[107]

In the meantime, Kosovo looked to be headed down the same path as Bosnia, with the same consequences for European freedom of action. On 25 October 1998, in private meetings at Pörtschach, Austria, British Prime Minister Tony Blair said that the EU's performance in the Balkans was "unacceptable," and defined by "weakness and confusion." Thus perhaps an EU defense could be compatible with NATO after all.[108] Six weeks later at St. Malo, he and Chirac announced their Joint Declaration on European Defense. This stated that "The European Union needs to be in a position to play its full role on the international stage" as envisioned in the Treaty of Amsterdam. "To this end, the Union must have the capacity for autonomous action, backed up by credible military forces, the means to decide to use them and a readiness to do so, in order to respond to international crises."

During 1999, the scope of what would become the EU's Rapid Reaction Force (RRF) took shape. At NATO's Washington Summit in April, the allies agreed that European forces would be "separable but not separate," from NATO, which didn't completely clarify matters.[109] In its Cologne Summit in June, the EU said its force would be one it would use "without prejudice to actions by NATO." Moving on to Helsinki in December, the EU agreed that it would create, by 2003, the ability to deploy a force of "60,000 servicemen within 60 days to conduct Petersberg tasks for up to one year." This "Headline Goal" was supplemented by an agreement to set up a Political and Security Committee for CFSP, a Military Committee of Defense Chiefs or militaries, and a Military Staff to support the Council. The Helsinki plan continued the agreement reached in Washington that the EU force—the

RRF—would be guaranteed access to NATO assets, but was less clear about the how much prior consultation would be conducted with NATO.[110]

Helsinki did not answer all the questions, but it did change the terms of the debate. The ESDP held out more hope for free action than the CJTFs, which British Foreign Minister Malcolm Rifkind said offered "as much autonomy as that enjoyed by an adolescent borrowing the family car to go out on Saturday night."[111] Even so, the ESDP wasn't strictly incompatible with the Berlin plan, as long as all the NATO states would agree to automatic access. Many of the RRF troops would not be separate from forces already assigned to NATO. No separate headquarters was established, leaving it dependant on sharing NATO facilities, including the Deputy SACEUR. The Headline Goal also left out details such as how the RRF would deploy, the opposition it could expect to face, provisions for an immediate smaller response, and basing facilities. The most critical question, however, was the NATO–EU relationship, in particular the role of non-EU members of NATO. In other words, Turkey.[112]

Turkey and other non-EU states had long had an associate membership in the WEU, able to participate in its decision-making. With the WEU rolled into the EU, the six European members of NATO were left out. The United States objected to any discrimination against any of these states, although in practice it came down to Turkey. The Visegrad states (Poland, Hungary, and the Czech Republic) expected to soon join the EU, Iceland provides NATO with bases rather than arms, and Norway was less concerned since it was unlikely to be affected by EU missions. Turkey, however, lies adjacent to several zones of conflict in which the RRF could potentially be used: the Aegean, the Balkans, Cyprus, the Caucasus, Iraq, and Israel. In addition, Turkey had contributed more than the other non-EU European members to the NATO assets that would now be available to the EU. Thus Turkey alone threatened to use its veto in NATO to block EU access unless it was it turn given the right to participate in planning for operations in areas of special interest. It described the EU's plans for the ESDP in 2000 as "far from being satisfactory," as they "have not taken into consideration the important points of the NATO's Summit and Council decisions." In particular, Turkey wanted "regular participation...in daily planning and consultations,...full and equal participation in operations under the leadership of the European Union where NATO capabilities will be used,...[and] full and equal participation in the decision-making process...where NATO capabilities will not be used."[113]

The Turkish position, as well as a lack of funding support, stalled the RRF for most of 2002. In September, in Warsaw, Rumsfeld proposed a NATO Rapid Reaction Force to the alliance's other defense ministers, warning that "If NATO does not have a force that is quick and agile, which can deploy in days or weeks instead of months or years, then it will not have much to offer the world in the 21st century."[114] NATO endorsed this concept in Prague on 21 November 2002, saying the "NATO Response Force (NRF)...will have its initial operational capability as soon as possible, but not later than

October 2004 and its full operational capability not later than October 2006." With respect to "the related work of the EU Headline Goal," NATO agreed the efforts "should be mutually reinforcing while respecting the autonomy of both organisations."[115]

While the NRF risked making the European RRF redundant, the European Council found a way to compromise on the deadlock between Turkey and Greece at Copenhagen in December 2002. Access to NATO facilities for ESDP purposes would "apply only to those EU Member States which are also either NATO members or parties to the 'Partnership for Peace,' and which have consequently concluded bilateral security agreements with NATO." This excluded Cyprus (and Malta), meeting Turkish concerns, in a way that could be seen as rational in Greece.[116] This made it possible for the EU to proceed with taking over the NATO peace mission in Macedonia and also with replacing NATO as the lead for the police mission in Bosnia.[117] As the latter began on 1 January 2003, Solana noted with evident pride, "we will see for the first time our European colours adorn the national uniforms of our police officers in a mission on the ground."[118] ESDP forces, led by Germany, took over Amber Fox in Macedonia on 31 March 2003, with all EU members except Denmark and Finland participating. Thirteen non-EU European states and Canada joined the operation.[119] In June 2003, the Council authorized an ESDP deployment to the Democratic Republic of the Congo under French leadership.[120] Also under consideration at that time was the possibility of the EU taking overall responsibility for SFOR, the NATO-led peacekeeping mission in Bosnia.[121]

Realist Approach

The American reaction to St. Malo strongly supports the realist expectation that the United States would seek to preserve its influence and freedom of action. Albright's official response became known as the "3 D's": "no discrimination against non-EU European NATO members, no duplication of effort or capabilities, and no decoupling of European security from North American allies."[122] U.S. officials responded more favorably to Helsinki, which seemed to answer Albright's concerns. U.S. Ambassador to NATO Alexander Vershbow said on 17 December 1999, "From the Washington perspective, the results of Helsinki were very positive...They certainly seem to have pointed the European enterprise in a direction that is a little more NATO-friendly."[123] Marc Grossman, Assistant Secretary of State for European Affairs, told the Senate on 9 March 2000, "we want ESDI, ESDP, to succeed, because...the ESDI will be good for the alliance, good for the United States, and good for U.S.-European relations." Grossman focused in particular on Helinski's assurance that "NATO remains the foundation of the collective defense of its members."[124] At several points in Grossman's testimony, however, he clearly equated Helsinki's ESDP—an EU effort for cooperative defense policy within that organization—with the ESDI—a NATO effort to promote action by European members of NATO without requiring American participation.

Evidence for American realism can also be found in its reaction to the Europeans' simultaneous attempts to develop a substitute satellite navigation system for the U.S. Global Positioning System. This system, known as Galileo, would allow the Europeans to be more independent of the Americans. In late 2001, Energy and Transport Commissioner Loyola de Palacio reported that despite initial support, "American pressure against the Galileo project has increased since September 11." American Deputy Secretary of Defense Paul Wolfowitz wrote the Commission of concerns that Galileo would "complicate" the U.S. ability to ensure its own support while denying adversaries similar information.[125]

We see most Europeans bandwagoning with the American preference, as realists would expect, and the French in particular promoting a different solution. While the United Kingdom, Netherlands, and Germany tended to support the U.S. position that Galileo represented spending money on a problem that did not exist, Chirac said that beyond military dependence, failure to support space programs like Galileo "would lead our country inevitably to a vassal status, first scientific and technical and then industrial and economic."[126] Even during his 1996 flirtation with NATO, Chirac set long-term goals for Europe of "strategic autonomy," and "for the Union gradually to assert itself as an active and powerful pole, on an equal footing with the United States."[127] Most famously, French Foreign Minister Hubert Védrine said on 7 November 1999, "We cannot accept a world that is politically unipolar or culturally uniform. Nor can we accept the unilateralism of the single hyperpower. This is why we are fighting for a multipolar, diversified and multilateral world."[128]

While the realist approach would not expect individual European states to attempt to directly balance American power, one must at least take note of this realist, balance-of-power rhetoric. It does not only come from the French. EU External Relations Commissioner Chris Patten commented on 3 December 1999 that the goal of the ESDP "is to make sure the European voice is heard at the same strong decibel level as when the European Union speaks as the world's biggest trade bloc and the biggest foreign aid donor."[129] Patten echoed this comment in a 15 June 2000 speech, in which he said, "A...goal the European Union should set itself is to become a serious counterpart to the United States...By working more effectively together, developing the CFSP so that it allows us better to project our combined potential, we my hope to contribute to a healthier global balance."[130] In June 2001, Swedish Prime Minister Goran Persson, then holding the Presidency of the European Council, said the EU is "one of the few institutions we can develop as a balance to U.S. world domination."[131] German Chancellor Gerhard Schröder said on 28 December 1999, the United States "lacked consideration for its allies...Whining about U.S. dominance doesn't help. We have to act."[132] It would appear that there was at least rhetorical interest in challenging NATO's dominance—and by extension, the role of the United States in Europe. In keeping with our hypotheses, we interpret these statements primarily as advocacy for institutional strength.

One must recall, however, that realism makes a different prediction if the EU does develop the ability to act as one. In that case, the world would be bipolar and the Union would be capable of directly balancing the United States. Support for multilateral institutions might then be seen as a more acceptable way to implement realism, especially since this institution is regional and exclusive, not global.

Liberal Institutional Approach

In concept, development of an EU RRF demonstrates the institutional pull of the EU. The Union provided a way to implement Blair's appeal to the French National Assembly in March 1998: "In defence we can and should do more together...We have without doubt the best equipped, most deployable, most effective military forces in Europe." Citing their cooperation on the ground in Bosnia, he said, "I would like this process of practical co-operation to advance much further and faster."[133] The Declaration at St. Malo said both NATO and WEU commitments would be maintained, as appropriate, but EU decisions would be made "within the institutional framework of the European Union." Finally, "the Union must be given appropriate structures and a capacity for analysis of situations, sources of intelligence and a capability for relevant strategic planning, without unnecessary duplication, taking account of the existing assets of the WEU and the evolution of its relations with the European Union." Both the use of NATO assets and the development of "national or multinational European means outside the NATO framework" were left open and ambiguous in the declaration.

The ESDP can also be seen as an effort to strengthen international institutions, rather than weaken them. After Albright issued her "3 D" demands, NATO Secretary General Lord George Robertson recast these more positively as the "3 I's": "improvements in European defence capabilities; inclusiveness of the non-EU NATO allies in common efforts; indivisibility of the transatlantic link."[134] ESDP, in this view, would allow the Europeans to carry more of their own burden for defense. Burden-sharing had long been a sticking point in NATO relations, especially since it was easier to measure dollars spent than the value of strategic location and specialized skills like minesweeping. Even so, the Europeans seemed to combine stinginess with inefficiency: working from a similar economic base, the European members of NATO spent about 60 percent as much on defense as the United States, but only obtained one-third of the equipment and conducted one-sixth of the research. The U.S. DoD stated officially, "such disparities in capabilities will seriously affect our ability to operate as an effective alliance over the long term."[135] The ESDP, if it narrowed this gap, would help NATO survive.

Beyond these goals, the institutional approach expects the European states to follow through with its own programs. The Europeans have not fully done so. The 2002 increase in U.S. defense spending—$48 billion—was larger than the entire defense budget of France or the United Kingdom.[136] In this context, the German proposal to increase defense spending by $1.5 billion seems less impressive.[137] Development of the RRF depends on having the men and materiel to fill out the force. In November 2001, the EU announced that it had met about 100 of 150 separate capability targets for the RRF—two-thirds of the goals in two-thirds of the time allotted. The gaps, however, included significant and long-lead items such as airlift, communications, and the ability to suppress air defenses.[138]

France would maintain its preference for a more independent ESDP, as shall be seen in the remaining cases. Along with Greece, it opposed Turkish access to European decisions.[139] It cited the principle of institutional integrity, but loss of access to NATO might also force the EU to develop a truly autonomous force. On 2 December 2001, the United States, United Kingdom, and Turkey had worked out a plan, which Turkish Prime Minister Bulent Ecevit said met "our justified expectations...to a very large extent." The agreement included assurances that NATO assets could not be used in an area of Turkish interest without Turkey's participation and agreement. Greece, however, immediately objected, with Foreign Minister George Papandreou insisting upon "the autonomy of the European Union regarding issues of foreign policy and defence," so "the fact that Turkey has agreed does not mean that Greece has agreed."[140] It would take another year to resolve this deadlock over Berlin Plus and French support for Turkey within NATO would be called into question again in 2003.

Overall, this case presents evidence that the EU promoted a defense policy that is not fully in accord with prior American preferences and that it had not been able to achieve without the Union. While not all of the Headline Goals have been met, the RRF has been successfully deployed. Most Europeans, however, are unwilling to support a fully separate ESDP. On 29 April 2003, Germany, France, and Luxembourg joined a Belgian initiative to develop a headquarters unit separate from NATO's, as well as to form a more unified military unit. Schröder insisted that "This is not directed against NATO. It's a reinforcement of NATO, because it will strengthen the European pillar." This was necessary, he added, because "In NATO we don't suffer from too much America; we suffer from not enough Europe."[141] This meeting occurred only days after Bush said, "It's very important that Europe not become fractured, to the point where the United States won't have relations with a united Europe whole, free and at peace. Hopefully, the past tensions will subside and the French won't be using their position within Europe to create alliances against the United States."[142]

The other 11 EU members were not invited to participate, and they repudiated the initiative. Given the lack of unity, it is difficult to say which group—the 4 or the 11—are acting counter to the European institution, especially since the opponents can argue that they support the NATO institutions. Blair said he would not support "anything that either undermines NATO or conflicts with the basic principles of European defense that we have set out."[143] Dutch Foreign Minister Jaap de Hoop Scheffer, who in 2004 would become NATO secretary general, offered a blunter evaluation of the plan: "Belgium and France will not guarantee our security. Germany will not guarantee the security of the Netherlands. I cannot imagine a world order built against the United States."[144]

If we cannot assess institutionalism with certainty, we can at least say that the majority of European states are following the realist expectation of bandwagoning. Schröder expressed agreement with Blair that transatlantic allies should work together as a "one polar world." The French more clearly saw the separate headquarters as an opportunity to match American power—although even Chirac placed this in terms of allied unity. He repeated the French position that

> Quite naturally a multipolar world is being created. For balance to exist there will have to be a strong Europe and a strong United States linked together by a strong cultural pact. That means our relations between the European Union and the United States will have to be relations of complementarity and partnership between equals. Otherwise it will be a different world, which is not what France observes and wants.[145]

Despite the opposition in other parts of the EU to join the initiative, Belgian Prime Minister Guy Verhofstadt, announced on 2 September 2003 that the headquarters would be built in 2004.[146] The United Kingdom initially indicated that it would oppose in Council any sub-European efforts on defense that followed the "enhanced cooperation" models allowed for the euro and the removal of internal border controls.[147] As European discussions on the new Constitution continued, however, the United States grew increasingly concerned that ESDP would develop into a NATO competitor despite British and French assurances to the contrary.[148]

Epistemic Approach

If we once again stretch the epistemic concept, we see that most of the countries involved in the ESDP debate adopted policies congruent with prior preferences. The United States wanted to retain its strong position in Europe via NATO. The United Kingdom wanted to maintain a strong transatlantic link. France wanted to promote European autonomy in defense issues. Greece and Turkey continued their feud. The only truly incongruous stance was the German, as they moved more toward the French position and away from the British. While this case thus seems to support epistemic expectations, the same caution applies as in the other cases: long-standing foreign policy preferences are not exactly the same as domestic legislation.

CASE 6.5: KOSOVO

Even as the Europeans worked to bring substance to their institutional goals, NATO aircraft were bombarding Serbia. In some ways, Kosovo had been the beginning of the wars of Yugoslav secession: it was there that Slobodan

Milosevic made his name, stoking Serb nationalism on the sixhundredth anniversary of their legendary defeat near Pristina. In December 1992, George H.W. Bush, while reluctant to commit troops to Bosnia, warned, "in the event of conflict in Kosovo caused by Serbian action, the United States will be prepared to employ military force against Serbians in Kosovo and in Serbia proper."[149] With an American peace presence in Macedonia, the southern Balkans remained relatively peaceful until March 1998, when Serb forces launched an offensive against armed opposition that had begun two years earlier. British Foreign Minister Robin Cook reacted by saying "We do not accept this as purely an internal affair," while Albright said, "We do not want a repetition of 1991." On 31 March, UNSC Resolution 1160 imposed a new arms embargo on Serbia, demanded that Milosevic withdraw special police, provide Red Cross access, and engage in dialog with Albanians aimed at the goal of restoring Kosovo's "enhanced status within the Federal Republic of Yugoslavia."[150]

Following more Serb attacks, the UNSC passed Resolution 1199 on 23 September 1998, which called the situation in Kosovo a "threat to international peace and security." Holbrooke returned to the Balkans and worked out an agreement with Milosevic to allow OSCE monitors into Kosovo, guarded, at a distance, by the NATO force in Macedonia. NATO was also authorized by UNSC Resolution 1203 to conduct flyovers to support monitoring. Despite these efforts, OSCE estimates suggested that by the end of 1998 there were 230,000 refugees in Kosovo. UN authorization of further action seemed unlikely, as both China and Russia regarded the Kosovo situation as an internal affair.[151]

In February 1999, the Contact Group (Russia, the United States, the United Kingdom, France, Germany, and Italy) convened peace talks at Rambouillet, France, with the EU's position represented by its special envoy for Kosovo, Wolfgang Petritsch. Its proposed terms were for a cease-fire, Serb withdrawal, demilitarization of the Kosovo Liberation Army, NATO peacekeeping, and autonomy for Kosovo. The Serbs rejected these terms out of hand as an infringement on their sovereignty, while the Kosovars argued that they should have a right to seek independence. The latter signed the agreement in mid-March, but Milosevic held firm despite a 22 March warning from Holbrooke that NATO would attack. Milosevic perhaps thought the threat was a bluff, given the range of allied views. Air operations began on 24 March, and within days, 1.4 million refugees had been created. Russia immediately demanded that the UNSC end the war, but its resolution was defeated 12-3.[152]

Operation Allied Force followed a model similar to that used in Bosnia in 1995, expanded now to include all of Serbia. The first phase of the war targeted deployed Serb forces and air defenses; followed by support targets in Serbia proper, followed in mid-April by strategic targets in Belgrade. France resisted stepping up to strategic targets early in the war, Italy called for bombing pauses, Greece had severe doubts about the whole operation, but no NATO member was willing to break unity and halt the action.

On 12 April, the NAC stated its goals as being in accordance with the prior UNSC resolutions, adding the "unconditional and safe return of all refugees" and the conditions set forth in Rambouillet. On 6 May, the G-8 added that the UNSC would determine an "interim administration" for Kosovo. The United Nations endorsed these goals in UNSCR 1239 on 14 May, effectively giving post hoc authorization to the NATO mission.[153]

The war lasted longer than expected—longer than NATO expected Milosevic to hold out, based on his capitulations in Bosnia and Croatia, and longer no doubt than Milosevic expected NATO to hold together. Early on, the United Kingdom argued for the introduction of ground troops, which Greece, Germany, Italy, and the United States resisted. On 27 May, the International Criminal Tribunal for the former Yugoslovia (ICTY) indicted Milosevic for crimes against humanity as rumors of an eventual ground attack grew. A week later, on 3 June, Russian Prime Minister Viktor Chernomyrdin and Finnish President Martti Ahtisaari (acting for the EU) secured Milosevic's agreement to a plan similar to the Rambouillet terms. The most significant differences were that no referendum on the future of Kosovo was to be held, and NATO operations would be limited to Kosovo itself. The UNSC endorsed the plan on 10 June, in Resolution 1244, assigning the tasks of peacekeeping and disarmament to NATO's Kosovo Force (KFOR) and setting up the UN Interim Mission in Kosovo (UNMIK), responsible for administration, relief, reconstruction, and refugee return.[154]

By summer 2001, conflict between ethnic Albanians and the Macedonian government increased in intensity. Combined effort by American James Pardew and the EU's special representative, François Leotard, brought about a cease-fire and a new NATO mission, Essential Harvest, in August. Under U.K. Command 3,500 NATO troops were deployed to collect weapons from the Albanian rebels. France, the Netherlands, Germany, and Greece also provided troops (along with non-EU member the Czech Republic), while the United States provided noncombat support.[155] The NATO mission would remain in Macedonia under German and then Dutch command until March 2003 when, as noted earlier, the EU took charge.

Liberal Institutional Approach

As the institutionalist approach would expect, the EU took the lead in formulating the international response. The Union had issued a common position on 19 March 1998 to support OSCE peace efforts in Kosovo, froze Serb assets and prohibited new investments and arms sales. In June, the EU added a ban on flights to Serbia, but did not ban oil sales until April 1999.[156] Blair invoked analogies to Munich and fascism in calling for intervention, telling *Newsweek International* during the war, "We tried [appeasement] 60 years ago. It didn't work then and shouldn't be tried now." Cook added, "Upholding international law is in our international interest" and linked Kosovo to NATO's credibility.[157] Even the United States invoked NATO unity as a cause, finding sufficient justification for action in the humanitarian emergency.

NATO also began to develop military plans over the summer of 1998, with the United States and United Kingdom arguing, unsuccessfully for the moment, that NATO did not need further UN authorization before issuing threats. On 15 June, 100 NATO aircraft buzzed Serbia's borders with Albania and Macedonia. Later in the year, a NATO Extraction Force went to Macedonia to provide intelligence for OSCE monitors and to evacuate them if needed. Two thousand French, British, German, and Italian troops participated in this mission, but no Americans did beyond those already monitoring the Macedonian situation. General Wesley Clark, Supreme Allied Commander Europe, wrote that here and in an earlier investigation of staging areas in northern Albania, "It was Pentagon policy to have the Europeans take on an ever larger role." NATO was also at this time worried that Milosevic would act against ethnic Hungarians in Vojvodina, creating an even greater problem for the alliance.[158]

The EU's role in Kosovo became reconstruction, as in Bosnia. As early as 26 May 1999, the Commission had proposed a Stabilization and Association Process, which was adopted at Cologne on 10 June. Its goals were "democratization and human rights, economic development and reconstruction, and external and internal security," and held out the prospect of eventual EU accession.[159] European states would play a stronger role in KFOR than in Allied Force, providing 65 percent of the forces by 2000, a percentage similar to their contribution to SFOR in Bosnia.[160] The Eurocorps took command of KFOR within NATO in April 2000. Europeans also manned the Kosovo sectors considered the most dangerous, leaving the United States in the southeastern region—although its proximity to Macedonia simply provided a different set of challenges for Americans than did reverse ethnic cleansing in the northern city of Mitrovica or tension in the Albanian-majority Presevo Valley in Serbia proper.[161]

We see in Kosovo both institutional leadership and institutional follow-through by the EU. The greatest problem for the institutional explanation is that the Union only weakly linked its actions to UN authorization. In the absence of a specific UN authorization, they used UNSCR 1199 to justify the use of force, and used NATO to follow through.

Realist Approach

While the Kosovo operation must be considered a transatlantic success—it met both its operational goals of securing the safety of Kosovars in the long run and its strategic goal of maintaining NATO as a credible force—it also reinforced the tensions from Bosnia that had contributed to St. Malo. Some NATO members, particularly the French, saw too many decisions being made by Clark or in Washington.[162] As in prior conflicts in Bosnia and Iraq, the United States provided the majority of the airstrikes, and also was responsible for collecting and analyzing intelligence data. The EU, or the

European portion of NATO, was reminded again that they relied on the United States for military power, and thus they must follow the American lead.[163]

Clark, for his part, emphasizes the premium Americans placed on multilateralism: "In the American channel there were constant temptations to ignore Allied reservations and attack the targets we wanted to strike...But though there was discussion in U.S. channels about striking unilaterally, we never did...No single target...was more important than NATO cohesion."[164] At the same time, he acknowledged that there was a trade-off to be made: "We paid a price in operational effectiveness by having to contain the nature of the operation to fit within the political and legal concerns of NATO member nations, but the price brought significant strategic benefits that future political and military leaders must recognize."[165] The American interest in preserving NATO—now in face of a possible competitor in the RRF—remained, but the United States now tried to do so in a more conciliatory manner.

Epistemic Approach

As in the Bosnian case, much of the epistemic evidence deals with state efforts to balance its national values. Germany was particularly split internally, as the Green party in the ruling coalition struggled with the value of pacifism in the face of human rights abuses. The Italian government faced a similar situation, torn also between its alliance commitments and fear of refugees. The United States actually has legislative action that one could compare with the operation, although the legislative message is unclear. In a series of votes on 28 April 1999, the U.S. House voted against declaring war, against the introduction of ground troops, against withdrawing U.S. forces and (in a tie vote) against approving the operation.[166] The air war continued for another month, undeclared, and ground troops were not introduced until the campaign was over.

CASE 6.6: AFGHANISTAN

One day after the 11 September 2001 terrorist attacks in the United States, NATO for the first time invoked its Article 5 collective defense provisions. Nevertheless, the United States conducted its response against Afghanistan, host for Osama bin Laden's main al-Qaeda training camps, outside NATO parameters. NATO's main contribution in the early days was to send AWACS to manage air defense over the United States, freeing up U.S. assets for Operation Enduring Freedom.[167] The EU met on 21 September in an "Extraordinary Council Meeting" in Brussels. Citing UNSCR 1368, the Council said "a riposte by the United States is legitimate," including action "directed against States abetting supporting or harbouring terrorists."[168] The EU also developed a European arrest warrant and a definition of terrorism by December 2001, and began work in April 2002 on "closer co-operation on extradition and mutual legal assistance," issues that had been hindered by death penalty concerns. After the war, the EU donated nearly 1 billion euros of humanitarian aid and reconstruction funds to Afghanistan by June 2002.[169]

Other than British Special Forces, the mission in Afghanistan did not include European military forces until Kabul had been captured. Once the Taliban was routed, Europeans began to play a larger role in Afghanistan. The United Kingdom took the lead on the International Security Assistance Force (ISAF) in Kabul, beginning in December 2001. This 19-country force was notable in that the United States retained operational control over it, but did not contribute forces to it.[170] All EU members except Luxembourg and Ireland contributed to ISAF, as did EU applicants Bulgaria, Romania, and the Czech Republic, as well as New Zealand and Norway. On 20 June 2002, command passed to Turkey, which had been the nineteenth member of the force.[171]

On 11 August 2003, command of ISAF transferred to NATO, operating for the first time outside its traditional area of responsibility. Germany and the Netherlands had led ISAF since February 2003, and a German general would be the initial operational commander of the NATO operation. This ended the ad hoc nature of the command structure, and aimed to bring continuity to the operation—as well as embed it in an international institution.[172] Almost immediately, Germany, which provided about 40 percent of the 5,000 ISAF troops, proposed that ISAF could extend operations beyond Kabul if so authorized by the United Nations.[173]

Realist Approach

The Afghan case strongly supports realist expectations. The United States declined to run its initial operations as part of an institution, perhaps due to its particular grievance, perhaps due to its greater ability to reach the first battlefields in Afghanistan, and perhaps due to frustration with war by committee in Kosovo. Secretary of Defense Donald Rumsfeld's comment "the mission determines the coalition, and we don't allow coalitions to determine the mission" suggested to many Europeans that the United States would continue to insist on freedom of action in military operations.[174] Rumsfeld also asserted the primacy of the American role in his comments about prisoners at Guantánamo Bay, as discussed in chapter 1.

Within the EU, its member states acted bilaterally with the United States in offering military support. This support was maintained despite concerns over international humanitarian law as applied to Afghan prisoners. Prior to the EU Council meeting on 19 October 2001, Blair, Chirac, and Schröder held a separate strategy meeting. They followed this up with a dinner meeting in London on 5 November, which was joined at the last minute by several other European leaders and EU officials. The Union, as such, was in disarray.[175]

Liberal Institutional Approach

The lack of unity speaks to the absence of evidence in support of institutionalism. Officially, the EU played no military role in Afghanistan, despite a premature announcement to that effect by Belgian Foreign Minister Louis Michel at the December 2001 Laeken Council. The United Kingdom, which would be leading the International Security Assistance Force in Kabul for three months, contested its characterization as an EU operation, saying "It's a United Nations-mandated international force which will have EU members. It will also have a range of other countries. Quite clearly it is not an EU force."[176]

The United Kingdom assisted U.S. plans in nonmaterial ways as well. Blair acted as an interlocutor between the United States and Europeans who were put off by Bush phrases like "dead or alive," and "smoke them out." While the United States declined to publish its proof of al-Qaeda involvement, Blair did so in the House of Commons.[177] Blair also engaged with the Arab publics, making the case that the West has protected Muslims in the Balkans, and that Osama bin Laden was just being punished for his admitted guilt. Blair promised the United States "We were with you at the first. We will stay with you to the last." Nevertheless, British support was not unconditional. While action in Afghanistan was justified, any further phase of the war—in Iraq, or perhaps Sudan or Somalia, would need further UN authorization, a wide coalition, and "100% proof of guilt."[178] This strong British support for the United States, apart from any EU position, did not please advocates of an EU CFSP, including Commission President Prodi.[179]

Epistemic Approach

While again the epistemic approach has little to say about the Afghan operation itself, the Union's actions on terrorism do not support these hypotheses. Development of a EU arrest warrant broke a long-standing impasse over such a policy. The EU also began to reconsider its position on mutual legal assistance, despite the death penalty issue. Public concern over Guantánamo Bay did not prevent cooperation from continuing.

CASE 6.7: IRAQ 2003

American attention next turned to Iraq once again, even as operations continued in Afghanistan (and Bosnia and Kosovo and Macedonia, and as the second round of NATO enlargement progressed). Action against Iraq is an ironic denouement for these cases: Americans tried to justify it not only on traditional security grounds—the danger Saddam Hussein posed to other states given his record of aggression—but also in terms of human rights abuses, weapons proliferation, and even the environmental devastation caused by draining the Shi'ite-inhabited wetlands around Basra. None of these considerations won favor with European publics, nor did the argument

Bush made to the United Nations on 12 September 2003 that it must defend international law as established in its own Security Council Resolutions. The United States sought multilateral approval, and made concessions to French (and Russian) preferences in wording 9 November's UNSCR 1441, which sent Hans Blix and the weapons inspectors back into Iraq.[180]

American military action received strong support in the Union from Blair, who faced dissent from within his own Labour party as well as from other EU leaders.[181] Schröder went to the other extreme in his re-election campaign, ruling out support for U.S. action against Iraq. He told the *New York Times*, "I would also be against such an intervention if—for whatever reasons and in whatever form—the Security Council of the United Nations were to say 'Yes,' which I cannot imagine happening in the present situation."[182] At least part of the opposition seems to have been based on doubts about the sincerity of Bush's sudden affection for the United Nations. At his 6 March 2003 press conference, as debate continued over a UNSC Resolution that would more clearly authorize the use of force, Bush said, "I want the United Nations to be effective. It's important for it to be a robust, capable body. It's important for its words to mean what they say." He preceded that, however, by saying, "when it comes to our security, if we need to act, we will act. And we really don't need United Nations approval to do so."[183] Four days later, Chirac ended the debate on a second resolution by announcing that he would veto it.[184]

Of the EU members, only the United Kingdom offered substantial support to the American invasion, which as in the other cases was dominated by U.S. forces. The conventional phase of the war in Iraq ended as quickly as had the war in Afghanistan. As the military effort turned to pacification and the search for weapons and Saddam's supporters, more European states joined the effort. EU invitee Poland took the lead, and by September 2003, the United States had begun working in earnest to obtain UN approval of its operations as an inducement for other states to contribute troops and money to the nation-building effort.

Liberal Institutional Approach

The EU did not develop a meaningful common stance how to address Iraq. On 17 February 2003, the Council issued its official position: "The union's objective for Iraq remains full and effective disarmament in accordance with the relevant United Nations Security Council resolutions, in particular Resolution 1441." They added, "We want to achieve this peacefully. War is not inevitable. Force should be used only as a last resort." Nevertheless, they also said, "It is for the Iraqi regime to end this crisis by complying with the demands of the Security Council... Iraq has a final opportunity to resolve the crisis peacefully. The Iraqi regime alone will be responsible for the consequences if it continues to flout the will of the international community." This position was not so different from the American position, with perhaps the key difference being how to interpret "Inspections cannot continue indefinitely in the absence of full Iraqi cooperation." The meaning of both "indefinitely" and "full" could be interpreted differently by different countries.

France, Germany, Belgium, and Luxembourg strongly opposed American action; the first two, members of the Security Council, opposed a UN authorization of force in March 2003. Their views were not publicly shared by the other members of the Union. On 30 January, eight European leaders, representing EU members Britain, Spain, Italy, Portugal, and Denmark as well as candidates Czech Republic, Hungary, and Poland, issued a joint statement supporting the United States. They argued, "Today more than ever, the transatlantic bond is a guarantee of our freedom...The transatlantic relationship must not become a casualty of the current Iraqi regime's persistent attempts to threaten world security." Citing UNSCR 1441, they said, "Our goal is to safeguard world peace and security by ensuring that this regime gives up its weapons of mass destruction." If disarmament does not proceed, "the Security Council will lose its credibility and world peace will suffer as a result."[185] Over the next few weeks, other EU candidates endorsed this letter, prompting Chirac to declare that the EU invitees had "missed a great opportunity to keep quiet," and advised Romania and Bulgaria that "If they wanted to reduce their chances of entering Europe, they could not find a better way." These two countries, as well as Turkey and the ten countries that had been invited to join the EU two months earlier, had not been permitted to join the Council debate. Blair countered Chirac by sending a letter to the others saying "As you know, I had argued that you should be present and able to contribute fully to the debate."[186]

The Council position immediately followed resolution of yet another dispute over Turkey. Turkey had requested NATO assistance so it would be prepared for an attack from Iraq. The aid would include Patriot air defense missiles, reconnaissance aircraft, and chemical and biological protection gear. France, Germany, and Belgium blocked this in the North Atlantic Council (NAC) on the grounds that aid to Turkey would suggest that the decision for war had already been made, and so reduce the chance of Iraqi cooperation. The dispute was resolved by taking it from the NAC to the Defense Planning Group, from which France continued to exclude itself. Germany and Belgium, unwilling to stand alone in the smaller group, decided not to block the request.[187] Ultimately, Turkey did not allow American troops to use its territory for the March invasion, and Iraq did not attack its neighbor.

Realist Approach

Evidence in support of the institutional approach is missing because we instead see many EU members states bandwagoning with the American position. In doing so, their leaders took positions counter to their own public opinion, and as we have seen were willing to break publicly with EU unity. American behavior continued to strongly support realism as well. While the

United States sought Security Council backing for the use of military force in Iraq, Bush's statements made it clear that he did not regard that as necessary. Ultimately, Iraq was invaded primarily by American forces, with significant help from the British around Basra. Once Saddam's regime was overthrown, other European states sent forces to serve under U.S. operational control. In September, Poland took command of a portion of Iraq, leading a force that included over 1,000 troops from Spain and Italy, contingents from Bulgaria, Hungary, Romania, Latvia, Slovenia, Lithuania, and staff officers from Denmark, Norway, and the Netherlands.[188] The Dutch had already sent over 1,000 troops to Iraq.[189] When the United States returned to the United Nations in September 2003 to ask for UNSC endorsement of its policies, it resisted turning control of the operation, especially its military aspects, over to the United Nations.

Epistemic Approach

As in the other wars, the best proxy for the epistemic hypothesis to look at public support for the war. Unlike in Bosnia, no country's leader resisted his people's call for invasion, but only the American and British publics offered such support. The leaders of the other EU members that supported American action defied public opinion to do so—suggesting once again that more than ideas and values influence the divergent positions.

SUMMARY

The contrasts between this chapter and the others are obvious. Each military operation was multilateral in principle, having been authorized by the UNSC or at least linked to UNSC resolutions. In practice, however, each warfighting operation was conducted in accordance with American preferences and with Americans providing the majority of the forces used. In each case, some European states argued for nonmilitary solutions, but were overruled by Washington. The one case where Europeans tried to take the military lead, in Bosnia, quickly slid over to NATO when major military action was contemplated. After the operations in the Balkans and Afghanistan were complete, Europeans provided the bulk of the peacekeeping forces, even moving to command them, and also the bulk of the reconstruction funding. NATO reorganization and enlargement proceeded along American terms, with the minor concession of creating a European Deputy SACEUR.

Perhaps even more noteworthy in this chapter is the relative absence of the EU as an independent actor. The EU is a constant presence in arms control, the environment, and human rights. European unity was more difficult to achieve on these issues of war and peace, except in the Balkans. From Slovenia to Srebrenica, the EU worked to resolve a crisis on its borders. The record here is more positive than popular perceptions might lead one to believe. Early on, EU negotiators did help to end the conflicts in Slovenia and Croatia, and proposed a Bosnian solution remarkably similar to Holbrooke's Dayton plan. The EU was handicapped, however, by U.S. opposition to its peace efforts and advocacy of air strikes, which contributed to Bosnian rejection of the partition plans and a reversal of the Croatian settlement. Nevertheless, the EU demonstrated a greater willingness to accept casualties in Bosnia than the stronger Americans would in other engagements, suggesting that if the will to create a more robust RRF develops, the will to use it would follow. EU member states also concluded after Srebrenica that passive peacekeeping would not suffice, and transformed their ground presence into an active role in Operation Allied Force. While the American solution was ultimately applied in Bosnia and Kosovo, it was only applied after the Europeans agreed that no other option could work.

Outside the Balkans, however, in Iraq and Afghanistan, the EU had no writ. Once matters passed to the UNSC, no unity was apparent between the United Kingdom and France, nor with other members of the EU who had been elected to the Security Council. This has also been apparent in NATO reorganization. For all the fears in the United States of a European caucus, it has not yet developed on security issues. Instead, we see the United Kingdom standing particularly close to the United States, but other states taking stands in support of U.S. preferences as well. In matters of military action, the United States has generally managed to achieve what it could not in the other issue areas. American resistance to multilateral institutions in other issue areas was not enough to block them from coming into being. European preference for multilateralism in security did not block U.S. action.

Throughout these cases, we find evidence that strongly supports realist expectations of American behavior. Most clearly, the Americans insisted on the primacy of NATO in Europe over a European defence capability that would exclude the United States. NATO expansion and reorganization also reflected American preferences over those of some Europeans. At Berlin, it worked to maintain the ESDI within NATO and at Madrid it blocked a greater European role in NATO decision-making. Albright's demands on the ESDP and American opposition to Galileo also fit this pattern. In the Balkans, the United States promoted its own solution to the crisis, in competition to the Europeans' efforts on the ground in Bosnia. While the Kosovo operation adhered more to multilateral practices, the United States retained the dominant role. Operations in Afghanistan were conducted under American control, and the United States asserted its own interpretation of how prisoners taken there should be treated under international law. Finally, in Iraq, the United States supported maintaining international sanctions, but determined for itself how to enforce those rules even to the point of the 2003 war.

European bandwagoning, as expected by realists, is slightly less consistent. There were always some states, most consistently the United Kingdom and Germany, that supported U.S. actions as expected. Yet there were other states, most often France and Belgium, that often opposed the U.S. position. The Union rarely acted as one, except in the Balkans. In Bosnia and Kosovo, the Europeans did work to ensure that the United States would follow the same policy—until in the Bosnian case the Europeans decided to change their approach to match the American preference. The EC also persuaded the United States to remain involved in Kurdish relief longer than it had preferred to. The aftermath of 11 September 2001 most clearly shows European states acting on their own to support the United States, ignoring EU procedures in the process. This began to change with the 2003 war in Iraq, when a few European states took a firm stance against American policy. In 2003, the EU RRF also became more active in the Balkans and in Africa. Even so, this does not run fully counter to realist expectations. The crisis over Iraq may mark the beginning of the first serious effort by the EU to balance American power rather than merely trying to restrain it.

Development of the ESDP supports the liberal institutionalist hypothesis that Union deepening will lead to greater support for multilateral solutions than the Americans would prefer. Likewise, the Union seems to have been critical on Kurdish relief, on peace efforts in Croatia and Bosnia, and in reaction to Kosovo. In all those cases, the EU led the world, including the UN, in proposing a course of action. The institutional approach expects that EU unity over multilateral approaches should increase over time as the Union deepens. This has not occurred, as the EU was not able to overcome internal differences to reach a strong position on Iraq. In some ways, its unity in cases of military cooperation was greater in 1991 than today. The stronger question for the institutional approach is the EU's view of the United Nations. The Kosovo operation began without UN approval, suggesting that the Union may define multilateralism to suit its own preferences rather than support a larger multilateral view. Divergence over Iraqi policy in 2003 also turned on the need for explicit UN authorization for American action, which many EU members decided was not needed. Thus the evidence is mixed for this first institutional hypothesis, especially since support for ESDP is not quite the same as support for an ICC. The Europeans support development of a regional capability, not a global military force.

The evidence is also mixed for the other institutional hypothesis: that the Union would support multilateral approaches even without American participation. The Union had difficulty in meeting its own goals on the ESDP, although it did ultimately command forces in Macedonia and Bosnia. The Union also took early action in Bosnia independently of the United States. At the same time, EU support for the Iraqi sanctions regime was inconsistent, but it did not advocate breaking with American preferences. The Union was unwilling to remain in Bosnia after Dayton without American participation. Most telling against this hypothesis is the maintenance of NATO primacy in Europe. Despite consistent French preferences, EU members have not taken clear steps to break free of American-controlled assets in their use of the ESDP forces.

The epistemic approach led to a hypothesis that states would try to internationalize their preexisting domestic legislation as it relates to global issues. There is little such legislation that applies in this issue area. The little we have to evaluate if we stretch the concept does not support the epistemic approach. Public opinion in Europe supported more action in Bosnia than the governments were willing to take, and less action in Iraq than most governments did take. The Germans overcame their aversion to military action in the Balkans, and the danger of terrorism led EU members to accelerate cooperation on criminal investigations. We do see consistency in foreign policy regarding the effectiveness of sanctions, as well as on the value of maintaining a strong NATO link to the United States. On the whole, the evidence does not support the epistemic approach, but this assessment is so tangential to the specific epistemic expectations that one could not in good faith interpret this as a rejection of that approach either.

The cases in this issue area once again provide evidence that supports realist expectations of American behavior. We also see once again little evidence that supports the epistemic approach for either the Americans or Europeans. While there is some evidence that supports both the realist and institutionalist expectations for European behavior, the realist evidence is stronger. On the realist side, the Europeans tend to bandwagon with the United States when they act as separate states. When they came together with a common position, they acted to maintain an American investment in their approach, limiting American ability to adopt a contrasting policy. Institutionalist expectations for developing a unified, multilateral position often are met in these cases. The Union did not reach a strong common stance on Iraq, and it stayed away from NATO expansion, but in general EU influence on European unity seems clear. The EU does not, however, consistently support the United Nations, and EU development of its own military capability fits realism more closely than liberalism. The Europeans also were reluctant to take unified action in the absence of American participation, and were reluctant to break free of American influence, through NATO, over the ESDP despite French urging.

Over these past four chapters, we have reviewed in detail 20 different international issues. We have gathered some initial impressions as to which approaches receive the most support with in an issue area. Now we are ready to make a final assessment of these hypotheses, and seek the answer to our puzzle: Why are the United States and the European Union so rarely able to agree on the means for addressing global issues?

7

CONCLUSIONS

Throughout these four issue areas, we see a common a pattern in U.S.–EU relations: the United States and the European Union share similar goals with respect to global issues, but are increasingly unable to reach agreement about how to proceed. The cases described in this book demonstrate that the EU consistently supports multilateral agreements to address global issues, while the United States opposes them with equal consistency unless it can ensure that the final agreement will precisely meet U.S. conditions. That is the puzzle from which we began: *Why, despite their professed similarity of goals, do the policy preferences of the European Union and United States diverge on so many multilateral issues?* This conclusion restates the evidence and then uses the hypotheses deduced in chapter 2 to assess American and European behavior. Overall, we will find that the realist approach is strongly consistent with the behavior of the United States. While the development of European positions is often consistent with liberal institutional expectations, European behavior in the end also tends to be consistent with realist expectations. Finally, we reflect on what these findings mean for the study of international politics and for the future of the U.S.–EU relationship.

SUMMARY OF EVIDENCE

Before developing those conclusions, let us go back and recall the evidence developed in each of the issue areas, and the hypotheses deduced from three approaches to the study of international politics.

Issue Areas

In the area of arms control, the United States supported three multilateral agreements since the structural change wrought by the end of the Soviet Union: the CWC, the NPT extension, and initially the CTBT. It opposed three other multilateral agreements, in addition to ultimately rejecting the CTBT: the MBT, the BWC Verification Protocol, and the Small Arms Program of Action. The EU reached a common position in support of the latter two agreements, as well as the NPT, and a near-common position in support of the MBT. EU support for the CTBT coalesced later than American support, but remained coherent after the United States rejected it. European states supported the CWC, but the Union as such could not take action until after Maastricht, when it moved to harmonize chemical exports. Europeans have ratified the MBT and the CTBT without the United States, but have not proceeded alone to control small arms or to verify the BWC.

In the environmental area, the United States promoted the Montreal Protocol and agreements on long-range air pollution, while it opposed the Kyoto Protocol. The European Union, for its part, strongly supported Kyoto. Earlier controls on air pollution and on ozone depletion were resisted within the EC, in particular by the United Kingdom and France. Germany and the Nordic states—mostly not yet members of the EU—led the fight in these earlier cases, ultimately leading to agreement with the United States. The Union later accelerated the Montreal limits, and has ratified the Kyoto Protocol. The EU is so far not on target to meet the Kyoto timetable.

In human rights, the United States has resisted all agreements, from the Genocide Convention to the ICC. The United States only accepted restrictions on Child Soldiers when the agreement was worded to allow the United States to maintain its current practices, and it remains the only state not to ratify the CRC and the only large Western democracy not to ratify the CEDAW. The United States has also opposed attempts to limit use of the death penalty. The EU experience has been the reverse. EU members have accepted all of these, most prior to the birth of the EU itself, and have brought their laws into compliance with optional protocols against the death penalty. The EU strongly supports the ICC, and resisted American attempts to exempt itself from its provisions.

In cases of military cooperation, the United States and Europeans supported multilateral solutions from the Balkans to Asia, and also supported collective forces within NATO and the EU. Military action with respect to Kuwait, Bosnia, and Afghanistan all conformed to UNSC Resolutions. The EU was particularly active in seeking a collective solution in the Wars of Yugoslav Secession, but in all these cases military action followed American preferences. The U.S.-led NATO intervention in Kosovo, like the ad hoc coalition that invaded Iraq in 2003, could be linked to UNSC wording but not to clear authorization. European states accepted this in Kosovo and were divided over Iraq. Both the United States and EU members supported the evolution and enlargement of NATO, and the United States eventually supported the EU efforts to build an RRF as part of its ESDP. Throughout this period, France advocated a stronger European role in security cooperation.

The Realist Approach

The realist approach to international politics focuses on power derived from material capabilities. This book uses the offensive interpretation of realism, which asserts that states seek power, not security, as their ultimate end. In the unipolar world of the moment, pending the development of a true rival to the United States, the realist expects the United States to seek to enhance its power where it is reasonable to do so. The United States cannot induce other states to bandwagon with its power, but it could try to discourage balancing by signing up to multilateral agreements and binding itself. Such steps cannot mask the visage of power, and so a realist would not expect that the United States would sacrifice power in pursuit of this end. A realist would expect the United States to reject multilateral agreements, unless they lock in a power advantage for the United States or prevent others from gaining an advantage over the United States. Given the realist disdain for the strength of institutions, this condition will rarely occur. The institution would only have the strength given it by the United States, so the United States would gain little in exchange for hindering its own freedom of action. The more common strategy for the United States would be to maintain its edge in power, seeking to increase it as appropriate.

Europeans, on the other hand, face two distinct options. To the extent they act as separate states, they cannot hope to balance U.S. power. In such situations, they would support or bandwagon with U.S. power. If they are able to overcome the difficulty of acting in unison, then they would seek to restrain U.S. power as a means of balancing it. Even if the EU cannot yet match U.S. power, this would ensure that the gap in power does not increase. The Europeans could use multilateral instruments as a way of limiting American power, but would have little interest in joining them—limiting their own power in the process—if the United States does not do so as well. From this, we deduce one hypothesis for the United States and one for the Europeans:

H1A: The United States will support multilateral agreements only if they limit other states' ability to challenge the United States at least as much as they limit American capabilities or autonomy of action.

H1B: When European states act in unison, they will accept multilateral agreements if they have a negative impact on American relative power or autonomy of action, as long as the United States has also agreed to follow them. When European states adopt policy as independent states, they should support or bandwagon with the U.S. position on multilateral agreements, which in practice means that once again they support such agreements if the United States agrees to them.

The Liberal Institutional Approach

The institutional approach focuses on the influence of institutions and norms of behavior. This suggests that the process of decision-making within the EU should lead it to support more regulation of international affairs, especially when a formal common position is reached. The institutionalist values institutions for creating a web of law that helps to create a more stable and secure world. Thus the value placed on the institutional solution would be unrelated to whether or not others join it. Even if the United States stands aside, the EU would see an advantage in moving to promote and implement the multilateral solution. In principle, the same behavior could be predicted for the United States, but we know before research begins that the cause of transatlantic divergence has not been excessive American promotion of multilateralism. We are left with two hypotheses for European behavior:

H2A: EU institutions, especially as the Union deepens its decision-making into a formal CFSP process, will lead the Union to favor more regulation and more multilateralism than the United States does.

H2B: EU support for a multilateral solution will be unrelated to whether or not the United States agrees to be bound by it as well.

The Epistemic Approach

The epistemic approach focuses on the influence of beliefs and ideas. We rejected hypotheses based on regime type, since both the United States and EU member states are liberal democracies (and even the EU as a whole can be linked to elected officials). We also rejected hypotheses based on different global interests, since the puzzle rests on the lack of cooperation despite similar interests. The epistemic hypotheses then must be linked to a deeper level of culture, following the questionable but vital assumption that there is a "European culture" shared among the EU members, distinct from "American culture." Under this model, no unified "Western culture" exists. We rejected the argument that the European Union and United States have cultural preferences for and against multilateralism, based on the historical record. The only remaining basis for the epistemic approach would be to assert that national policies reflect a cultural preference, and that each side would want to export its model to the rest of the world. This analysis produced the following hypothesis, applicable for both actors:

H3: In both the United States and the European Union, support for multilateral policies will reflect their congruence with national policies already adopted.

Assessment

It seems clearest to assess the behavior of each actor in turn. After doing so, this section briefly explores, and rejects, two other explanations for these transatlantic differences. American behavior matches the expectations of the realist approach more closely than those of the epistemic. We easily reject the epistemic explanation of European behavior. While there is certainly evidence in favor of an institutional understanding of European positions, especially in their formulation, the bulk of the evidence favors a realist interpretation on that side of the Atlantic as well.

American Behavior

Throughout these issue areas, American behavior closely matches the realist approach in its strongest, power-seeking version. In arms control, the United States accepted the NPT, which gave it an advantage, and the CWC, which it concluded was verifiable and would prevent other states from obtaining weapons that could make American military planning more difficult. The United States rejected agreements that would have either limited its ability to use its power, such as the MBT and the Small Arms Program of Action, or that it did not believe would prevent others from obtaining new weapons, such as the CTBT or the BWC Verification Protocol. A similar pattern holds for environmental agreements. The United States favored the Montreal Protocol, which would apply to all countries and could be verified relatively easily, and opposed the Kyoto Protocol, which would not apply to developing countries and which would be difficult to verify. The costs of compliance with Montreal, where replacement chemicals had been developed, were also lower than the perceived costs of reducing greenhouse gas emissions. With human rights agreements, the United States rejected giving other states any ability to judge its actions. This is seen in its insistence that it be exempt from the ICC—either by leaving prosecutions subject to a UNSC veto or by Article 98 agreements—in its reservations and understandings applied to the Genocide Convention and the ICCPR, and in its non-ratification of other human rights agreements. The United States advocated the supremacy of NATO over European defense efforts, and ensured that operations in the Balkans and Asia were conducted according to its preferences. This included asserting a right to interpret UNSC resolutions in Kosovo and Iraq.

There is very little evidence that speaks against the realist interpretation of American behavior. Ultimately, the United States accepted the European RRF, and independent European action in Macedonia; but these actions meshed with American interest in reducing troop presence in the Balkans. The United States conducted the Kosovo operation as part of a coalition in NATO. The United States ratified the Child Soldiers Protocol, even though it might be difficult to verify—although here it is difficult to think that the Americans are concerned that a future rival will gain an advantage through using adolescent soldiers. Finally, the Americans agreed to an OPCW structure that placed it outside its full control. These examples do not come close to balancing out the evidence in favor of the realist approach.

Our accepting realism does not logically exclude the possibility that the epistemic approach also explains American behavior. American behavior, however, does not support that approach as well as it supports the realist approach. At times, the United States did work to internationalize its domestic legislation, as the epistemic approach expects. For example, its positions on nuclear, biological, and chemical weapons non-proliferation were supported in agreements, and the change with respect to the CWC closely follows its decision to eliminate such weapons. Even the American position on land mines can be seen as epistemic, since it proposed that it be allowed to continue to follow its existing policies. The United States resisted controls on small arms that would go beyond its existing laws. American positions on environmental agreements also align with the epistemic approach. The United States actively sought to internationalize its position on ozone-depleting chemicals, and encouraged pollution restrictions in the LRTAP that would lead other states to adopt its own air quality standards. American opposition to Kyoto also meshes with its domestic policies.

It is in the area of human rights that we see the most evidence against the epistemic approach. American reservations to human rights agreements have included provisions that were already included in its Constitution or in Supreme Court precedents. The ICC matches fairly well with American jurisprudence, and the United States already allows extradition to courts that are more alien to the American judicial system than the ICC is. U.S. support for the International Criminal Tribunals suggests that the United States is not opposed to enforcing human rights, but that it opposes subjecting itself to the scrutiny of other states. The United States sees very little gain from the ICC. It can try its own criminals, while the court is unlikely to protect American victims because they will not exist—and if they do, the United States can use its own power to punish them rather than drag them into court.[1] The United States also opposed the CTBT, despite its own moratorium on nuclear tests. American efforts to change its laws to meet the requirements of the CWC also go against what the epistemic approach expects.

Since for each case that supports the epistemic approach one finds that it equally supports the realist approach, and since there are several cases that correspond well to the realist and not to the epistemic, one must conclude that the best explanation for American behavior—for the western half of the transatlantic divergence—is a realist preference for maintaining the freedom and power to act in America's self-defined material interests. It is not completely fair to say that "The U.S. . . . has never been willing to place itself at the mercy of a system it did not trust. And it has never been willing to trust a system it did not control."[2] The United States did support and join the OPCW, as well as other institutions relating to trade. Such cases are rare, however, and overwhelmed by the cases where the United States places the highest value on its sovereignty.

European Behavior

The European side of the transatlantic divergence must be compared to the expectations of all three approaches. We begin with the epistemic approach, because it can be rejected in the European case even more easily than in the American. European evidence that matches that approach can most often be seen in the agreements they opposed, and in human rights. The Europeans resisted international limits on ozone-depleting chemicals and air pollution when they were first proposed, in part because they went beyond their current domestic policies. Where relevant, they also placed reservations against the CEDAW to protect monarchic rules of succession. They advocate abolition of the death penalty now that they have abolished it themselves. These examples are overwhelmed by those against the epistemic approach.

Contrary to epistemic expectations, the EU frequently accepted multilateral agreements that required its member states to change their domestic legislation. For example, the Europeans had to restrict chemical exports to comply with the CWC and would have had to enact stricter limits on small arms transfers had that Program been enacted. Even support for the NPT extension required a policy change by the non-NATO members of the Union, and French support for the CTBT did not match its concurrent enthusiasm for nuclear testing. Ratification of the Kyoto Protocol requires the Europeans to adjust their energy consumption patterns, which they have done to a limited extent. They have adjusted domestic legislation to coincide with the CRC and the norm against executions, and support the ICC despite national laws against extradition of citizens. While there was little evidence for or against the epistemic approach in matters of military cooperation, we do see German support for new NATO missions despite prior constitutional interpretations as well as movement toward common arrest warrants for terrorist cases.

One can think of the epistemic hypothesis and the first institutional hypothesis as answering the question of what the Europeans will advocate, while the other institutional hypothesis and the realist approach are directed more at the intensity of that support. We find far more evidence for the first institutional hypothesis than for the epistemic approach. In general, stronger Union institutions corresponded with greater European unity in support of multilateral agreements, and this support extended beyond American preferences. This is very clear in the arms control cases, where EU unity increased in the later cases, and this unity on BWC verification, small arms, and the CTBT went beyond what the Americans would support. A similar dynamic applied to the mine ban, even though Finland held out against a strong Union position. Qualified majority voting led directly to Union support for tougher air pollution standards, and we see a strong link between a deeper Union and support for both Montreal and Kyoto. Agreement on greenhouse gas targets and timetables would not have been possible without the Union being able to create a bubble allowing different targets for different members. Once again, environmental proposals went beyond the American preferences, although the latter went along with European proposals to accelerate the elimination of ozone-depleting chemicals. The Union also helped to develop a common position in favor of the ICC, while the independent CoE has led the way on the death penalty and other human rights agreements. As the Union has deepened, it has created the RRF as part of its CFSP. Both of these also went beyond American preferences, as did the Europeans' initial work in the Balkans.

The more recent cases of military cooperation argue against this first institutional hypothesis. The Europeans did not develop a unified policy on Iraq, from 1996 onward, nor are they unified on NATO and the EU's relationship to it. While British support was crucial to forming the RRF, the British have also worked to ensure that European initiatives did not exceed American limits. The French have consistently been the strongest advocates of European defense, but they have not won many followers beyond francophone Europe. The relationship between the Union and the United Nations in this area has also been inconsistent. In the other three issue areas, the EU supported or even led UN initiatives, as it also did in Bosnia. Europeans supported the Kosovo operation, preempting the UN preference for further negotiations. Most European governments supported the America and British operation in Iraq in 2003, once again despite the UN (and French, Belgian, Luxembourg, and German) preference for continuing inspections. The ESDP creates a local capability, an alternative to American forces, but does not necessarily help to create a global web of rules. Despite this, we can see that the institutional approach anticipates the content of the EU's proposed solutions to global issues much more closely than the epistemic approach does.

Support for the institutional approach is less consistent when we look at the second hypothesis. This stated that the Europeans, recognizing the value inherent in moderating anarchy with a web of international rules, would adopt multilateral agreements even in the absence of American adherence. There are some examples of this. The Europeans have ratified the CTBT, Mine Ban, and Kyoto Protocol even though the United States has not, as well as the ICC and the whole suite of human rights agreements. They also worked to develop independent policy in the Balkans. Most of those examples occurred during the mid-1990s. More recently, the Europeans did not proceed with either the Small Arms Program of Action or BWC verification without the United States. The Europeans compromised on American demands for UNSC immunity from the ICC in the face of veto threats, and have been slow to follow through on the threat to expel the United States from CoE observer status. European pressure on Belgium to amend its universal jurisdiction laws was parallel to American pressure. The institutional approach would expect the Europeans to support the UN's interpretation of its rulings rather than generally sharing the American interpretation.

When we look more closely at the examples of European adherence to multilateralism in the Americans' absence, support for the institutional approach seems even weaker. EU adherence to the CTBT came at a time when American ratification was believed probable. European ratification of Kyoto came after it was clear that the United States would opt out, but the Union is so far not on schedule to meet its targets. While the RRF has been sent to Macedonia and Congo, the Europeans have hesitated to break free of NATO either in Europe or even now Afghanistan. The best case for multilateralism without the United States is in human rights, where the Europeans have limited their domestic options without limiting the Americans. The ICC has come into existence without the United States, and EU members resisted the 2002 American push for indefinite exemption from the UNSC. The EU has been less closely united on the question of Article 98 bilateral exemptions for the United States, ultimately granting parts of what the United States had asked for in the name of preserving some of the ICC's integrity. Outside the area of human rights, the Union only adopted policies separate from the Americans during a narrow window in the mid-1990s, and even those policies may reasonably have been based on a belief that the United States would ultimately accept Kyoto, the CTBT, the MBT, and the ICC.

The evidence is stronger in support of the realist approach. Realists expect Europe to bandwagon with, or adopt the same polices as, the United States. If the Union is not acting as one, this bandwagoning would occur through individual states' support for the American position. If the Union is acting as one, then the Union should support multilateral policies that would limit American power or sovereignty, but only adopt the policy if the Americans do so as well. We see independent bandwagoning in the early arms control cases, and we see the Union later conceding to American preferences on small arms and BWC verification. Bandwagoning is slower on the early environmental agreements, but eventually the American lead is followed on ozone and air pollution. The Europeans accepted the American position on age limits for child soldiers, but otherwise do not seem to match realist expectations in the human rights area. Most European states joined with American preferences in military cooperation, and often worked against Union unity. This view applies to NATO restructuring and enlargement, and its relationship to the EU, and the means of military action in the Balkans and Afghanistan. Even France moved to bandwagon with the United States in the mid-1990s, only returning to its previous stance in the wake of the AFSOUTH command dispute and U.S. missile attacks in Iraq. Most European states again acted to show their solidarity with the United States over Iraq, including providing troops once the initial phase of fighting was complete. Development of the RRF suggests movement toward a deeper phase of realism: rather than merely supporting multilateral agreements that would limit American power, the ESDP would directly enhance European political power.

The major cases where the Europeans seem to act contrary to realist expectations are the same ones noted earlier as support for the institutional approach. Once again, however, when these are examined more closely, they do not seem to be so strongly divergent from realist expectations. The Europeans supported the CTBT without the United States, but in the expectation that the Americans would ratify it. Furthermore, only France and the United Kingdom are European nuclear powers, the United States has its own domestic moratorium—and without American ratification the CTBT has not entered into effect in any case. The primary limit of the Mine Ban on the Europeans who have accepted it is on arms sales; once again, the Americans have imposed a moratorium on mine sales as well so they have not obtained an advantage over Europe. The Kyoto Protocol offers a potentially stronger argument against realist bandwagoning, since it imposes real limits on European action with no comparable limits on the Americans, and the Europeans knew at ratification that the Americans would not join soon. European noncompliance with Kyoto takes some of the force away from this argument, however. Since most of the human rights agreements also do not penalize the Europeans—the Americans gain little advantage in international politics by executing criminals—only the ICC offers a fairly pure counter-example to realist expectations. Even here it remains to be seen how strongly the Europeans resist American pleas for exemptions and how much their own freedom of action is restricted by the Court—and one case (two if we accept Kyoto) contrary to realism does not overbalance the rest of the evidence.

There is another set of cases that are in apparent variance with the realist approach. The Europeans did not quickly bandwagon with the United States on the early environmental agreements. This could be interpreted as a bid to retain a comparative advantage over the United States, especially in the area of ozone-depleting chemicals. While realism would argue that it is futile for a European state to try to balance the Americans, realists would expect Europeans to try to retain an advantage if one develops. In any case, these environmental cases do not support the institutional approach either.

If we compare the two hypotheses that most directly compete with each other—how does the Union react when the United States abstains from an international agreement?—we find that the more common foreign policy behavior is for the EU to not follow through if it would impose real costs on them. While it appears that European behavior corresponds to institutional expectations in developing European policy preferences, the EU rarely moves ahead with a costly institutional solution if the United States does not. The ICC stands as the major exception to this pattern, along with Kyoto if we assume that the Union will meet its targets and timetables for emissions reductions. This trend in favor of the realist approach is more robust than the liberal institutional interpretation. French advocacy of an independent European military, and opposition to U.S. action in Iraq, could be inter-preted as evidence in favor of the institutional approach. One could also cat-egorize those policies as motivated by realism and a drive to balance the United States—a succession of French leaders have advocated that. Furthermore, the ESDP does not develop global institutions, but is directed at least in part at creating a European alternative to U.S. power. The evi-dence in favor of the realist approach thus seems even stronger. Advocacy of multilateral solutions may simply be the most palatable way to bring about limits to American power.

Alternative Approach 1: European Identity

One can develop a fairly plausible hypothesis that some of these differences might flow from a European quest to establish a separate identity. Without fully developing the theoretical basis for this approach, it would argue that the EU leadership would want to try to enhance Europeans' identification with the EU as a whole.[3] This would help build support for deepening the EU,[4] for collective action in defense areas,[5] and for becoming a more significant world power. Building such an identity requires a target to identify oneself against.[6] The only logical target would be the United States. Thus one would expect, first, that when divergence between an American and common EU position develops, the divergence will be stated by the EU using value-laden language that focuses on how the European position is more progressive or more civilized than the American position. Furthermore, European leaders should use appeals to European solidarity, and distinction from America, when addressing their domestic constituency on the underlying issue.

This theory attributes rather cynical motives to the European leadership, for it suggests that the divergence has been manufactured and maintained for domestic reasons (if one may use the term "domestic" to refer to EU politics).[7] This is quite different from political leaders merely reaping political advantage from a situation that exists on its own, as in the 2002 German reelection campaign. In case there is some tendency for an American reader to be willing to assume such manipulation by Europeans, these hypotheses are akin to suggesting that the Bush administration forced a confrontation with France over Iraq in the belief that latent anti-French sentiment in the United States would cause Americans to rally around the invasion. As one senior state department official has said, "There's an aspect of building Europe, which means distinguishing Europe from the United States of America. Europe is not junior of the United States. Europe is a full-fledged power in its own right. And that requires distinguishing it from the United States." He does not argue, however, that these differences are in any way contrived or insincere.[8]

Nevertheless, we cannot reject an approach because it seems too cynical— or else realism itself could hardly survive. Instead we turn to the evidence, and find that there is very little that supports this approach. There are a few comments denigrating the United States, in particular relating to Kyoto and the death penalty, but many of these are from a national, not European, basis. Even more often, it has been representatives of NGOs and the media that condemned the United States, not European political leaders. Official EU statements tend to be rather moderate. Statements by EU officials after the breakdown of BWC verification talks emphasized the process—that they had thought the United States had agreed not to end the AHG—as opposed to suggesting that the Americans supported biological weapons. The president of the Environmental Council, Kjell Larsson of Sweden, said after Bush officially rejected Kyoto that "we cannot accept this," while the official EU statement accepted that "the US wants to seriously address the threats of climate change."[9] At ratification, Wallström said, "The United States is the only nation to have spoken out against and rejected the global framework for addressing climate change. The European Union urges the United States to reconsider its position."[10]

Harsher language on Kyoto came from national leaders, speaking apart from the Union. German Chancellor Gerhard Schröder announced he would personally try to counter American diplomacy with the Japanese, saying "Any attempt to prevent this internationally crucial agreement from getting under way in Bonn and making it ratifiable for everyone would be a serious political mistake."[11] Belgian energy minister Olivier Deleuze described Bush's Kyoto alternative as "a policy that's not very moral...It's a bit like saying: 'Wealth is for us today in 2002 and we will leave the problems for our children or for people in Africa or Asia.'" German Environment Minister Juergen Trittin called for the United States to join Kyoto rather than follow this "disappointing" plan: "We must not let the country with the biggest emissions of greenhouse gases worldwide escape responsibility for protecting the global climate."[12] The leader of a French commission on global warming said the Bush plan "lacks credibility," and further suggested that the U.S. problem was that it wanted to address climate change "at no cost and in a way that would not in any way challenge the American lifestyle and especially its consumption."[13]

Human rights is the one area where harsh language about the United States is commonly found. European states lodged objections to American reservations to human rights agreements, including the Genocide Convention and the CRC. On the other hand, much of the anti-death penalty momentum has come from the CoE and the ECHR. Official European discussion of the ICC unsigning has, as in other such cases, seemed aimed more at cajoling the Americans to go along than at condemning them. Human rights does, however, seem to be an area where European leadership argues that its record is superior to the American, even to the point of calling American practices "barbaric."

The official EU commentary on the United States tends to stick to one primary critique: the United States is unilateral when Europeans believe it should not be. Such statements would then be indistinguishable from the expectations of the institutional approach. There is no evidence to suggest a deeply-rooted cultural divergence between the United States and EU member states exists with respect to multilateralism. The strong European resistance to environmental agreements in the 1980s suggests that any preference for multilateralism is recent, although it was seen as common by the late 1990s.[14] Development of a European military capacity and disregard for the UNSC in Kosovo suggest that the preference for multilateralism remains secondary to Europe's own interests.

Alternative Approach 2: Blame Bush

The other common explanation for these difficulties in the transatlantic relationship has been to blame President George W. Bush, or Republicans in general.[15] While it cannot be denied that Bush is less popular in Europe than his predecessor, nor that comments from members of his administration have irritated European leaders, this explanation is not only simplistic, it is wrong. The divergence between the United States and EU began in the 1990s. It was the Clinton administration that emphasized NATO supremacy after St. Malo and placed conditions on the ICC, Kyoto Protocol, and MBT that

Europe could not accept. Democratic Senators, including John Kerry, were as loud in their opposition to these agreements as Republicans were. The Bush administration took Clinton's policies to their logical conclusion, unable and perhaps also unwilling to maintain the diplomatic process with no intent of ratifying—even Clinton, in his final days in office, recommended against ratification of the ICC. The puzzle at the heart of this book was posed to the author by a senior British diplomat in March 2001, not as if this divergence was sudden, but as if these cumulative disagreements were common knowledge. As an EU spokesperson more recently said,

> I think that Europe was slow in grasping the reality of the turn away from multilateralism because of eight years of the Clinton Administration and excellent Clinton public relations. That shaped our view of U.S. foreign policy. It was not so much the reality of Capitol Hill and the most influential lobby groups. Now with the Bush administration, this is the true reflection of the feeling of the great majority of people on Capitol Hill. It is a more truthful representation of majority feelings.[16]

A somewhat more sophisticated version of this argument attributes the divergence to a Right–Left political division. Thus it would not be Bush, but Republicans in general, who create the trouble. If one notes that the divergence existed under Clinton, this argument could respond by blaming Republicans in Congress, claiming that the divergence was less under Clinton, or noting that the American political spectrum is to the right of the European. This more sophisticated argument also does not hold up under closer analysis. Republicans and Democrats alike opposed Kyoto and the ICC, and we have already noted that the divergence was significant under Clinton.

If this argument were correct, then we should see the European Right supporting the United States, especially under Bush, and the Left opposing it. While Right-of-Center governments in Italy and Spain supported the U.S. position on Iraq, they have supported the other agreements that the Americans oppose. Blair's Labour government has supported both American administrations, and has been the leading note of caution on the ESDP. The German Left opposed the United States on Iraq, but has led Europe in support of operations in Afghanistan. Finally, the Right-of-Center government of Jacques Chirac has led the European search for alternatives to American power. The transatlantic divergence runs deeper than partisanship.

CONCLUSION

The realist approach best explains U.S. behavior with respect to Europe. The United States consistently tries to maintain its freedom of action and sovereignty even in areas like human rights, about which realism would not generally speak. The epistemic or cultural approach could have been an alternative, but it is rejected by the evidence. Instead, the United States declines to make its own national policies multilateral and binding. Consistent with realism, the United States seeks to retain its autonomy of action, its freedom to change its policies at will. This is a significant conclusion for the study of international politics, as is discussed in the next section.

EU behavior is only slightly more difficult to assess. We can easily reject the epistemic approach to explaining its behavior. The institutional approach receives its greatest support from the fate of a few major initiatives. The EU proceeded with support for Kyoto, Ottawa, and Rome in the face of American opposition. The EU worked to bring these into effect despite the fact that they were binding themselves, not the United States and not other powers that are relevant to those global issues. With St. Malo, the Union developed a new capability for its own institution against a negative initial reaction from the United States.

Despite this evidence in support of the institutional explanation, on closer inspection, one must also note significant reasons to reject institutionalism. The self-binding efforts on climate change, land mines, and war crimes are less dramatic than they appear. The EU member states that supported the MBT were not giving up a capability they believed they needed. Finland's abstention in suspicion of future Russian intentions is significant in this light, revealing the limits of institutional consensus building. In other areas of arms control, the same pattern holds. Most EU states were not following chemical or nuclear weapons programs, and France resisted limits on its testing program. The EU has not followed through with an Ottawa-like process for verification of bio- logical weapons or small arms transfers. Kyoto represents a significant inde- pendent step for the EU, but the Protocol was constructed with built-in advantages for EU states, including the regional bubble and the German hot air. While the EU has ratified Kyoto, it has not implemented the measures needed to meet its targets. European resistance to earlier environmental accords can perhaps be explained away as a lack of institutional capability, but certainly they do not support the institutional approach. The Rome Statute has taken effect, and the ICC exists, but the Europeans' exposure to it may not be significantly greater than the Americans'. U.S. forces remain vulnerable to acts committed where no Article 98 agreement has been reached, while EU forces remain as immune as the American so long as they conduct legitimate investi- gations of allegations. Other human rights areas, from racism to the death penalty, do not represent significant new commitments on the Europeans' part. Finally, European support for the official UN position on Iraq has been equivocal, and the ESDP supports itself, not the United Nations.

EU behavior across these cases provides stronger support for the realist approach. While the EU sometimes proceeds without the United States, it does not give up very much in the process. As long as NATO remains, its members do not need land mines. Kyoto is a paper commitment, unenforce- able. Europeans can work with the ICC. The Europeans are developing a military capability that will serve themselves, not the international community as a whole.

Further support for realism can be found if we look more closely at the impact of the agreements on the United States and the European Union. While the EU may not be giving up very much in its agreements, the

United States is bound in practice despite its non-ratification—just as a European realist would prefer. The United States reserves the right to use land mines, but its NATO allies will not permit their deployment from bases in their states. As a practical matter, the United States could not use land mines in the former Yugoslavia, even if it wished to do so. Some in the U.S. State Department are concerned that this process may continue with other types of conventional weapons, such as cluster bombs or depleted uranium shells. Likewise, the United States remains vulnerable to ICC prosecution, despite its efforts to avoid it. The United States has moved closer to support of an EU RRF complementing NATO than it originally envisioned, even if the force never comes into operation. Even in the case of Kyoto, if ratifiers implement emissions standards to aim at compliance, American exporters may find they must absorb the economic cost of adjusting as well.

Furthermore, to the extent that the EU continues to advocate multilateralism, it remains consistent with a corollary of the realist hypotheses. One recalls the realist view that it would be futile for the United States to encourage bandwagoning, since the capability gap is too large to be ignored for long as a potential danger. The EU faces no such constraint, however, as it represents a lower threat to other states. The EU as a great power would seek to have smaller powers bandwagon with it, rather than with the United States. The EU's very model of governance promotes Kupchan's model of self-binding: power in Europe is distributed among several states, reducing its ability to threaten its neighbors. Nevertheless, the very presence of the EU induces its neighbors to adjust their policies to conform to those of the EU.[17]

In addition, realism expects to find national self-interest blocking EU cooperation as it does so often: Greek resistance to pollution controls and to compromising with Turkey over the RRF; French resistance to the CTBT and its angling for favorable NATO restructuring; Finland's abstention from the MBT; the British military links to the United States, joined by many member states acting alone after 11 September 2001; and the jostling for favorable positions in the Kyoto bubble. These issues relate more closely to deepening EU integration than to transatlantic relations, but they signal a resistance to sacrificing national interest in hard cases and thus expose the realist tendency for coalitions to break down over distribution of gains.

By advocating multilateral agreements, the EU may achieve a propaganda goal. This point is not strictly in the realist tradition, since it addresses non-material sources of power—although Carr does include power over opinion as one of the three varieties of power.[18] As more and more states are drawn to the EU's model of international behavior, the United States may be induced to adopt a more multilateral approach as well, suggesting that the EU approach could modify American behavior.

Significance for the Study of International Politics

Before discussing the significance of finding realism in this relationship, let us note some consequences that should not be drawn. Support for realism in this case does not directly denigrate the utility of the other approaches in other areas. The epistemic approach may be relevant to cases where cultural and other differences of ideas and values are more extreme than in this case. The institutional approach might yet explain other areas of international politics, although this appeared *a priori* to be an easier case for that approach than some of the others. Furthermore, deepening of the EU may produce EU policies that break from realism in favor of institutional expectations.

This book's finding for realism, however, is robust, particularly on the American side. This is not a question of Republican versus Democrat, of Bush versus Clinton. The Clinton administration laid the groundwork for rejection of the BWC Verification Protocol, rejected the MBT outright, and responded to St. Malo with suspicion and demands. Clinton signed the ICC while recommending against its ratification and never submitted Kyoto to the Senate for ratification. Likewise in the Senate, we see the unanimous preemptive rejection of Kyoto unless restrictions are placed on developing states, a resounding rejection of the CTBT, and Senators Biden and Helms side-by-side congratulating Scheffer for voting against the Rome Statute.

On the EU side, the finding is also robust, although slightly less so than for the Americans. One can plausibly imagine that EU external relations would be guided by institutionalism more than realism at some point in the future. The tide of institutionalism seems, however, to have crested in 1998 on the coast of St. Malo. While the Commission rejected the idea of ICC Article 98 agreements with the United States, the Council demonstrated a more open perspective on U.S. opposition. The EU has not proceeded to follow the Ottawa model in other areas beyond land mines, and supported the unprecedented removal of Bustani from leadership of the OPCW. One can construct "institutionalist" arguments for all of these steps: preservation of the ICC even in less-effective form, the expense of developing institutions without the United States, the need to save the OPCW from itself—but these examples fit realism better than institutionalism. Kyoto stands as a potential contradiction to realism, but even if member states meet its targets on time, that one example cannot support an institutionalist explanation of the overall pattern of disagreement.

This finding in support of realism is unexpected on several levels. First, realism generally looks more to traditional areas of statecraft and security. Here we find realism supported by state behavior both on environmental issues and in human rights. In this particular case, Kyoto can be linked to economic growth and the ICC to military flexibility, but the other human rights cases are further removed from the realist realm.

Second, some suggest that realism may have very little to say about relations between postindustrial market democracies where the cost of coercion is very high relative to the degree of conflict of interest.[19] While the possibility of transatlantic war remains vanishingly small, realism continues to permeate the relationship. If realism can interfere with the possibility of cooperation between states that share cultural, political, and economic values; are generally satisfied with the status quo; and have collaborated militarily for a half-century, then there would seem to be few if any areas of international politics where realism is not relevant.

Third, there was strong reason to expect that institutionalism would explain the EU's actions. Solana has said, for example,

> A common thread [to our disagreements] is that we Europeans are instinctively multilateralists and want the U.S. to be more committed to multilateral solutions...Because of our tradition of shared sovereignty, we believe in collective action...For us, multilateralism is a tool to master our own destiny.[20]

Or we could take the words of Patten, who asked, "What is so wrong or so dangerous?" about American unilateralism. "My answer is not that the unilateralist urge is wicked but that it is ultimately ineffective and self-defeating." Multilateralism, he says, drives one toward nonmilitary solutions, avoiding the danger of thinking "that the projection of military power is the only basis of true security."[21] Thus his goal was "to apply our experience of multilateral cooperation to a wider stage."[22]

While it would be foolish to deny that such a motivation exists, expressed as it has been by EU decision-makers themselves, this preference for multilateralism does not exist in a vacuum. Just as a power-seeking realist state may find a use for tactical collaboration, even sacrifice of power, in the face of significant system-level competition, the multilateral institutionalist will collide with the realism of others. It is a new form of the old security dilemma. Rather than prompting suspicion through weapons intended for defense, the multilateralist creates suspicion through attempts to limit the flexibility of all. The traditional security dilemma eroded the military edge of the most capable; the new sovereignty dilemma erodes the autonomy of the most sovereign. In both cases, the initiator of change finds unexpected hostility, which leads to questions about the intentions of the stronger state, and then enhanced efforts to close the gap between them. This may not lead to war—the dreadnought race did not lead immediately to war—but it could have as corrosive effect on transatlantic relations as the dreadnoughts did on a century of British–Prussian cooperation.[23] We have seen this in 2003 in the battle over the Iraqi provisional government, leading Thomas Friedman—hardly a xenophobic conservative—to declare "It is time we Americans came to terms with something. France is not just our annoying ally. It is not just our jealous rival. France is becoming our enemy."[24] Realist behavior does that, even to friends. This aspect of these findings—the real world application of these results—influences whether the United States and the European Union will be at odds, will be allies, or manage to be allies while also at odds.

Significance for the Future of Transatlantic Relations

This book began by avoiding the assumption that U.S.–European relations are in a crisis. They are not in a crisis, but they are also not in good condition.

Current transatlantic problems are more severe than prior problems because the structural imperative of the Soviet threat is gone, so there is no external drive to keep the alliance together. Nor is there as much internal glue to the relationship: common values and ideas have come into question. The growth and development of the EU has led its leadership to value multilateral approaches. Rather than overcoming realism, this adds to their misgivings about American assertions of independence from multilateral approaches.[25]

Nevertheless, the relationship is not in a crisis. The worldwide gap in capabilities is too great for a crisis because the EU cannot directly oppose or replace the United States, and the interests of the EU remain closer to those of the United States than they do to other centers of world power. The EU does not support anti-Western terrorism (or any other form of terrorism). The EU has no interest in the proliferation of weapons of mass destruction. The EU cannot conduct distant peace interventions without the support of American logistics. For now, the EU lacks the institutional capability for a sustained, unified foreign policy. The greatest contribution of the EU is its willingness to spend money on nation building after conflict, or on efforts to build peace, which complements American military and diplomatic efforts and American reluctance to spend that money. Another great contribution of the EU is to keep dialogues open with individual states like Iran or on global issues as at Durban.

The relationship is not in a crisis, yet. There is a slow erosion of trust in the United States on the European side, a cumulative dysfunctional spillover of noncooperation.[26] Each new disagreement is coming to be seen in Europe as part of a pattern of opposition to its goals. Thus American arguments against the ICC, or against the BWC Verification Protocol, begin to be assessed not on their merits but as a repeat of the same arguments used before, as noted by an EU spokesperson:

> What is bad is the ever-growing list of withdrawals by the United States from global problem solving: the ICC, landmines, biological weapons, small arms, climate, test ban. It's getting ever longer and it is clearly perceived here as a pattern and Patten sees it as a pattern and Solana sees it the same way. We have to say that there is a mutually reinforcing effect of the repeated withdrawals from international commitments.[27]

The relationship is not in a crisis, but that is not a reason for the United States to be complacent. The danger is not so much that the EU will actively oppose U.S. actions, but that it will stand aside when asked to cooperate. French independence is long-standing. The German election campaign of September 2002 demonstrated the electoral appeal of declining to join a U.S. policy, even if endorsed by the United Nations. The EU's purse strings may eventually be drawn shut against rebuilding states after a U.S. intervention, as we have seen to some extent with Iraq. As the EU deepens its governance and develops more of a common foreign and security policy, a U.S. Secretary of State will know what number to dial to get Europe—but Europe may not answer the phone. From this lack of cooperation, and from slow institution building and identity building to overcome the realist imperative to bandwagon with the United States, the EU may eventually develop the capabilities to match the United States as a world power. The most important elements missing for Europe are the will do to so, and then a short amount of time to build up its power.

The relationship is not in a crisis, but there remain concerns for the United States even now. While the United States can avoid direct participation in multilateral agreements, it retains an interest in shaping them. As matters stand, the MBT prevents American deployment of certain weapons because the countries hosting American forces will not permit it. The ICC exposes American forces to its reach, unless the United States spends diplomatic capital on bilateral exemption agreements. This trend could continue, if future arms control agreements are reached to ban cluster bombs or depleted uranium, or if a protocol is implemented to the Convention on Torture to mandate challenge inspections of any prison, including those on American bases in states parties. Despite this interest in the outcome, American and NGO observers note that U.S. arguments are increasingly being rejected during multilateral negotiations, and the United States finds its changes of position damaging its credibility.[28] This extends beyond Europe, as other states bandwagon with the EU example.

> All those who share the basic values which remain in common to the United States and Europe—be it Philippines, be it Brazil, be it Argentina, be it Poland—all those who have become democracies over the last 15 years, basically share European attitudes toward these sorts of things, which makes it perhaps even worse from the U.S. point of view.[29]

Realists recognize the danger of provoking counter-balancing. U.S. national security policy argues

> The United States must and will maintain the capability to defeat any attempt by an enemy...to impose its will on the United States, our allies, or our friends...Our forces will be strong enough to dissuade potential adversaries from pursuing a military build-up in hopes of surpassing, or equaling, the power of the United States.[30]

As has already been discussed, a realist would concur with this strategy, although with concern that it could fuel others' urge to counter the United States in small ways while waiting to build enough power to overcome the American edge. In the meantime, the United States still needs NATO, and its bases in Europe, even if just as a staging ground for conflicts in other areas, which potentially gives Europeans some leverage over the United States.[31]

Assertions that the United States is the "indispensable nation" are sometimes perceived by Europeans as arrogant: "such language grates unnecessarily on the nerves of our allies and reduces their enthusiasm to stand by us in a crisis."[32] U.S. behavior, such as rejecting the CTBT or pulling out of the ABM treaty, leads to "concerns that the United States was acting unilaterally to maintain its global military dominance."[33] The Economist in that context referred to the United States as a "rogue state," a concern voiced also by Huntington.[34] Nevertheless, there are those who argue, "The maintenance of a decent and hospitable international order requires continued American leadership," adding, "The American-led world that emerged after the Cold War is a more just world than any imaginable alternative."[35] While U.S. power makes organized opposition difficult, they go on to say,

> The unwillingness of other powers to gang up on the United States also has something to do with the fact that it does not pursue a narrow, selfish defini-tion of its national interest, but generally finds its interests in a benevolent international order. In other words, it is precisely because American foreign policy is infused with an unusually high degree of morality that other nations find they have less to fear from its otherwise daunting power.[36]

If morality is thus manifested in part in "a benevolent international order," then it would seem to serve U.S. interests to sacrifice some of its autonomy in service of benevolence. Yet Kristol and Kagan advocate "a for-eign policy premised on American hegemony, and on the blending of prin-ciple with material interest."[37] The international order is unipolarity, not multilateralism, and a policy of restrained hegemony is consistent with offen-sive realism. This tension in realism between sacrificing current power for a better future position will be difficult to resolve. Although burden-sharing with Europe to develop a partnership with more equal capabilities would help advance U.S. goals, the United States is "likely to react negatively to perceived European attempts to build...an identity in opposition to the United States."[38] A meaningful ESDI or ESDP would "mean a great diminution in Washington's dominance of the transatlantic relationship, but such an outcome is probably inevitable no matter what policy the United States pursues."[39] Realism suggests, however, that the United States will continue to try to maintain a preeminent role in Europe, as elsewhere in the world, until it is incapable of doing so at an acceptable cost.[40]

The finding for realism on the American side means that there is no rea-son to expect that a change in the presidency will result in anything more than a change in the rhetoric and marginal changes in behavior. There are deep differences between the shores of the Atlantic, and if realism best explains past behavior, then changes in behavior will require a change in material reality—new threats, new capabilities, or new interests. On the other hand, such changes can also occur without a change in leadership. Either Europe or America, or both, may conclude that their goals can only be achieved through cooperation. Less dramatically, either side may recognize that excessive exuberance for either multilateralism or the preservation of sovereignty may get in the way of other national goals.

On the European side, meanwhile, realist tendencies compete with insti-tutionalist tendencies. So far, realism is evident in European unwillingness to incur high costs for the sake of institutions. The long European reluctance to enforce UNSC resolutions against Iraq, for example, suggests a limit to its willingness to support that global institution. With the partial exceptions of Kyoto and the ICC, the EU has not supported costly multilateral measures without the United States. If this trend continues, we can expect to continue to see inconclusive diplomatic battles between the United States and the European Union over global issues. The United States will not join a multi-lateral solution except on its own terms, and the EU will reject terms that are more favorable to the United States.

This manifestation of realism is complemented within the EU by its states' resistance to deeper integration in foreign policy. As shown by the U.S.–EU example, realism can operate even among the economically advanced democracies of the world. Nevertheless, one cannot rule out the Union's gradual deepening toward a single international actor. The European states have accomplished far too much over the past half-century to claim that there is a limit to such deepening. Furthermore, realism would advise the European states to recognize that their only hope for accumulating power is through acting together. If the EU were to develop a single voice, and develop the military and diplomatic capabilities to match its economy, then it could stand equal to the United States. At that point, we might find another interesting test for realism. If the EU so develops, the world would be bipolar. Realism would expect bipoles to be rivals: Could liberal concepts such as economic ties or common democratic values overcome that ten-dency? On the other hand, by the time the EU achieves such unity, other powers may also have risen, and the European Union and United States might simply resume their alliance against other threats.

The EU faces a tension between enlargement and deepening. Realism suggests that states should retain their sovereignty and yet also suggests that these small states bandwagon together to gain power as a group. Realism also suggests that the EU bring in new members, to expand its reach and increase its potential power. Yet enlargement can undermine deepening, as more member states resist collective positions. Not only do the new mem-bers present more opportunities for sovereignty to be asserted, but also the new members will dilute a European identity and be less accustomed to the diffuse reciprocity required to maintain the institution and to overcome the collective-action problems. While a larger EU will have more potential power, enlargement most likely would delay the day when the EU is able to realize that power as an international actor.

The relationship is not in a crisis, because there is no crisis that requires the relationship. The United States remains free to act as it prefers— multilaterally if others will join it in ad hoc coalitions, unilaterally if it must. For the United States, as threats recede from Europe, EU members will become allies of convenience and preference, but not of necessity. The EU is less free to act as it prefers, since it will face intermittent American pressure on issues important to the United States, such as terrorism. The EU is unlikely to maintain the unity required to resist such pressure. This pressure on the EU and its members will not, however, be to act against its interests, but rather to simply allow the United States to follow its own methods toward what remain common interests. If new shared threats arise through a change in the international distribution of power, the European Union and United States will overcome these differences and cease to be at odds. If and when the EU is able to develop enough unity to act as a single power, the European Union and United States will cease to be allies in the way they have been since mid-century—although a new form of cooperation could not be ruled out. Unless and until those changes occur, the United States and the European Union will remain allies at odds.

NOTES

1 THE UNITED STATES AND THE EUROPEAN UNION: ON THE BRINK OF THE TRANSATLANTIC RIFT?

1. Elaine Sciolino, "France Will Use Veto, Chirac Says," *The New York Times*, 11 March 2003, http://www.nytimes.com.
2. Donald Rumsfeld, Briefing at the Foreign Press Center, 23 January 2003. Transcript at http://www.defenselink.mil/news/Jan2003/t01232003_t0122 sdfpc.html.
3. This pattern is also noted in Kagan, "Power and Weakness" and *Paradise and Power*, and van Ham and Kugler, *Western Unity*, to name only three recent examples.
4. Treaty on European Union, 7 February 1992, Article J.1.2.
5. Christopher Patten, "A European Foreign Policy: Ambition and Reality," speech to the Institut Français des Relations Internationales, Paris, 15 June 2000.
6. Clinton, *National Security Strategy 1999*, iii.
7. Ibid., 5. The 2000 version of this document is less succinct in its restatement of the same vision and goals.
8. Richard Haass, "Multilateralism for a Global Era," speech to the Carnegie Endowment for International Peace Conference, 14 November 2001.
9. Richard Haass, "Defining U.S. Foreign Policy in a Post-Post-Cold War World," Arthur Ross Lecture to the Foreign Policy Association, 22 April 2002.
10. Bush, *National Security Strategy 2002*, 1.
11. Ibid., 14–30.
12. "Revolt at the U.N.," *The New York Times*, 5 May 2001, A12; William Safire, "Slavery Triumphs," *The New York Times*, 7 May 2001, A17.
13. Statement by William F. Schulz, Executive Director of Amnesty International USA, 4 May 2001.
14. Barbara Crossette, "For First Time, U.S. Is Excluded from U.N. Human Rights Panel," *The New York Times*, 4 May 2001, A1.
15. Christopher Marquis, "Washington Arguing over Losing Rights Seat," *The New York Times*, 4 May 2001, A13.
16. "Error of Commission," *The New Republic*, 21 May 2001, 11.
17. For an excellent treatment of the development of Common Foreign and Security Policy, see Eliassen, ed., *Foreign and Security Policy*; Regelsberger, de Schoutheete, and Wessels, ed., *Foreign Policy of the European Union*; Duke, *Elusive Quest*; Smith, *European Union Foreign Policy*; Guay, *Political Economy of a Relationship*; Soetendorp, *Foreign Policy in the European Union*; Holland, *European Union Common Foreign Policy*; and Peterson and Sjursen, eds., *Competing Visions*. For a more general look at EU policy-making, see Peterson and Bomberg, *Decision-Making in the European Union*. For the first years of European integration, see Haas, *Uniting of Europe*.
18. *Costa v. ENEL*, cited in Wallace, "Sharing of Sovereignty," 510.

19. Ibid., 505–6.
20. Ibid., 518. While the EU may not exercise sole control over all its inhabitants, this is also true of many "failed states," particularly in Africa (Somalia, Sierra Leone, Congo) but also in Colombia and Iraq. Perhaps recognition as a state today requires only the inhabited territory and the "ability to enter into relations with other states," as suggested by Dugard, *Recognition and the United Nations*, 7.
21. Maggie Farley, "U.S. Regains Seat on Rights Panel," *Los Angeles Times*, 30 April 2002, http://www.latimes.com.
22. "Secretary Rumsfeld Roundtable with Radio Media," Department of Defense News Transcript, 15 January 2002.
23. "Secretary Rumsfeld Media Stakeout at NBC," Department of Defense News Transcript, 20 January 2002.
24. "EU Presses U.S. on Prisoner Rights," *BBC News*, 21 January 2002, http://news.bbc.co.uk/hi/english/world.
25. T.R. Reid, "British Find No Abuse of U.S. Captives At Cuba Base," *The Washington Post*, 22 January 2002, A08.
26. "Britain Questions Treatment of Prisoners by U.S.," *The Washington Post*, 21 January 2002, A07.
27. "Germany Criticizes U.S. Over Prisoners' Treatment," *The Washington Post*, 22 January 2002, http://www.washingtonpost.com.
28. "U.S. 'Rewriting Rules on Prisoners,'" *BBC News*, 8 February 2002, http://news.bbc.co.uk/hi/english/world.
29. "Detainee Operations," DoD Talking Points, 10 May 2002.
30. Todd Pitman, "British Won't Give Captured Enemies to U.S.," *The Washington Times*, 30 April 2002, http://www.washingtontimes.com.
31. Tom Malinowski (Advocacy Director, Human Rights Watch) and David Bowker (Attorney Adviser, Department of State), and American government officials, in discussion with the author, June 2002.
32. U.S. Mission to the United Nations Press Release # 87 (02) June 30, 2002.
33. Colum Lynch, "Dispute Threatens UN Role In Bosnia," *The Washington Post*, 1 July 2002, A01.
34. Richard Beeston, David Charter, James Bone and Rory Watson, "Britain Seeks U.S. Truce to Save Peace Missions," *The Times (London)*, 2 July 2002, http://www.thetimes.co.uk.
35. Judy Dempsey, "EU to Speed Action on Bosnia Police," *The Financial Times*, 4 July 2002, http://news.ft.com/world.
36. "U.S. Offers Court Veto Deal," *BBC News*, 3 July 2002, http://news.bbc.co.uk/hi/english/world.
37. Colum Lynch, "U.S. Wins 1-Year Shield From War Crimes Court," *The Washington Post*, 13 July 2002, A16.
38. H.R. 4775, 2002 Supplemental Appropriations Act for Further Recovery From and Response To Terrorist Attacks on the United States, Title II—American Service-Members' Protection Act
39. P5_TA-PROV(2002)0367.
40. Statement of the U.S. Embassy to the Netherlands, 12 June 2002, www.usemb.nl/061202.htm. Dutch colleagues of the author, spoken to during this period, did not find this statement fully reassuring.
41. Lee Dembart, "U.S. and Global Criminal Court: How Much Leeway for Washington?" *International Herald Tribune*, 25 September 2002, http://www.iht.com.

42. Judy Dempsey, "Accords with U.S. 'Will Violate' ICC Treaty," *Financial Times*, 27 August 2002, http://news.ft.com/world.

43. Robert Wielaard, "EU Panel Disputes Immunity at ICC," *The Washington Times*, 29 August 2002, http://www.washingtontimes.com.

44. Elizabeth Becker, "European Union Urges Aspirants to Rebuff U.S. on World Court," *The New York Times*, 14 August 2002, http://www.nytimes.com.

45. Elizabeth Becker, "U.S. Issues Warning to Europeans in Dispute Over New Court," *The New York Times*, 26 August 2002, http://www.nytimes.com; Peter Slevin, "U.S. Presses Allies on War Crimes Court," *The Washington Post*, 26 August 2002, http://www.washingtonpost.com.

46. Judy Dempsey, "UK to Back U.S. on War Crimes Court," *Financial Times*, 31 August 2002, http://news.ft.com/world/; "EU to Consider Exempting U.S. from ICC," *The Washington Times*, 1 September 2002, http://www. washingtontimes.com.

47. Judy Dempsey, "Europe Retreats over Criminal Court Accords," *Financial Times*, 30 September 2002, http://news.ft.com/world.

48. Javier Solana, "A Partnership with Many Missions," speech at the German Marshall Fund Peter Weitz Awards Dinner, Washington, 20 May 2002.

49. Haass, "Defining U.S. Foreign Policy."

50. For more, see Smith, *European Union Foreign Policy*; Holland, *European Union Common Foreign Policy*; Soetendorp, *Foreign Policy in the European Union*; Bronstone, *European Union-United States Security Relations*; and Krenzler and Wiegand, "EU-U.S. Relations."

51. Treaty on European Union, Article B. This language has been retained in Article 2 of the Treaty, as amended at Amsterdam and at Nice.

52. Right Honourable Henry McLeish (Member of Scottish Parliament), in discussion with the author, April 2002.

53. The only mention Bush made of Europe, as opposed to generic references to "our allies," was near the end, when he said, "Together with friends and allies from Europe to Asia, and Africa to Latin America, we will demonstrate that the forces of terror cannot stop the momentum of freedom." *State of the Union Address*, 29 January 2002.

54. This division of topics into different "issue areas" follows the model of Brecher, Steinberg, and Stein, "Framework for Research," although the specific issue areas differ from what they specify on pages 91–2. Following Potter, "Issue Area," 419, this division implies the possibility that foreign policy behavior could be different in these issue areas. This work was pioneered by Lowi, "American Business."

55. The classic work is Olsen, *Logic of Collective Action*. See also Sandler, *Collective Action*, or Barkin and Shambaugh, *Anarchy and the Environment*.

56. For a full discussion of multilateralism, see chapter 2; in particular Ruggie, "Multilateralism," and *Multilateralism Matters*.

57. Patrick J. Haney and Walt Vanderbush, "The Helms-Burton Act: Congress and Cuba Policy," in *Contemporary Cases*, ed. Carter, 270–90; for a description of diplomatic efforts between the United States and EU to resolve the issue see Richard A. Nuccio, "Cuba: A U.S. Perspective," in *Transatlantic Tensions*, ed. Haass, 7–28 and Joaquín Roy, "Europe: Cuba, the U.S. Embargo, and the Helms-Burton Law," in *Transatlantic Tensions*, ed. Haass, 29–47.

58. Roy, "Europe," 30–9.

59. Marco Gestri, "Control by States Parties over Private Extraterritorial Activities: Issues of Jurisdiction and International Responsibility," in *The New Chemical Weapons Convention*, ed. Bothe, Ronzitti, and Rosas, 476–8.

60. For example, Bonser ed., *Security, Trade, and Environmental Policy*; Telò ed., *European Union and New Regionalism*; Calleya ed., *Regionalism in the Post-Cold War World*; Bergsten, "America and Europe"; and Krenzler and Wiegand, "EU-U.S. Relations."

61. Soetendorp, *Foreign Policy in the European Union*, 88.

62. Guay, *Political Economy of a Relationship*, 78.

63. "Trade War Looms over Steel Dispute," *BBC World*, 6 March 2002, http://news.bbc.co.uk/hi/english/world.

64. Helmut Bünder and Claus Tigges, "Transatlantic Tete-a-Tete Hardens Over U.S. Tariffs for Steel Imports," *Frankfurter Allgemeine Zeitung*, 2 May 2002, http://www.faz.com/IN/INtemplates/eFAZ.

65. Bronwen Maddox, "EU Throws Down Gauntlet to Bush as Steel Wars Hot Up," *The Times* (London), 17 May 2002, http://www.thetimes.co.uk.

2 INTERNATIONAL RELATIONS APPROACHES AND TRANSATLANTIC RELATIONS

1. This concept of evaluating existing and competing research programs follows the design of Imre Lakatos, "Falsification and the Methodology of Scientific Research Programs," in *Criticism and the Growth of Knowledge*, ed. Lakatos and Musgrave, 115.

2. Thorough discussion of the differences between realism and liberalism can be found in Niou and Ordeshook, "Realism versus Neoliberalism"; Wendt, "Anarchy is What States Make of It"; Baldwin, *Neorealism and Neoliberalism*; Hellmann and Wolf, "Future of NATO"; Powell, "Anarchy in International Relations Theory"; Kegley, *Controversies in International Relations Theory*; Mearsheimer, "False Promise"; Doyle, *Ways of War and Peace*; and Mowle, "Worldviews in Foreign Policy."

3. Walt, "One World, Many Theories."

4. Mearsheimer, "False Promise."

5. Legro and Moravcsik, "Is Anybody Still a Realist?" 5–55. They use the term "paradigm" where others use "theory," or "school," or "worldview." This book is not concerned with the precise definition of these terms. Whatever we call them, they lead to different hypotheses about our puzzle.

6. Ibid., 12.

7. Ibid., 10.

8. Ibid., 11.

9. The latter limit is suggested by Ibid., 49–50.

10. Mearsheimer, "False Promise," 9–12.

11. Among the first to make this observation was Mueller, *Retreat from Doomsday*. Kaysen, "Is War Obsolete?" supports Mueller's observation, but argues that it is caused primarily by the changing basis of economics and the resulting unprofitability of warfare. The division is made more explicit in works like Jervis, "Future of World Politics," and Singer and Wildavsky, *The Real World Order*. Most recently, the concept of two world tiers has become the major organizing principle of a standard textbook, Snow and Brown, *International Relations*.

12. Legro and Moravcsik, "Is Anybody Still a Realist?" 49–50.

13. Waltz, *Theory of International Politics*. His own critique of classical or "traditional" realism permeates the book, but is most sustained on 60–73.

14. Morgenthau, *Politics Among Nations*, 5.

15. Doyle, *Ways of War and Peace;* Thucydides, *Peloponnesian War;* Hobbes, *Leviathan;* Machiavelli, *Prince;* Carr, *Twenty Years' Crisis.*

16. Morgenthau, *Politics Among Nations,* 12–13.

17. For a brief summary of the critiques of classical realism, see Robert O. Keohane, "Neorealism and World Politics," in *Neorealism and Its Critics,* ed. Keohane, 1–26. More detailed critiques can be found in Waltz, *Man, the State, and War,* and Claude, *Power and International Relations,* 25–7. Classical realism's assumptions of rationality have also been criticized, including Allison, *Essence of Decision,* and Snyder and Diesing, *Conflict Among Nations,* but these aspects of the critique are less important for this study since each of these approaches retains the rationality assumption.

18. Legro and Moravcsik, "Is Anybody Still a Realist?" 12–17.

19. Mearsheimer, *Tragedy of Great Power Politics.*

20. Grieco, "Anarchy and the Limits of Cooperation."

21. Waltz, *Theory of International Politics,* 118. Schweller proceeds as well from the assumption that some states may be security seekers while others are the power maximizers that drive change in the system—"Neorealism's Status Quo Bias," 98–100.

22. Schweller, "Neorealism's Status Quo Bias," 117–18.

23. See Van Evera, "Causes of War."

24. Among the evidence in support of this assumption is Labs, "Beyond Victory." Labs looks at Prussian, American, and British war aims in five wars and finds that the expansion of war aims was consistently considered when states saw an opportunity to do so after a decisive victory, although the war aims did not expand if the costs were judged too high. If defensive realism were correct, then the active discussion of war aims should not have taken place (48).

25. Waltz, *Theory of International Politics,* 118.

26. Walt, *Origins of Alliances.*

27. Brooks, "Dueling Realisms," 456–62.

28. Waltz, *Theory of International Politics,* 126.

29. Schweller, "Bandwagoning for Profit," 80–3, 92–9.

30. Waltz, *Theory of International Politics,* 127.

31. Claude, *Power and International Relations,* 90–3; Morgenthau, *Politics Among Nations,* 209–12.

32. But that debate is not for this book: see Waltz, *Theory of International Politics,* 161–93; Kaplan, *System and Process,* 22–50; Gaddis, "International Relations Theory," 23–5, 29–34; Mearsheimer, "Cold War and After"; Kaysen, "Is War Obsolete"? Van Evera, "Primed for Peace"; Gaddis, "Long Peace"; Kegley and Raymond, *Multipolar Peace?*

33. Huntington, "Lonely Superpower," who describes the system as "uni-multipolar," is among the most prominent. Huntington defines unipolarity as a situation in which the unipole can act at will even against the entire rest of the world. In the current system, a second tier of powers, including "the German-French condominium" (not the EU!), Brazil, and Nigeria are present. This definition of unipolarity seems extreme, unless Huntington were to concede that the world of the 1970s and 1980s was "bi-multipolar," which he does not. Huntington concludes, however, that American unilateralism is likely to prompt balancing by the rest of the world. This balancing is tempered insofar as it is difficult to construct, and further tempered if the United States pays more heed to European interests in particular. These conclusions are parallel to the hypotheses drawn from assuming that the world is unipolar at the moment.

34. Wohlforth, "Unipolar World," 17.
35. Ibid., 20. This observation was first made clear in Krauthammer, "Unipolar Moment," published even before the final collapse of the Soviet Union; Krauthammer, in "Bush Doctrine," continues to find it valid while Kagan in "Power and Weakness" and *Paradise and Power* has argued at length on its consequences for the transatlantic relationship.
36. Wohlforth, "Unipolar World," 30–1.
37. Layne, "Unipolar Illusion."
38. "Excerpts from Pentagon's Plan: 'Prevent the Re-Emergence of a New Rival,'" *New York Times*, 8 March 1992, A14.
39. Elman, "Horses for Courses," argues that it is legitimate to apply neorealism to foreign policy, despite Waltz's admonitions not to. Waltz himself makes such policy predictions in "America as a Model?" 667 and "Emerging Structure," 45–6. Mearsheimer, "Back to the Future" and "Future of the American Pacifier," and Layne, "Unipolar Illusion," go beyond their systemic predictions to predict the behavior of Germany and other states. This use of realism to look at foreign policy behavior has taken on the label "neoclassical realism." See Rose, "Neoclassical Realism."
40. Wohlforth, "Unipolar World," Layne, "Unipolar Illusion," Huntington, "Lonely Superpower."
41. Labs, "Beyond Victory," 15–16. This is in fact a central dilemma for the offensive realist: if the pursuit of hegemony is self-defeating because it provokes a balancing response, then is it rational to pursue such a policy? See Glaser, "Realists as Optimists." One response to this dilemma would be to distinguish manual, or intended, expansion (which perhaps is not rational in the long run) from the automatic expansion that occurs as a state fills a power vacuum, as in Elman, "Horses for Courses," 29, and Labs, "Beyond Victory," 11–16. Schweller, "Neorealism's Status Quo Bias," 107–8, reminds us that, rational or not, there are many examples of leaders seeking expansion despite the risk it poses to the very survival of the state.
42. Some even argue for a short of glorious isolationism: Gholz et al., "Come Home America"; discussed also by Ruggie, "Past as Prologue?" 90–2, and Posen and Ross, "Competing Visions," 13–15.
43. Taliaferro, "Security Seeking," 128–61.
44. Labs, "Beyond Victory," 28–34, 47.
45. Kupchan, "After Pax Americana," 77.
46. Taliaferro, "Security Seeking," 159. On the security dilemma, see Jervis, "Cooperation Under the Security Dilemma."
47. Schweller, "Neorealism's Status Quo Bias," 111.
48. Mastanduno, "Preserving the Unipolar Moment," 88. A concurring argument that unilateralism tends to be self-defeating, even for powers strong enough to contemplate it, is Bertele and May, "Unilateralism."
49. Posen and Ross, "Competing Visions," 40.
50. Wohlforth, "Unipolar World," 23–8, 38.
51. Noted by Mearsheimer, "Future of the American Pacifier," 50.
52. Examples include Snyder, "Averting Anarchy"; Mearsheimer, "Back to the Future"; and Van Evera, "Primed for Peace." Wohlforth, "Unipolar World," 31–2, does acknowledge that a unitary EU would greatly change the system, but this will be taken up in the third section of this chapter. Mearsheimer, on the other hand, continues to ignore the EU entirely in "Future of the American Pacifier."

53. See Grieco, "State Interests," and Grieco, "Maastricht Treaty."
54. Wohlforth, "Unipolar World," 31.
55. The Americans and Soviets used similar techniques of appealing to the moral high ground as part of their Cold War competition, as noted by Hall, "Moral Authority," 619, as he brings his assessment of feudal power relations into the state era.
56. Doyle, *Ways of War and Peace*, 230–300; Krasner, *International Regimes*, 361.
57. Nye, "Neorealism and Neoliberalism," 246.
58. Stephen D. Krasner, "Regimes and the Limits of Realism: Regimes as Autonomous Variables," in Krasner, ed., *International Regimes*, 361; Keohane, "Multilateralism," 737.
59. Jervis, "Understanding the Debate," 60–1.
60. Stein, "Coordination and Collaboration."
61. Jervis, "Understanding the Debate," 58–9.
62. A thorough discussion of the differences between realism and neoliberal institutionalism can be found in Niou and Ordeshook, "Realism versus Neoliberalism"; Wendt, "Anarchy is What States Make of It"; Baldwin, ed., *Neorealism and Neoliberalism*; Hellmann and Wolf "Neorealism"; Powell, "Anarchy in International Relations Theory"; Kegley, ed., *Controversies*; and Mearsheimer, "False Promise."
63. Wendt, "Anarchy is What States Make of It," 399.
64. Ruggie, "Multilateralism," 562; he refers here to a sharp contemporaneous debate: Mearsheimer, "Back to the Future"; Snyder, "Averting Anarchy"; Van Evera, "Primed for Peace."
65. Ruggie, "Multilateralism," 563.
66. Ibid., 568.
67. Ibid., 571. Keohane, "Multilateralism," offers a similar definition.
68. Caporaso, "Search for Foundations," 603.
69. Carr, *Twenty Years' Crisis*, 41–88.
70. Caporaso, "Search for Foundations," 601.
71. Ibid., 617–19.
72. Keohane, *After Hegemony*, 129.
73. Keohane, "Reciprocity," 4.
74. Ibid., 20–1; Keohane, *After Hegemony*, 122–31.
75. Jervis, "Realism, Neoliberalism, and Cooperation," 54.
76. Caporaso, "Search for Foundations," 605–6.
77. Martin, "Interests, Power, and Multilateralism," 775–6.
78. Taylor, *Possibility of Cooperation*, 83.
79. Wendt, "Anarchy is What States Make of It," 399–400. Kocs, "Explaining the Strategic Behavior of States," argues that this relationship in fact underlies the entire structure of international politics.
80. Friedrich Kratochwil, "Norms v. Numbers: Multilateralism and the Rationalist and Reflexivist Approaches to Institutions—A Unilateral Plea for Communicative Rationality," in *Multilateralism Matters*, ed. Ruggie, 471.
81. Jupille, "International Outcomes."
82. Ibid., 409.
83. Ibid., 414.
84. For more on epistemic networks and communities, see Haas, "Epistemic Communities" and the entire special issue of *International Organization*, Winter 1992.

85. Vlahos, "Culture and Foreign Policy," 59.
86. Huntington, "Clash of Civilizations?" 24.
87. Desch, "Culture Clash," 150–5.
88. Lake, "Powerful Pacifists"; Russett, *Grasping the Democratic Peace;* and Maoz and Russett, "Normative and Structural Causes."
89. Schweller, "Domestic Structure."
90. Wendt, "Anarchy is What States Make of It," 397.
91. Schweller, "Neorealism's Status Quo Bias," 108.
92. Walt, *Origin of Alliances.*
93. Schimmelfennig, "Community Trap," 59.
94. Ibid., 62–73.
95. Vlahos, "Culture and Foreign Policy," 60–1.
96. Smith, *European Union Foreign Policy*, 48. Smith does, however, regard the EC as, in this context, part of a "West-West system," 17. A similar argument about divergent values and culture is made by Cromwell, *The United States and the European Pillar.* Earlier, Smith, *Western Europe and the United States,* saw some ideological divergence, although he placed less importance on it.
97. Huntington, "Clash of Civilizations?" 25.
98. Serfaty, *Stay the Course*, 48; Guay. *The United States and the European Union,* 13.
99. This is part of the argument made in Kagan, "Power and Weakness." See also Javier Solana, "A Partnership with Many Missions," speech at the German Marshall Fund Peter Weitz Awards Dinner, Washington, 20 May 2002; Christopher Patten, "Comment and Analysis." *The Financial Times*, 15 February 2002, http://news.ft.com/world; Christopher Patten, "A European Foreign Policy: Ambition and Reality," speech to the Institut Français des Relations Internationales, Paris, 15 June 2000.
100. Ruggie, "Past as Prologue?" 111. See in general Ruggie, "The Past as Prologue?" 89–125; also Wittkopf, "Foreign Policy Beliefs"; Wittkopf, "Elites and Masses"; Judith Goldstein, "Creating the GATT Rules: Politics, Institutions, and American Policy," in *Multilateralism Matters*, ed. Ruggie, 201–32; Peter F. Cowhey, "Elect Locally—Order Globally: Domestic Politics and Multilateral Cooperation," in *Multilateralism Matters*, ed. Ruggie, 157–200; and Anne-Marie Burley, "Regulating the World: Multilateralism, International Law, and the Projection of the New Deal Regulatory State," in *Multilateralism Matters*, ed. Ruggie, 125–56.

3   ARMS CONTROL

1. John D. Holum, "The Clinton Administration and the Chemical Weapons Convention: The Need for Early Ratification," in *Ratifying*, ed. Roberts, 8.
2. Michael Moodie, "Evaluating the CWC in the Post–Cold War Security Context," in *Ratifying*, ed. Roberts, 13.
3. Lieber Code of Conduct, 24 April 1863, Article 70.
4. (Second) Hague Convention, 1907, Article 23.
5. Jonathan B. Tucker, "From Arms Race to Abolition: The Evolving Norm Against Biological and Chemical Warfare," in *New Terror*, ed. Drell et al., 163–6.
6. Ibid., 167–70.
7. Vogel, *Chemical Weapons Convention*, 5.

8. Julian Perry Robinson, "The Negotiations on the Chemical Weapons Convention: A Historical Overview," in *New Chemical Weapons Convention*, ed. Bothe et al., 21.

9. Tucker, "From Arms Race to Abolition," 171–7.

10. Ibid., 184.

11. Robinson, "Origins of the Chemical Weapons Convention," in *Shadows and Substance*, ed. Morel and Olson, 47–8.

12. Tucker, "From Arms Race to Abolition," 182–7.

13. Trapp, *Verification*, 7–9.

14. Michael Bothe, "The Chemical Weapons Convention: A General Overview," in *New Chemical Weapons Convention*, ed. Bothe et al., 2–4.

15. Tucker, "From Arms Race to Abolition," 197.

16. Bothe, "National Implementation of the CWC: Some Legal Considerations," in *New Chemical Weapons Convention*, ed. Bothe et al., 550.

17. David A. Koplow, "The Shadow and Substance of Law: How the United States Constitution will Affect the Implementation of the Chemical Weapons Convention," in *Shadows and Substance*, ed. Morel and Olson, 163.

18. Robinson, "Origins," 50–1; United States Department of Defense Annual Report, 1992, 12.

19. Holum, "Clinton Administration," 6.

20. James E. Goodby, "Arms Control in Changing Times," in *Shadows and Substance*, ed. Morel and Olson, 264–5.

21. Trapp, *Verification*, 1–13.

22. Goodby, "Arms Control in Changing Times," 273.

23. Jennifer E. Sims, "The U.S. Domestic Context," in *Arms Control*, ed. Larsen and Rattray, 66–73; Bothe, "General Overview," 9.

24. Koplow, "Shadow and Substance," 169.

25. Trapp, *Verification*, 15.

26. Michael P. Scharf, "Enforcement Through Sanctions, Force, and Criminalization," in *New Terror*, ed. Drell et al., 448–9.

27. John C. Yoo, "BCW Treaties and the Constitution," in *New Terror*, ed. Drell et al., 272–82.

28. Ibid. 289–92; Bothe, "National Implementation," 564–5; Tucker, "From Arms Race to Abolition," 222.

29. Koplow, "Shadow and Substance," 174–5.

30. Yoo, "BCW Treaties," 284–6.

31. Ibid., 293–5.

32. Thilo Marauhn, "National Regulations on Export Controls and the Chemical Weapons Convention," in *New Chemical Weapons Convention*, ed. Bothe et al., 501–31.

33. Marauhn, "Implementing the Chemical Weapons Convention in the EU Context," in *New Chemical Weapons Convention*, ed. Bothe et al., 572–7.

34. Regulation 3381/94, accompanied by Joint Action 94/942, 19 December 1994.

35. Andrea de Guttry, "The Organization for the Prohibition of Chemical Weapons," in *New Chemical Weapons Convention*, ed. Bothe et al., 121–33.

36. Bothe, "General Overview," 10.

37. Trapp, *Verification*, 59–62, 92–3.

38. Marauhn, "The EU Context," 571.

39. Dates taken from the CWC homepage, www.opcw.org.

40. Michael Binyon, "America Forces Out UN Arms Director," *The Times (London)*, 23 April 2002, http://www.thetimes.co.uk.
41. Shaun Gregory, "France, the Nuclear Weapons Test Moratorium and the NPT and CTBT Processes," in *France*, ed. Chafer and Jenkins, 104.
42. William K. Domke, "Proliferation, Threat, and Learning: The International and Domestic Structures of Export," in *Future of the International Nuclear Non-proliferation Regime*, ed. van Leeuwen, 211.
43. Joachim Krause, "The Future of the NPT: A German Perspective," in *1995*, ed. Pilat and Pendley, 136.
44. Fischer and Müller, *United Divided*, 7–9.
45. Ibid., 3–5.
46. Harald Müller, "Beyond 1995: The NPT and Europe," in *1995*, ed. Pilat and Pendley, 154–7.
47. Jayantha Dhanapala, "Extending the Nuclear Non-Proliferation Treaty: A Case History of a Multilateral Disarmament Conference," in *Arms Control*, ed. Brown, 14–18; Fischer and Müller, *United Divided*, 19–21; Miguel Marin-Bosch, "The NPT's Indefinite Extension: Carrot or Stick?" in *Arms Control*, ed. Brown, 34–5.
48. Fischer and Müller, *United Divided*, 35.
49. Bidwai and Vanaik, *New Nukes*, 38.
50. Tertrais, *Nuclear Policies in Europe*, 15–18.
51. Jacques Chirac, speech to the Institut des Hautes Etudes de Défense Nationale in Paris, 8 June 96.
52. Tertrais, *Nuclear Policies*, 55–8.
53. Fischer and Müller, *United Divided*, 13–17.
54. Tertrais, *Nuclear Policies*, 13.
55. Fischer and Müller, *United Divided*, 31.
56. "Towards a Nuclear-Weapon-Free World: The Need for a New Agenda," posted on http://www.basicint.org/8nation.htm.
57. *Legality of the Use by a State of Nuclear Weapons in Armed Conflict*, International Court of Justice, 8 June 1996.
58. Gregory, "France," 104–5.
59. Department of Defense Annual Report, 1992, 12.
60. Marin-Bosch, "Carrot or Stick?" 35–7; Dhanapala, "Extending the Nuclear Non-Proliferation Treaty," 20–1; Eric Arnett, "The Comprehensive Test Ban Negotiations and the Non-Proliferation Treaty," in *Arms Control*, ed. Brown, 52.
61. Jan Th. Hoekma, "CTBT and NPT: An Essential Linkage?" in *Future of the International Nuclear Non-proliferation Regime*, ed. van Leeuwen, 236.
62. Rebecca Johnson, "Nuclear Arms Control through Multilateral Negotiations," in *Arms Control*, ed. Gallagher, 88.
63. Arnett, "Comprehensive Test Ban Negotiations," 53.
64. Rebecca Johnson, "Advocates and Activists: Conflicting Approaches on Nonproliferation and the Test Ban Treaty," in *Third Force*, ed. Florini, 74.
65. Ratification status taken from the CTBT Organization, www.ctbto.org.
66. Department of Defense Annual Report, 2001, 93.
67. Richard Butler, "Nuclear Testing and National Honor," *The New York Times*, July 13, 2001, http://www.nytimes.com/.
68. Colum Lynch, "U.S. Boycotts Nuclear Test Ban Meeting: Some Delegates at U.N. Session Upset at Latest Snub of Pact Bush Won't Back," *Washington Post*, November 12, 2001, A06.

69. Walter Pincus, "U.S. to Seek Options On New Nuclear Tests: White House Worries About Arsenal's Reliability," *The Washington Post*, 8 January 2002, A04.
70. "U.S. denies nuclear test rethink," BBC News, 8 January 2002, http://news.bbc.co.uk/hi/english/world.
71. Department of Defense Annual Report, 1992, 15–16.
72. Department of Defense Annual Report, 1995, 77.
73. Johnson, "Advocates and Activists," 56.
74. Johnson, "Nuclear Arms Control," 100–1.
75. Final Communiqué, Ministerial Meeting of the Defence Planning Committee and the Nuclear Planning Group, 5 December 2000, paragraph 9.
76. Final Communiqué, Ministerial Meeting of the North Atlantic Council Held in Budapest, 29 May 2001, paragraph 80.
77. Common position 1999/533/CFSP, 29 July 1999.
78. Council Decision 2001/286/CFSP, 9 April 2001.
79. (First) Hague Convention, 1899, Article 23. The (Second) Hague Convention, 1907, here reads "unnecessary suffering."
80. (First) Hague Convention, 1899, Article 22.
81. Fourth Geneva Convention, 1949, Article III.
82. Maresca and Maslen, *Banning of Anti-Personnel Landmines*, 9–13.
83. Winslow, *Sowing the Dragon's Teeth*, 142; Stuart Maslen, "The Role of the International Committee of the Red Cross," in *Walk Without Fear*, ed. Cameron et al., 83.
84. Motoko Mekata, "Building Partnerships Toward a Common Goal: Experiences of the International Campaign to Ban Landmines," in *Third Force*, ed. Florini, 144.
85. Jody Williams and Stephen Goose, "The International Campaign to Ban Landmines," in *Walk Without Fear*, ed. Cameron, et al., 22–6.
86. Mekata, "Building Partnerships," 149.
87. Michael Dolan and Chris Hunt, "Negotiating in the Ottawa Process: The New Multilateralism," in *Walk Without Fear*, ed. Cameron et al., 401.
88. Mekata, "Building Partnerships," 158.
89. Williams and Goose, "International Campaign," 33.
90. David Long and Laird Hindle, "Europe and the Ottawa Process: An Overview," in *Walk Without Fear*, ed. Cameron et al., 248–54.
91. "Towards a Global Ban on Anti-Personnel Mines Declaration of the Ottawa Conference," Canadian Department of Foreign Affairs and International Trade.
92. Williams and Goose, "International Campaign," 134–6. Brian W. Tomlin, "On a Fast Track to a Ban: The Canadian Policy Process," in *Walk Without Fear*, ed. Cameron et al., 205, argues that the director-general of the Canadian International Security Bureau, Ralph Lysyshyn, deserves credit for the boldness of Axworthy's statement.
93. Mekata, "Building Partnerships," 162; Mary Wareham, "Rhetoric and Policy Realities in the United States," in *Walk Without Fear*, ed. Cameron et al., 227–9; Williams and Goose, "International Campaign," 141.
94. Wareham, "Rhetoric and Policy Realities," 231–3; Dolan and Hunt, "Negotiating in the Ottawa Process," 411–12; Williams and Stephen Goose, "International Campaign," 44.
95. Williams and Goose, "International Campaign," 44–6.
96. Hampson et al., *Madness in the Multitude*, 94.
97. Joint Action 95/170/CFSP, 12 May 1995.

98. EU Press Statement on Anti-Personnel Landmines, 13 May 1996.
99. Joint Action 96/588/CFSP.
100. Philippe Chabasse, "The French Campaign," in *Walk Without Fear*, ed. Cameron et al., 61–2.
101. Williams and Goose, "International Campaign," 26.
102. EU Joint Action 97/817/CFSP. Also Long and Hindle, "Europe and the Ottawa Process," 266–7.
103. National Defense Authorization Act for Fiscal Year 1993, Section 1365.
104. Wareham, "Rhetoric and Policy Realities," 218–19.
105. Winslow, *Sowing the Dragon's Teeth*, 135–6.
106. Mekata, "Building Partnerships," 156.
107. Foreign Operations, Export Financing, and Related Programs Appropriations Act, 1996, Section 580.
108. Chabasse, "The French Campaign," 64.
109. "U.S. Announces Anti-Personnel Landmine Policy," The White House, 16 May 1996.
110. Long and Hindle, "Europe and the Ottawa Process," 256–7; Robert J. Lawson, Mark Gwozdecky, Jill Sinclair, and Ralph Lysyshyn, "The Ottawa Process and the International Movement to Ban Anti-Personnel Landmines," in *Walk Without Fear*, ed. Cameron et al., 164.
111. Dolan and Hunt, "Negotiating in the Ottawa Process," 404; Lawson, "The Ottawa Process: Fast-Track Diplomacy and the International Movement to Ban Land Mines," in *Leadership and Dialogue*, ed. Hampson and Molot, 85.
112. "Statement by the Press Secretary: United States Announces Next Steps on Anti-Personnel Landmines," The White House, 17 January 1997.
113. Wareham, "Rhetoric and Policy Realities," 224–31.
114. Renner and Peterson, *Small Arms, Big Impact;* Michael Klare, "An Overview of the Global Trade in Small Arms and Light Weapons," in *Small Arms Control*, ed. Dhanapala, 4–8.
115. Hampson et al., *Madness in the Multitude*, 109–11.
116. Statement by John R. Bolton to the UN Conference on Illicit Trade in Small Arms and Light Weapons, 9 July 2001.
117. Loretta Bondi (Advocacy Director, The Fund for Peace) and Tamar Gabelnick (Director, Arms Sales Monitoring Project, Federation of American Scientists), in discussion with the author, June 2002.
118. "Small Arms Issues: U.S. Policy and Views," ACDA Fact Sheet, 11 August 1998.
119. Jayantha Dhanapala, "Epilogue: Recent Governmental, Trans-governmental and Nongovernmental Efforts to Curb the Spread of Small Arms," in *Small Arms Control*, ed. Dhanapala, 289–91.
120. Ian Anthony, "Causation and the Arms Trade, with Reference to Small Arms," in *Small Arms Control*, ed. Dhanapala, 70–1.
121. 1999/34/CFSP, 17 December 1998.
122. Statement by John R. Bolton to the UN Conference on Illicit Trade in Small Arms and Light Weapons, 9 July 2001.
123. Goldblat and Bernauer, *Third Review*, 15–16.
124. Chevrier, "Towards a Verification Protocol," 201.
125. Tibor Tóth, "Negotiating a Compliance Protocol for the Biological Weapons Convention," in *New Terror*, ed. Drell et al., 228–9.
126. Pearson, *UNSCOM Saga*, 11–15; Deaver, *Disarming Iraq*, 71, 91–5.

127. Ritter, *Endgame*, 176–7; Butler, *Greatest Threat*, 91–104;

128. Butler, *Greatest Threat*, 132. For the contrary view, see Ritter, *Endgame*, 20, 193–4; and Wurmser, *Tyranny's Ally*, 32–7.

129. Butler, *Greatest Threat*, 188–212.

130. Ibid., 227.

131. Final report of the Special Conference of the States Parties to the BWC, 19–30 September 1994.

132. Moodie, and others who preferred to remain off the record, in discussion with the author, June 2002.

133. Graham S. Pearson, "The Prohibition of Chemical and Biological Weapons," in *Verification*, ed. Dando et al., 23–4.

134. Tucker, "From Arms Race to Abolition," 214.

135. Woollett and Radcliffe, "Bioweapons," 8.

136. "Germ Warfare Talks Open in London; U.S. is the Pariah," *New York Times*, 23 July 2001, http://www.nytimes.com.

137. Statement by Ambassador Donald A. Mahley, United States Special Negotiator for Chemical and Biological Arms Control Issues, to the AHG of the BWC, 25 July 2001.

138. Ambassador Don Mahley (Special Negotiator for Chemical and Biological Arms Control, U.S. Department of State), in discussion with the author, June 2002.

139. Press Briefing by National Security Advisor Condoleezza Rice, on the APEC Meeting, 15 October 2001.

140. Mike Allen, "U.S. Seeks To Stiffen Treaty on Germ War: Pact's Enforcement Mechanism Faulted," *Washington Post*, 17 October 2001, A21.

141. John R. Bolton, U.S. Under Secretary of State for Arms Control and International Security, Statement to the Fifth Review Conference of the Biological Weapons Convention, 19 November 2001. Note that Bolton and Rice both refer to the "draft protocol," as the United States did not consider the labels "compliance" or "verification" to be accurate.

142. Jenni Rissanen, "Endgame in Earnest: First Draft of Final Declaration Issued on Penultimate Day," *BWC Review Conference Bulletin*, The Acronym Institute, 6 December 2001.

143. Emma Jane Kirby, "Bio-Weapons Talks Suspended: The U.S. Says Work on the Ban will Continue," *BBC News*, 7 December 2001, http://news.bbc.co.uk/hi/english/world; Rissanen, "Calm After the Storm: General Debate Concludes as The Hard Work Begins," *BWC Review Conference Bulletin*, The Acronym Institute, 26 November 2001; Rissanen, "Differences and Difficulties as Delegates Consider Wide Range of Proposals," *BWC Review Conference Bulletin*, The Acronym Institute, 30 November 2001.

144. European Union official, in discussions with the author, June 2002.

145. *Final Document, Fifth Review Conference of the States Parties to the BWC*, 3–4.

146. Richard Guthrie, "Technological Aspects of Verification: Declarations, Managed Access and Confidential Proprietary Information," in *Verification*, ed. Dando et al., 155–6.

147. Michael Moodie (president, Chemical and Biological Arms Control Institute), in discussion with the author, June 2002. Also Amy Sands (deputy director, Center for Nonproliferation Studies, Monterey Institute of International Studies), in discussion with the author, May 2002.

148. "Summary of PhRMA's Position on a Compliance Protocol to the Biological Weapons Convention"; "Compliance Protocol to the Biological Weapons

Convention: A Joint Position of European, United States and Japanese Industry."

149. Marie Isabelle Chevrier, "Towards a Verification Protocol," in *Verification*, ed. Dando et al., 202–10.

150. Goldblat and Bernauer, *Third Review*, 5.

151. Sands was the only such interviewee using that term willing to be quoted by name; Moodie more delicately referred to the "difficulties of the Iraq inspections."

152. Mahley, discussions.

153. 1999/346/CFSP, 17 May 1999.

154. Mahley, discussions.

155. Fred Tanner, "The Euro-Mediterranean Security Partnership: Prospects for Arms Limitation and Confidence-Building," in *Barcelona Process*, ed. Vasconcelos and Joffé, 200.

156. For more on the Russian–American negotiations on the ABM Treaty, see Thomas S. Mowle, "Arms Control after the Cold War," in *Milestones*, ed. Smith and Hall, 179–208.

157. Steven Erlanger, "Bush's Move on ABM Pact Gives Pause to Europeans," *The New York Times*, 13 December 2001, http://www.nytimes.com/.

158. Alton Frye, "The New NATO and Relations with Russia," in *NATO Enters the 21st Century*, ed. Carpenter, 99–100.

159. David Charter, "Straw Backs Missile Defence," *The Times (London)*, 21 November 2001, http://www.thetimes.co.uk; David R. Sands, "Germany: Missile Defense Won't Hurt Ties," *The Washington Times*, 27 July 2001, http://www.washingtonpost.com.

4 ENVIRONMENT

1. William C. Clark, Jill Jäger, Jeannine Cavender-Bares, and Nancy M. Dickson, "Acid Rain, Ozone Depletion, and Climate Change: An Historical Overview," in *Global Environmental Risks, Vol. 1*, Social Learning Group, 25–31.

2. Brian Wynne and Peter Simmons with Claire Waterton, Peter Hughes, and Simon Shackley, "Institutional Cultures and the Management of Global Environmental Risks in the United Kingdom," in *Global Environmental Risks, Vol. 1*, Social Learning Group, 97.

3. William C. Clark and Nancy M. Dickson, "Civic Science: America's Encounter with Global Environmental Risks," in *Global Environmental Risks, Vol. 1*, Social Learning Group, 262.

4. Gehring, *Dynamic International Regimes*, 63–8.

5. Clark and Dickson, "Civic Science," 264.

6. William L. Schroeer, "Progress Toward Canadian-U.S. Acid Rain Control," in *Nine Case Studies*, ed. Susskind et al., 179–84.

7. Gehring, *Dynamic International Regimes*, 105–19.

8. Michael Huber and Angela Libertore, "A Regional Approach to the Management of Global Environmental Risks: The Case of the European Community," in *Global Environmental Risks, Vol. 1*, Social Learning Group, 295–6.

9. Weale et al., *Environmental Governance*, 2–3, 32–4.

10. Ibid., 56–9.

11. Jeannine Cavender-Bares and Jill Jäger with Renate Ell, "Developing a Precautionary Approach: Global Environmental Risk Management in Germany," in *Global Environmental Risks, Vol. 1*, Social Learning Group, 63–4.

12. Weale et al., *Environmental Governance*, 94–7.

13. Miranda A. Schreurs et al., "Issue Attention, Framing, and Actors: An Analysis of Patterns across Arenas," in *Global Environmental Risks, Vol. 1*, Social Learning Group, 355.

14. Weale et al., *Environmental Governance*, 399–400.

15. Mark Corrales and Tony Dreyfus, "Negotiations over Auto Emissions Standards in the European Economic Community 1983–1989," in *Nine Case Studies*, ed. Sússkind et al., 47–50.

16. Weale et al., *Environmental Governance*, 4–5, 42–7.

17. Single European Act, Articles 6 and 7.

18. Corrales and Dreyfus, "Auto Emissions Standards," 50–1.

19. Weale et al., *Environmental Governance*, 127, 400–2.

20. Gehring, *Dynamic International Regimes*, 64–5.

21. Cavender-Bares and Jäger with Ell, "Developing a Precautionary Approach," 61–5, 78–80.

22. Weale et al., *Environmental Governance*, 388–92.

23. Wynne et al., "Institutional Cultures," 93–9.

24. 88/609/EEC.

25. Angela Liberatore, "The European Union: Bridging Domestic and International Environmental Policy-Making," in *Internationalization of Environmental Protection*, ed. Schreurs and Economy, 195.

26. Litfin, *Ozone Discourses*, 62–4.

27. Robert Falkner, "Business Conflict and U.S. International Environmental Policy: Ozone, Climate, and Biodiversity," in *Environment*, ed. Harris, 164.

28. Clark et al., "Historical Overview," 39.

29. Gehring, *Dynamic International Regimes*, 203–15.

30. Litfin, *Ozone Discourses*, 74–6.

31. Srini Sitaraman, "Evolution of the Ozone Regime: Local, National, and International Influences," in *Environment*, ed. Harris, 122.

32. Gehring, *Dynamic International Regimes*, 237–9.

33. Edward A. Parson, "The Montreal Protocol: The First Adaptive Global Environmental Regime?" in *Protecting the Ozone Layer*, ed. Le Prestre et al., 128.

34. Gehring, *Dynamic International Regimes*, 260.

35. Litfin, *Ozone Discourses*, 114.

36. Granda, "Montreal Protocol," 39.

37. Michael J. Glennon and Alison L. Stewart, "The United States: Taking Environmental Treaties Seriously," in *Engaging Countries*, ed. Weiss and Jacobson, 193.

38. Huber and Libertore, "Regional Approach," 301.

39. Wynne and Simmons et al., "Institutional Cultures," 93.

40. Litfin, *Ozone Discourses*, 128, 149–51.

41. Gehring, *Dynamic International Regimes*, 284–5.

42. Litfin, *Ozone Discourses*, 168–76; Gehring, *Dynamic International Regimes*, 312–13.

43. Alberta M. Sbragia with Philipp M. Hildebrand, "The European Union and Compliance: A Story in the Making," in *Engaging Countries*, ed. Weiss and Jacobson, 225–6.

44. Rodney Dobell et al., "Implementation in the Management of Global Environmental Risks," in *Global Environmental Risks, Vol. 2*, Social Learning Group, 125.
45. Neil E. Harrison, "From the Inside Out: Domestic Influences on Global Environmental Policy," in *Climate Change*, ed. Harris, 93–4.
46. Huber and Libertore, "Regional Approach," 297.
47. Miranda A. Schreurs, "Domestic Institutions and International Environmental Agendas in Japan and Germany," in *Internationalization of Environmental Protection*, ed. Schreurs and Economy, 143.
48. Josee van Eijndhoven with Gerda Dinkelman, Jeroen van der Sluijs, Ruud Pleune, and Cor Worrell, "Finding Your Place: A History of the Management of Global Environmental Risks in the Netherlands," in *Global Environmental Risks, Vol. 1*, Social Learning Group, 118.
49. Cavender-Bares and Jäger with Ell, "Precautionary Approach," 68; Wynne et al., "Institutional Cultures," 99.
50. Marc A. Levy et al., "Goal and Strategy Formulation in the Management of Global Environmental Risks," in *Global Environmental Risks, Vol. 2*, Social Learning Group, 94.
51. Litfin, *Ozone Discourses*, 110–13; Schreurs, "Domestic Institutions," 145–6.
52. Joanne M. Kauffman, "Domestic and International Linkages in Global Environmental Politics: A Case-Study of the Montreal Protocol," in *Internationalization of Environmental Protection*, ed. Schreurs and Economy, 78–9.
53. Falkner, "Business Conflict," 165.
54. Quote from Litfin, *Ozone Discourses*, 83; stance also reported in Schreurs et al., "Issue Attention, Framing, and Actors," 357, and Alberta M. Sbragia with Philipp M. Hildebrand, "The European Union and Compliance: A Story in the Making," in *Engaging Countries*, ed. Weiss and Jacobson, 224.
55. Gehring, *Dynamic International Regimes*, 233.
56. Richard Elliot Benedick, "The Montreal Protocol as a New Approach to Diplomacy," in *Protecting the Ozone Layer*, ed. Le Prestre et al., 82.
57. Litfin, *Ozone Discourses*, 87.
58. Harrison, "From the Inside Out," 90–7.
59. Litfin, *Ozone Discourses*, 93; Kauffman, "Domestic and International Linkages," 81; Falkner, "Business Conflict," 166; Chris Granda, "The Montreal Protocol on Substances that Deplete the Ozone Layer," in *Nine Case Studies*, ed. Susskind et al., 37.
60. Duncan Brack, "The Use of Trade Measures in the Montreal Protocol," in *Protecting the Ozone Layer*, ed. Le Prestre, Reid, and Morehouse, 100–5.
61. Gehring, *Dynamic International Regimes*, 253–8.
62. Litfin, *Ozone Discourses*, 114.
63. Mostafa K. Tolba, "The Story of the Ozone Layer: Lessons Learned and Impacts on the Future," in *Protecting the Ozone Layer*, ed. Le Prestre, Reid, and Morehouse, 20–3.
64. Benedick, "Montreal Protocol," 87.
65. Gehring, *Dynamic International Regimes*, 291–5.
66. Litfin, *Ozone Discourses*, 153–5.
67. Sitaraman, "Evolution of the Ozone Regime," 124.
68. Litfin, *Ozone Discourses*, 108.
69. Ibid., 113.

70. Gehring, *Dynamic International Regimes*, 244–8.
71. Tolba, "Story of the Ozone Layer," 21.
72. Huber and Libertore, "Regional Approach," 311–14.
73. Elizabeth Cook, "Lessons from the CFC Phase-out in the United States," in *Protecting the Ozone Layer*, ed. Le Prestre, Reid, and Morehouse, 180–3.
74. Bodansky, "The History of the Global Climate Change Regime," in *International Relations*, ed. Luterbacher and Sprinz, 24–9.
75. Clark and Dickson, "Civic Science," 270.
76. Cavender-Bares and Jäger with Ell, "Precautionary Approach," 69.
77. Barrett, "Political Economy," 117.
78. Roderick Ogley, "Between the Devil and the Law of the Sea: The Generation of Global Environmental Norms," in *Environment*, ed. Vogler and Imber, 165; Paul G. Harris, "International Environmental Affairs and U.S. Foreign Policy," in *Environment*, ed. Harris, 13; Linda C. Reif, "Environment Policy: The Rio Summit Five Years Later," in *Leadership and Dialogue*, ed. Hampson and Molot, 267–84.
79. Oberthür and Ott, *Kyoto Protocol*, 33–6.
80. Bodansky, "International Law," 207.
81. Oberthür and Ott, *Kyoto Protocol*, 8–14.
82. Jacob Park, "Governing Climate Change Policy: From Scientific Obscurity to Foreign Policy Prominence," in *Climate Change*, ed. Harris, 80.
83. Oberthür and Ott, *Kyoto Protocol*, 40–7.
84. Ibid., 24–8.
85. Ibid., 17–23; Frank Grundig, Hugh Ward, and Ethan R. Zorick, "Modeling Global Climate Negotiations," in *International Relations*, ed. Luterbacher and Sprinz, 168.
86. Paul G. Harris, "Climate Change and American Foreign Policy: An Introduction," in *Climate Change*, ed. Harris, 12–13.
87. Oberthür and Ott, *Kyoto Protocol*, 103–4.
88. Ibid., 52–4.
89. Ibid., 55–7.
90. Ibid., 120–9.
91. Harris, "Introduction," 10.
92. Moore, *Sickness or Health*; Shogren, *Benefits and Costs*, 14–23.
93. Detlef F. Sprinz and Martin Weiss, "Domestic Politics and Global Climate Policy," in *International Relations*, ed. Luterbacher and Sprinz, 69–90; Grundig, Ward, and Zorick, "Modeling Global Climate Negotiations," 165–76; Halucha, "Climate Change Politics," 293–5.
94. Oberthür and Ott, *Kyoto Protocol*, 88–91.
95. Ibid., 270.
96. Ibid., 85–7, 137, 268–9.
97. Balakrishnan, "Kyoto Protocol," 332.
98. Missbach, "Regulation Theory," 145.
99. Oberthür and Ott, *Kyoto Protocol*, 197–204, 288–9.
100. Harris, "Introduction," 13–5.
101. Park, "Governing Climate Change Policy," 85–6.
102. Posted on www.climnet.org.
103. Oberthür and Ott, *Kyoto Protocol*, 261–3.
104. European Council Declaration on Climate Change, Annex II to the Presidency Conclusions of the Stockholm European Council, 24 March 2001.

105. "President Bush Discusses Global Climate Change," *White House Press Release*, 11 June 2001.
106. Eric Pianin, "Koizumi Strengthens Bush's Hand On Kyoto," *The Washington Post*, 2 July 2001, A02.
107. Doug Struck, "Japan's Leader Stuck in the Middle on Kyoto," *The Washington Post*, 12 July 2001, A23.
108. William Drozdiak, "U.S., Japan Are Pressed On Kyoto," *The Washington Post*, 17 July 2001, A11.
109. Drozdiak, "U.S. Left Out of Warming Treaty: EU-Japan Bargain Saves Kyoto Pact," *The Washington Post*, 24 July 2001, A01; Eric Pianin and Dana Milbank, "Climate Agreement Leaves U.S. Out in the Cold," *The Washington Post*, 24 July 2001, A16; "Breakthrough in Bonn?" *Economist.com*, 23 July 2001; Andrew C. Revkin, "178 Nations Reach Climate Accord: U.S. Only Looks On," *The New York Times*, 24 July 2001, http://www.nytimes.com/; Carol J. Williams, "Nations Adopt Climate Pact Without U.S." *The Los Angeles Times*, 24 July 2001, http://www.latimes.com/; Williams, "Environmentalist Claim Global Bid to Reduce "Greenhouse Gases" Instead Cuts Expectations," *The Los Angeles Times*, 25 July 2001, http://www.latimes.com/.
110. Pianin, "Warming Pact a Win for European Leaders," *The Washington Post*, 11 November 2001, A02.
111. Revkin, "Bush Offers Plan for Voluntary Measures to Limit Gas Emissions," *The New York Times*, 15 February 2002, http://www.nytimes.com/; Pianin, "Bush Unveils Global Warming Plan," *The Washington Post*, 15 February 2002, A09.
112. Alexandra Zavis, "Approval of Kyoto Pact Said to be Near," *The Washington Times*, 4 September 2002, http://www.washingtontimes.com.
113. Paul Georgia, "Global-Warming Minefield," *National Review Online*, 15 February 2002.
114. European Environment Agency, *Annual European Community Greenhouse Gas Inventory 1990–2001 and Inventory Report 2003* (Technical report No. 95), 5 May 2003. Posted at http://reports.eea.eu.int/technical_report_2003_95/en.
115. *Greenhouse Gas Inventory 1990–2001*, 6–7.
116. Oberthür and Ott, *Kyoto Protocol*, 67–8.
117. Ibid., 65–8, 147–9.
118. Shogren, *Benefits and Costs*, 31.
119. Paul G. Harris, "International Norms of Responsibility and U.S. Climate Change Policy," in *Climate Change*, ed. Harris, 231–5.
120. Burniaux and O'Brien, *Action Against Climate Change*, 78.
121. Oberthür and Ott, *Kyoto Protocol*, 228–9.
122. Ibid., 65–8.
123. Ibid., 293–4.
124. Morlot, *National Climate Policies*, 51.
125. Josee van Eijndhoven et al., "Finding Your Place," 120.
126. Remarks of U.S. Ambassador to the EU Richard Morningstar to The European Policy Center's Environment Conference, Brussels, 2 May 2001.
127. *Greenhouse Gas Inventory 1990–2001*, 7.
128. Scott Barrett, "Political Economy of the Kyoto Protocol," in *Environmental Policy*, ed. Helm, 117.
129. Huber and Libertore, "Regional Approach," 302.
130. Wynne et al., "Institutional Cultures," 103.

131. Scott Barrett, "Political Economy," 118–20.

132. Urs Luterbacher and Carla Norrlöf, "The Organization of World Trade and the Climate Regime," in *International Relations*, ed. Luterbacher and Sprinz, 284–88.

133. Harrison, "From the Inside Out," 101–2.

134. Rodney Dobell with Justin Longo, Jeannine Cavender-Bares, William C. Clark, Nancy M. Dickson, Gerda Dinkelman, Adam Fenech, Peter M. Haas, Jill Jäger, Ruud Pleune, Ferenc L. Tóth, Miranda A. Schreurs, and Josee van Eijndhoven, "Implementation in the Management of Global Environmental Risks," in *Global Environmental Risks, Vol. 2*, Social Learning Group, 129–30; Clark and Dickson, "Civic Science," 278.

135. Bryner, "Congress and the Politics of Climate Change," in *Climate Change*, ed. Harris, 121.

136. Oberthür and Ott, *Kyoto Protocol*, 126–8.

137. Barrett, "Political Economy," 124.

138. Victor, *Collapse of the Kyoto Protocol*, 48.

139. Burniaux and O'Brien, *Action Against Climate Change*, 44–61.

140. Ronald B. Mitchell, "Institutional Aspects of Implementation, Compliance, and Effectiveness," in *International Relations*, ed. Luterbacher and Sprinz, 227; Barrett, "Political Economy," 123–7; Burniaux and O'Brien, *Action Against Climate Change*, 9–18; Victor, *Collapse of the Kyoto Protocol*, 8–11; Oberthür and Ott, *Kyoto Protocol*, 131–6, 151–197.

141. Karen Fisher-Vanden, "International Policy Instrument Prominence in the Climate Change Debate," in *Climate Change*, ed. Harris, 160–6.

142. Media Roundtable With Timothy Wirth, U.S. Under Secretary Of State For Global Affairs, Tokyo, Japan, 10 November 1997.

143. Uma Balakrishnan, "The Kyoto Protocol: A Balance of Interests," in *Contemporary Cases*, ed. Carter, 329; Victor, *Collapse of the Kyoto Protocol*, 42.

144. Barrett, "Political Economy," 112–16, 137–8; Ian H. Rowlands, "Classical Theories of International Relations," in *International Relations*, ed. Luterbacher and Sprinz, 56–8; Daniel Bodansky, "International Law and the Design of a Climate Change Regime," in *International Relations*, ed. Luterbacher and Sprinz, 204–17.

145. Falkner, "Business Conflict," 158–69; Clark and Dickson, "Civic Science," 271–8.

146. Huber and Libertore, "Regional Approach," 306.

5 HUMAN RIGHTS

1. Lawrence Weschler, "Exceptional Cases in Rome: The United States and the Struggle for an ICC," in *United States and the International Criminal Court*, ed. Sewall and Kaysen, 110.

2. Hampson et al., *Madness in the Multitude*, 64–5.

3. Ball, *Prosecuting War Crimes and Genocide*, 21.

4. Leila Nadya Sadat, "The Evolution of the ICC: From The Hague to Rome and Back Again," in *United States and the International Criminal Court*, ed. Sewall and Kaysen, 34.

5. Miskowiak, *International Criminal Court*, 44.

6. Ball, *Prosecuting War Crimes and Genocide*, 49.

7. Sadat, "Evolution of the ICC," 35.

8. Hampson et al., *Madness in the Multitude*, p. 66.

9. Samantha Power, "The United States and Genocide Law: A History of Ambivalence," in *United States and the International Criminal Court*, ed. Sewall and Kaysen, 165.

10. LeBlanc, *United States and the Genocide Convention*, 11–12; 220–1; Catherine Redgwell, "The Law of Reservations in Respect of Multilateral Conventions," in *Human Rights as General Norms*, ed. Gardner, 3.

11. Ralph G. Carter and Donald W. Jackson, "The International Criminal Court: Present at the Creation?" in *Contemporary Cases in U.S. Foreign Policy*, ed. Carter, 367–8.

12. LeBlanc, *United States and the Genocide Convention*, 201–9, 228. Spain made a similar reservation, 211.

13. Ibid., 135, 146.

14. Ibid., 153–70.

15. Ibid., 176–99.

16. Accession and ratification status from www.unhchr.ch/html/menu3/b/ treaty1gen.htm. New EU member Malta had not ratified as of 9 October 2001.

17. LeBlanc, *United States and the Genocide Convention*, 144.

18. Power, "United States and Genocide Law," 167–9.

19. LeBlanc, *United States and the Genocide Convention*, 106.

20. Ibid., 25–97.

21. Sadat, "Evolution of the ICC," 37–8.

22. Adriaan Bos, "The Experience of the Preparatory Committee," in *Challenge to Impunity*, ed. Nesi and Politi, 20.

23. Hampson et al., *Madness in the Multitude*, 69.

24. Robertson, *Crimes against Humanity*, 72–6.

25. "Dutch Government Quits over Srebrenica," *BBC World*, 16 April 2002, http://news.bbc.co.uk/hi/english/world/.

26. Robertson, *Crimes against Humanity*, 285–96.

27. Spyros Economides, "The International Criminal Court," in *Ethics and Foreign Policy*, ed. Smith and Light, 114–15.

28. Ball, *Prosecuting War Crimes and Genocide*, 171–2.

29. Richard J. Goldstone and Gary Jonathan Bass, "Lessons from the International Criminal Tribunals," in *United States and the International Criminal Court*, ed. Sewall and Kaysen, 51.

30. Sadat, "Evolution of the ICC," 38–9.

31. Robertson, *Crimes against Humanity*, 336.

32. Miskowiak, *International Criminal Court*, 17.

33. Weschler, "Exceptional Cases," 107.

34. Rome Statute, Article 8-2-b-xx.

35. Elizabeth Wilmshurst, "The International Criminal Court: The Role of the Security Council," in *Challenge to Impunity*, ed. Nesi and Politi, 41; Bartram S. Brown, "The Statute of the ICC: Past, Present, and Future," in *United States and the International Criminal Court*, ed. Sewall and Kaysen, 67.

36. Rome Statute, Article 8-2-b-viii.

37. Economides, "International Criminal Court," 118.

38. Rome Statute, Article 8. See Herman von Hebel and Darryl Robinson, "Crimes within the Jurisdiction of the Court," in *Making of the Rome Statute*, ed. Lee, 107–12.

39. Economides, "International Criminal Court," 120.

40. David Scheffer, "The United States and the ICC," in *International Crimes, Peace, and Human Rights*, ed. Shelton, 204–5.

41. Wilmshurst, "Jurisdiction of the Court," in *Making of the Rome Statute*, ed. Lee, 132.

42. Weschler, "Exceptional Cases," 97–99.

43. Miskowiak, *International Criminal Court*, 26–8.

44. Quotes from Robertson, *Crimes against Humanity*, 325. For the decisions of different groups, see Hampson et al., *Madness in the Multitude*, 71; Miskowiak, *International Criminal Court*, 14–15; and Schabas, *Introduction to the International Criminal Court*, 15.

45. Carter and Jackson, "International Criminal Court," 365. Miskowiak, *International Criminal Court*, 15, goes against the consensus on Yemen, suggesting that India cast the seventh vote against the court.

46. Weschler, "Exceptional Cases," 110.

47. Carter and Jackson, "Present at the Creation?" 379.

48. McNerney, "Issues for Consideration," 190.

49. Bolton, Senate testimony, 23 July 1998.

50. Ruth Wedgwood, "The Irresolution of Rome," in *United States and the International Criminal Court*, ed. Morris, 201–8.

51. Statement by the President on the Signature of the International Criminal Court Treaty, 31 December 2000.

52. Weschler, "Exceptional Cases," 104–7; Robertson, *Crimes against Humanity*, 304; Ball, *Prosecuting War Crimes and Genocide*, 191.

53. Hans-Peter Kaul, "The International Criminal Court: Trigger Mechanism and Relationship to National Jurisdictions," in *Challenge to Impunity*, ed. Nesi and Politi, 61.

54. Miskowiak, *International Criminal Court*, 25–30, 36–7; Scheffer, "The U.S. Perspective on the ICC," in *United States and the International Criminal Court*, ed. Sewall and Kaysen, 116.

55. Michael P. Scharf, "The ICC's Jurisdiction over the Nationals of Non-Party States," in *United States and the International Criminal Court*, ed. Sewall and Kaysen, 213–25.

56. Sadat, "Evolution of the ICC," 39.

57. Brown, "Statute of the ICC," 63.

58. Carter and Jackson, "Present at the Creation?" 371–6; Bolton, "Risks and Weaknesses," 173.

59. Fernández de Gurmendi, "The Role of the International Prosecutor," in *Making of the Rome Statute*, ed. Lee, 180–1.

60. Morris, "Complementarity and Conflict: States, Victims, and the ICC," in *National Security and International Law*, ed. Sewall and Kaysen, 198–204; Miskowiak, *International Criminal Court*, 41.

61. Morris, "Complementarity and Conflict," 196.

62. Economides, "International Criminal Court," 124; Weschler, "Exceptional Cases in Rome," 92.

63. Sadat, *Justice for the New Millennium*, 70.

64. Scheffer, "The U.S. Perspective," 115–17.

65. Weschler, "Exceptional Cases," 95.

66. Robertson, *Crimes against Humanity*, 407.

67. Morris, "High Crimes and Misconceptions," 236–41.

68. Lietzau, "International Criminal Law after Rome: Concerns from a U.S. Military Perspective," in *United States and the International Criminal Court*, ed.

Morris, 122, 133; Bolton, "Risks and Weaknesses," 172; Patricia McNerney, "The International Criminal Court: Issues for Consideration by the United States Senate," in *United States and the International Criminal Court*, ed. Morris, 186.

69. Power, "The United States and Genocide Law," 171.

70. John R. Bolton, Hearing before the Senate Subcommittee on International Operations of the Committee on Foreign Relations, 23 July 1998.

71. Robinson O. Everett, "American Service Members and the ICC," in *United States and the International Criminal Court*, ed. Sewall and Kaysen, 138–42; Roger S. Clark, "The ICC Statute: Protecting the Sovereign Rights of Non-Parties," in *International Crimes, Peace, and Human Rights*, ed. Shelton, 217; William L. Nash, "The ICC and the Deployment of U.S. Armed Forces," in *United States and the International Criminal Court*, ed. Sewall and Kaysen, 155–7.

72. Ruth Wedgwood, "The Constitution and the ICC," in *National Security and International Law*, ed. Sewall and Kaysen, 123–9.

73. Rome Statute, Article 17-1-a.

74. Weschler, "Exceptional Cases," 96.

75. Steve Vogel, "Military Jury Acquits Pilot In Cable Car Tragedy Case," *The Washington Post*, 5 March 1999, http://www.washingtonpost.com.

76. "Italian Anger Over Cable Car Sentence," *BBC News*, 3 April 1999, http://news.bbc.co.uk/hi/english/world/.

77. Participants at the Salzburg Seminar, in discussion with the author, March 2001.

78. Morris, "High Crimes and Misconceptions," 221, 233.

79. Everett, "American Service Members," 139; Darryl Robinson, "Case Study: The International Criminal Court," in *Human Security and the New Diplomacy*, ed. McRae and Hubert, 175; Wedgwood, "Constitution and the ICC," 120.

80. Weschler, "Exceptional Cases," 100–1.

81. Miskowiak, *International Criminal Court*, 80.

82. Bolton, Senate Testimony, 23 July 1998.

83. Madeline Morris, "High Crimes and Misconceptions: The ICC and Non-Party States," in *International Crimes, Peace, and Human Rights*, ed. Shelton, 243.

84. John R. Bolton, "The Risks and Weaknesses of the International Criminal Court from America's Perspective," in *United States and the International Criminal Court*, ed. Morris, 171; Scheffer, "United States and the ICC," 206.

85. Wedgwood, "Irresolution of Rome," 194.

86. Amnesty International, *NATO/Federal Republic of Yugoslavia*, 2–3, 19.

87. Senator Jesse Helms, address to the United Nations Security Council, 20 January 2000, in *The Future of U.S.-UN Relations: A Dialogue between the Senate Foreign Relations Committee and the United Nations Security Council*, 9.

88. David Travers, "The UN: Squaring the Circle," in *Kosovo Crisis*, ed. Weymouth and Henig, 268.

89. Gabriella Venturini, "War Crimes in International Armed Conflicts," in *Challenge to Impunity*, ed. Nesi and Politi, 101; Schabas, "Follow up to Rome: Preparing for Entry into Force of the Statute of the International Criminal Court," in *Challenge to Impunity*, ed. Nesi and Politi, 209.

90. Miskowiak, *International Criminal Court*, 59–69.

91. Brown, "Statute of the ICC," 77–8.

92. Medard R. Rwelamira, "Composition and Administration of the Court," in *Making of the Rome Statute*, ed. Lee, 162.

93. Schabas, "The Penalty Provisions of the ICC Statute," in *International Crimes, Peace, and Human Rights*, ed. Shelton, 120.

94. Robertson, *Crimes against Humanity*, 370–4; Stefanie Grant, "The United States and the International Human Rights Treaty System: For Export Only?" in *Future of UN Human Rights Treaty Monitoring*, ed. Alston and Crawford, 325.

95. Robertson, *Crimes against Humanity*, 387.

96. Bolton, "Risks and Weaknesses," 170.

97. Bolton, Senate Testimony, 23 July 1998.

98. Philippe Kirsch, Q.C., "The International Criminal Court: Current Issues and Perspectives," in *United States and the International Criminal Court*, ed. Morris, 5–10.

99. Brown, "Statute of the ICC," 63.

100. Robertson, *Crimes against Humanity*, 329.

101. Kaul, "Trigger Mechanism," 62.

102. "Views and Comments by Governments," in *Making of the Rome Statute*, ed. Lee, 574 5.

103. Council Common Position 2001/443/CFSP on the International Criminal Court, 11 June 2001.

104. Arvonne S. Fraser, "The Convention on the Elimination of All Forms of Discrimination Against Women (The Women's Convention)," in *Women, Politics, and the United Nations*, ed. Winslow, 78–84.

105. Virginia R. Allan, Margaret E. Galey, and Mildred E. Persinger, "World Conference of International Women's Year," in *Women, Politics, and the United Nations*, ed. Winslow, 35–8.

106. Fraser, "The Women's Convention," in *Women, Politics, and the United Nations*, ed. Winslow, 88.

107. Charlotte G. Patton, "Women and Power: The Nairobi Conference, 1985," in *Women, Politics, and the United Nations*, ed. Winslow, 70.

108. Deirdre Fottrell, "One Step Forward or Two Steps Sideways? Assessing the First Decade of the United Nations Convention on the Rights of the Child," in *Revisiting Children's Rights*, ed. Fottrell, 1–2.

109. Jenny Kuper, "Children and Armed Conflict: Some Issues of Law and Policy," in *Revisiting Children's Rights*, ed. Fottrell, 105.

110. Fottrell, "One Step Forward?" 8.

111. LeBlanc, *Convention on the Rights of the Child*, 150–4.

112. Ross Snyder, "Case Study: The Optional Protocol on the Involvement of Children in Armed Conflict," in *Human Security*, ed. McRae and Hubert, 154–6.

113. Christine Chinkin, "Reservations and Objection to the Convention on the Elimination of All Forms of Discrimination Against Women," in *Reservations and Objections*, ed. Gardner, 71.

114. Drinan, *Mobilization of Shame*, 36; James Dao, "Senate Panel Approves Treaty Banning Bias Against Women," *The New York Times*, 31 July 2002, http://www.nytimes.com.

115. LeBlanc, *Convention on the Rights of the Child*, 68–84.

116. Doug Ireland, "U.S. and Evil Axis—Allies for Abstinence," *The Nation*, May 2002.

117. Goonesekere, *Women's Rights and Children's Rights*, 8, 37.

118. LeBlanc, *Convention on the Rights of the Child*, 161–79.

119. Peter Newell, "Ending Corporal Punishment of Children," in *Revisiting Children's Rights*, ed. Fottrell, 116–21.
120. Kilkelly, *Child and the European Convention on Human Rights*, 15.
121. Thomas A. Johnson, "Involvement of the Child in Armed Conflict," in *Children's Rights in America*, ed. Cohen and Davidson, 331–2; Cohn and Goodwin-Gill, *Child Soldiers*, 63–9.
122. Abraham Rabinovich, "Israel sees Victory in Conference Declaration," *The Washington Times*, 10 September 2001, http://www.washingtontimes.com.
123. Michael Dynes and Richard Beeston, "Jospin Leads EU Threat to Quit Racism Meeting," *The Times (London)*, 6 September 2001, http://www.thetimes.co.uk.
124. Dennis Brutus and Ben Cashdan, "Reflections on Durban," *The Nation*, September 2001.
125. "Crossfire Over Middle East and Slavery," *The New York Times*, 9 September 2001, http://www.nytimes.com/.
126. For more on Durban, see Lantos, "Durban Debacle."
127. Erik Prokosch, "The Death Penalty versus Human Rights," in *Abolition in Europe*, Council of Europe, 23.
128. "Facts and Figures on the Death Penalty," Amnesty International website, 2002.
129. *Council of Europe Press Release*, 11 June 2001.
130. Article 3. "Pursuit of happiness" did not make the cut for the UDHR, although Article 24 provides for "the right to rest and leisure."
131. Schabas, *Abolition of the Death Penalty*, 24, 42; Goldman and Lin, *Capital Punishment*, 158.
132. Schabas, *Abolition of the Death Penalty*, 7–10, 47–72.
133. Bedau, "Background and Developments," in *Death Penalty in America*, ed. Bedau, 78–81.
134. Philippe Toussaint, "The Death Penalty and the 'Fairy Ring,'" in *Abolition in Europe*, Council of Europe, 30.
135. Caroline Ravaud and Stefan Trechsel, "The Death Penalty and the Case-Law of the Institutions of the European Convention on Human Rights," in *Abolition in Europe*, Council of Europe, 82.
136. Bedau, "Background and Developments," 8–9.
137. Goldman and Lin, *Capital Punishment*, 16.
138. Banner, *Death Penalty*, 244–9.
139. Goldman and Lin, *Capital Punishment*, 17, 43.
140. Michel Forst, "The Abolition of the Death Penalty in France," in *Abolition in Europe*, Council of Europe, 109–14.
141. Banner, *Death Penalty*, 268–75.
142. Bedau, "Background and Developments," 8–9.
143. Goldman and Lin, *Capital Punishment*, 4, 13, 17–18, 48, 60; Prokosch, "Death Penalty versus Human Rights," 21.
144. Caroline Ravaud and Stefan Trechsel, "The Death Penalty and the Case-Law of the Institutions of the European Convention on Human Rights," in *Abolition in Europe*, Council of Europe, 87–90; Schabas, *Abolition of the Death Penalty*, 230–7.
145. For a thorough review of death penalty issues between the landmark cases and more recent events, see Bruce Shapiro, "Dead Reckoning," *The Nation*, 6 August 2001.
146. Schabas, *Abolition of the Death Penalty*, 148–51.

147. Ibid., 168–75.

148. Ibid., 188–9.

149. Roberto Toscano, "The United Nations and the Abolition of the Death Penalty," in *Abolition in Europe*, Council of Europe, 95–101.

150. Goldman and Lin, *Capital Punishment*, 159, 170–1, 183.

151. Schabas, *Abolition of the Death Penalty*, 83–8; Markus G. Schmidt, "Reservations to United Nations Human Rights Treaties: The Case of the Two Covenants," in *Human Rights as General Norms*, ed. Gardner, 22–6.

152. Hugo Adam Bedau, "International Human Rights Law and the Death Penalty in America," in *Death Penalty in America*, ed. Bedau, 246–7.

153. Schabas, *Abolition of the Death Penalty*, 89–90.

154. Suzanne D. Strater, "Death is Never in the 'Best Interest' of a Child," in *Death Penalty*, ed. Mitchell, 273–6; LeBlanc, *Convention on the Rights of the Child*, 74.

155. Prokosch, "Death Penalty versus Human Rights," 21.

156. Linda Greenhouse, "Ruling Barring Execution of Retarded May Not Lead to Further Restrictions," *The New York Times*, 22 June 2002, http://www.nytimes.com; Harvey Weistein, "Killer's Sentence of Death Debated," *Los Angeles Times*, 19 February 2002, http://www.latimes.com.

157. Anne Gearan, "High Court: Executing Mentally Retarded Unconstitutional," *The Washington Post*, 20 June 2002, http://www.washingtonpost.com; David Stout, "Supreme Court Bars Executing the Mentally Retarded," *The New York Times*, 20 June 2002, http://www.nytimes.com.

158. Sue Anne Pressley, "Mentally Ill Inmate's Fate Draws Protest," *The Washington Post*, 25 February 2002, A02.

159. Michel Forst, "Abolition in France," 113–14.

160. Goldman and Lin, *Capital Punishment*, 165.

161. Marshall, "Death in Venice"; Banner, *Death Penalty*, 301; Goldman and Lin, *Capital Punishment*, 166–8.

162. Beinart, "New Life."

163. Banner, *Death Penalty*, 304; Beinart, "New Life"; Kari Lydersen, "Death Penalty Foes See Progress in Illinois," *The Washington Post*, 11 March 2002, A02.

164. Jodi Wilgoren, "Governor Assails System's Errors as He Empties Illinois Death Row," *The New York Times*, 11 Jan 2003, http://www.nytimes.com/.

165. Katty Kay, "Death Penalty is Unlawful, Rules Judge," *The Times (London)*, 2 July 2002, http://www.thetimes.co.uk; Charles Lane, "Judge Says Executions Violate Constitution," *The Washington Post*, 2 July 2002, A01; Goldman and Lin, *Capital Punishment*, 183.

166. Schabas, *Abolition of the Death Penalty*, 221, 248; Hans Christian Krüger, "Protocol No. 6 to the European Convention on Human Rights," in *Abolition in Europe*, Council of Europe, 69–71.

167. Peter Sisler, "EU's death-penalty objection divides Turkey," *The Washington Times*, 19 February 2002, http://www.washingtontimes.com.

168. Renate Wohlwend, "The Efforts of the Parliamentary Assembly of the Council of Europe," in *Abolition in Europe*, Council of Europe, 55–7.

169. Interview with Renate Wohlwend, 14 April 2003, released by Council of Europe Press Service as "Death Penalty: Council of Europe Keeps up Pressure on Washington." Posted at http://www.coe.int/T/E/Communication_and_Research/Press/Theme_Files/Death_penalty/e_interview_wohlwend2.asp#TopOf Page.

170. Amnesty International USA, *Cases of Europeans*, 2–4. Quotations taken from International Court of Justice, *Summary of Court's Holding, LaGrand Case, (Germany v. United States of America)*, posted on www.globalpolicy.org/wld-court/icj/2001/german.htm. Also Jeremy Zucker, (clerk at the ICJ during the LaGrand case), in discussions with the author, October 2002.
171. Grant, "For Export Only?" 318.
172. Amnesty International USA, *Cases of Europeans*, 5.

6 MILITARY COOPERATION

1. Gaddis, "Long Peace."
2. Hereafter referenced simply as "Bosnia."
3. Cited in Blainey, *Causes of War*, 108.
4. Niblock, *Pariah States*, 99–104.
5. Litwak, *Rogue States*, 129–30; White, *Crises after the Storm*, 21–39.
6. White, *Crises after the Storm*, 40–8; Litwak, *Rogue States*, 131–2.
7. Litwak, *Rogue States*, 133.
8. Pearson, *UNSCOM Saga*, 56.
9. Litwak, *Rogue States*, 138–9; White, *Crises after the Storm*, 56–60; Kenneth I Juster, Iraq: "An American Perspective," in *Transatlantic Tensions*, ed. Haass 112–13.
10. Peter Viggo Jakobsen, "The Twelve and the Crises in the Gulf and Northern Iraq," in *European Approaches*, ed. Jørgensen, 26–9; Graham-Brown, *Sanctioning Saddam*, 25–37; Pelletiere, *Managing Strains*, 3; Deaver, *Disarming Iraq*, 63.
11. Katzman, *International Support*, 6.
12. Butler, *Greatest Threat*, 220.
13. Litwak, *Rogue States*, 131; Kenneth I. Juster, "Iraq: An American Perspective," Niblock, *Pariah States*, 111–21 details the shift in oil export limits.
14. Katzman, *International Support*, 2.
15. Ibid., 2.
16. Butler, *Greatest Threat*, 200; Niblock, *Pariah States*, 124–6.
17. Prados, *Iraq Crisis*, 2–4.
18. Dominique Moïsi, "Iraq," in *Transatlantic Tensions*, ed. Haass, 134–6; Graham-Brown, *Sanctioning Saddam*, 60–78; Katzman, *International Support*, 2.
19. Litwak, *Rogue States*, 3–12, 42, 68–85.
20. Ibid., 84
21. Anton Tus, "The War in Slovenia and Croatia up to the Sarajevo Ceasefire," in *War in Croatia and Bosnia-Herzegovina*, ed. Magaš and Žanić, 45–6; Sonia Lucarelli, "Europe's Response to the Yugoslav Imbroglio," in *European Approaches*, ed. Jørgensen, 36; Susan L. Woodward, "International Aspects of the Wars in Former Yugoslavia: 1990–1996," in *Burn This House*, ed. Udovički and Ridgeway, 224; Bert, *Reluctant Superpower*, 139; Holbrooke, *To End a War*, 21.
22. Tus, "Slovenia and Croatia," 48–54; Lucarelli, "Europe's Response," 39–40; Woodward, "International Aspects," 228.
23. Lucarelli, "Europe's Response," 37, 41; Woodward, "International Aspects," 225–8; Burg and Shoup, *War in Bosnia-Herzegovina*, 96.

24. Rieff, *Slaughterhouse*, 17–23.
25. Holbrooke, *To End a War*, 32.
26. Lucarelli, "Europe's Response," 44–5; Woodward, "International Aspects," 235–7; Douglas C. Foyle, "Public Opinion and Bosnia: Anticipating Disaster," in *Contemporary Cases*, ed. Carter, 33.
27. Burg and Shoup, *War in Bosnia-Herzegovina*, 146–9.
28. Daalder, *Getting to Dayton*, 31–2.
29. Lucarelli, "Europe's Response," 53.
30. Foyle, "Public Opinion and Bosnia," 44.
31. Ozren Žunic, "Operations Flash and Storm," in *War in Croatia and Bosnia*, ed. Magaš and Žanić, 69–75.
32. Rohde, *Endgame*, 77–159; Drew, *Berlin to Bosnia*, 15; Holbrooke, *To End a War*, 69–70.
33. Rohde, *Endgame*, 290–301; Bert, *Reluctant Superpower*, 221.
34. Dittman and Dawkins, *Deliberate Force*, 12.
35. Ripley, *Operation Deliberate Force*, 196–221; Daalder, *Getting to Dayton*, 114; Glenny, *Balkans*, 650–1.
36. Ripley, *Operation Deliberate Force*, 228–74.
37. Ibid., 281–97; Holbrooke, *To End a War*, 143–4.
38. Holbrooke, *To End a War*, 200–4; Bert, *Reluctant Superpower*, 224–5.
39. Richard Holbrooke, Statement at Field Hearing on Implementation of United Nations Reform, *The Future of U.S.—UN Relations: A Dialogue between the Senate Foreign Relations Committee and the United Nations Security Council*, 21 January 2000, 19.
40. Beverly Crawford, "Bosnian Road to NATO Enlargement," in *Explaining NATO Enlargement*, ed. Rauchhaus, 54–6; Bert, *Reluctant Superpower*, 227.
41. Sophia Clément, "Introduction," in *Issues Raised*, ed. Clément, 4.
42. Burg and Shoup, *War in Bosnia-Herzegovina*, 99–124; Jasminka Udovicki and Ejub Štitkovac, "Bosnia and Hercegovina: The Second War," in *Burn This House*, ed. Udovicki and Ridgeway, 185.
43. Holbrooke, *To End a War*, 318.
44. Lucarelli, "Europe's Response," 39.
45. Ripley, *Operation Deliberate Force*, 26, 107–38; Crawford, "Bosnian Road," 51; Lucarelli, "Europe's Response," 56; Daalder, *Getting to Dayton*, 41–5.
46. Holbrooke, *To End a War*, 143.
47. Bert, *Reluctant Superpower*, 65–123.
48. Holbrooke, *To End a War*, 23.
49. Cited by Jovan Divjak, "The First Phase, 1992–1993: Struggle for Survival and Genesis of the Army of Bosnia-Herzegovina," in *War in Croatia and Bosnia-Herzegovina*, ed. Magaš and Žanić, 166.
50. Baker, *Politics of Diplomacy*, 637.
51. Owen, *Balkan Odyssey*; Bert, *Reluctant Superpower*, 193–210.
52. Holbrooke, *To End a War*, 318.
53. Senior European Commission officials, in discussions with the author, May 2002.
54. Sikavica, "The Army's Collapse," in *Burn This House*, ed. Udovicki and Ridgeway, 147–8.
55. Daalder, *Getting to Dayton*, 15–19.
56. Rieff, *Slaughterhouse*, 28.
57. Holbrooke, *To End a War*, 65–7.

58. Nicole Gnesotto, "Prospects for Bosnia after SFOR," in *Issues Raised*, ed. Clément, 24–6; Jane Sharp, "Prospects for Peace in Bosnia: The Role of Britain," in *Issues Raised*, ed. Clément, 33; Susan Woodward, "The U.S. Perspective: Transition Postponed," in *Issues Raised*, ed. Clément, 46.
59. "U.S. Peacekeeping Contributions," *The New York Times*, 3 July 2002, http://www.nytimes.com/.
60. Natalie La Balme, "Constraint, Catalyst, or Political Tool? The French Public and Foreign Policy," in *Glass House*, ed. Nacos et al., 295; Pierangelo Isernia, "Where Angels Fear to Tread: Italian Public Opinion and Foreign Policy," in *Glass House*, ed. Nacos et al., 292; Crawford, "The Bosnian Road," 46; Richard Sobel, "To Intervene or Not to Intervene in Bosnia: That was the Question for the United States and Europe," in *Glass House*, ed. Nacos et al., 123–7.
61. Daalder, *Getting to Dayton*, 63.
62. Smith, *First Decade*, 139.
63. Menon, *Politics of Ambivalence*, 9–12.
64. Cogan, *Forced to Choose*, 125.
65. Quinlan, *European Defense Cooperation*, 17–19.
66. Ronald D. Asmus, "Double Enlargement: Redefining the Atlantic Partnership after the Cold War," in *America and Europe*, ed. Gompert and Larrabee, 39.
67. Juliet Lodge, "The EU: From Civilian Power to Speaking with a Common Voice—The Transition to a CFSP," in *Transatlantic Relationship*, ed. Wiener, 73–86.
68. Frédéric Bozo, "Continuity or Change? The View from Europe," in *After Fifty Years*, ed. Papacosma et al., 55–61; Fierke and Wiener, *Constructing Institutional Interests*, 7.
69. Sir Timothy Garden, "The United Kingdom: Making Strategic Adjustments," in *Enlarging NATO*, ed. Mattox and Rachwald, 76; Cornish, *Partnership in Crisis*, 32–43; Brenner and Parmentier, *Reconcilable Differences*, 1–14; Menon, *Politics of Ambivalence*, 40–69; James A. Thomson, "A New Partnership, New NATO Military Structures," in *America and Europe*, ed. Gompert and Larrabee, 85–8.
70. Smith, *First Decade*, 73; Cornish, *Partnership in Crisis*, 32; Menon, *Politics of Ambivalence*, 43–7; Janet Bryant, "Changing Circumstances, Changing Policies? The 1994 Defence White Paper and Beyond," in *France*, ed. Chafer and Jenkins, 90; Quinlan, *European Defense Cooperation*, 23.
71. Smith, *First Decade*, 107.
72. Smith and Timmins, *Building a Bigger Europe*, 92.
73. Paul Gallis, "France: NATO's 'Renovation' and Enlargement," in *Enlarging NATO*, ed. Mattox and Rachwald, 57.
74. Gallis, "France," 67–9; Menon, *Politics of Ambivalence*, 58–9; Asmus, *Opening NATO's Door*, 167–9.
75. Smith, *First Decade*, 111–13; Smith and Timmins, *Building a Bigger Europe*, 22–8.
76. Tewes, *Germany, Civilian Power*, 166–72, 193; Smith, *First Decade*, 120.
77. Tewes, *Germany, Civilian Power*, 175–81; Smith and Timmins, *Building a Bigger Europe*, 37; Ronald J. Bee, "Boarding the NATO Train: Enlargement and National Interests," in ed. *Explaining NATO Enlargement*, ed. Rauchhaus, 152; Gale A. Mattox, "The United States: Stability Through Engagement and Enlargement," in *Enlarging NATO*, ed. Mattox and Rachwald, 20.
78. Roberto Menotti, "Italy: Uneasy Ally," in *Enlarging NATO*, ed. Mattox and Rachwald, 98–101; Garden, "United Kingdom," 80; Menon, *Politics of*

Ambivalence, 58; Hyde-Price, *Germany and European Order*, 152; Whiteneck, "Germany," 48–50; Mattox, "United States," 21; Tewes, *Germany*, 192–5; Gallis, "France," 66–9; Gale A. Mattox and Daniel Whiteneck, "The ESDI, NATO, and the New European Security Environment," in *Two Tiers or Two Speeds?* ed. Sperling, 132; Smith and Timmins, *Building a Bigger Europe*, 47–8; Borawski and Thomas-Durell Young, *NATO after 2000*, 74.

79. Prague Summit Declaration, 21 November 2002, paragraph 2.
80. Ibid., paragraph 6.
81. Paul Gallis, "France: NATO's 'Renovation' and Enlargement," in *Enlarging NATO*, ed. Mattox and Rachwald, 58; Cornish, *Partnership in Crisis*, 81–6.
82. Brenner and Parmentier, *Reconcilable Differences*, 52–5; Gallis, "France," 62; Menon, *Politics of Ambivalence*, 56–7; Roberto Menotti, "Italy: Uneasy Ally," in *Enlarging NATO*, ed. Mattox and Rachwald, 98.
83. Cornish, *Partnership in Crisis*, 92–3.
84. Menon, *Politics of Ambivalence*, 138–46; Thomas-Durell Young, "NATO's Double Expansion and the Challenge of Reforming NATO's Military Structures," in *Two Tiers or Two Speeds?* cd. Sperling, 105–11.
85. Daniel J. Whiteneck, "Germany: Consensus Politics and Changing Security Paradigms," in *Enlarging NATO*, ed. Mattox and Rachwald, 36–41; Tewes, *Civilian Power*, 160–4; Bee, "Boarding the NATO Train," 159; Hyde-Price, *Germany and European Order*, 150–1.
86. Garden, "United Kingdom," 77–87.
87. Brenner and Parmentier, *Reconcilable Differences*, 45–59; Menon, *Politics of Ambivalence*, 49–53; Smith, *First Decade*, 94.
88. Duignan, *NATO: Its Past, Present, and Future*, 69; Menon, *Politics of Ambivalence*, 139; Gallis, "France," 64–6.
89. Borawski and Young, *NATO after 2000*, 20–1; Jeffrey Simon, "The Next Round of Enlargement," in *NATO Enlargement and Peacekeeping*, ed. Crisen, 12; Ted Galen Carpenter, "NATO's Search for Relevance," in *Fifty Years*, ed. Papacosma, et al., 30–2.
90. Asmus, *Opening NATO's Door*, 134–74, 238–45.
91. Jolyon Howorth, "France and European Security 1944–94: Re-Reading the Gaullist 'Consensus,'" in *France*, ed. Chafer and Jenkins, 18–20.
92. Pierre-Henri Laurent, "NATO and the European Union: The Quest for a Security/Defense Identity," in *Fifty Years*, ed. Papacosma, et al., 142.
93. Quinlan, *European Defense Cooperation*, 2.
94. Howorth, "France," 23.
95. Ibid., 22–8; Soetendorp, *Foreign Policy in the European Union*, 138–42.
96. Vanke, "Impossible Union."
97. Kjell A. Eliassen, "Introduction: The New European Foreign and Security Policy Agenda," in *Foreign and Security Policy*, ed. Eliassen, 3.
98. Williams and Jones, *NATO and the Transatlantic Alliance*, 73; Cornish, *Partnership in Crisis*, 35.
99. Antonio Missiroli, "Towards a European Security and Defense Identity? Record—State of Play—Prospects," in *European Security Integration*, ed. Jopp and Ojanen, 24.
100. Quinlan, *European Defense Cooperation*, 21.
101. Ibid., 20–1.
102. Smith and Timmins, *Building a Bigger Europe*, 30.
103. Rome Declaration on Peace and Cooperation, 8 November 1991.

104. Laurent, "NATO and the European Union," 148; Martin A. Smith, *NATO in the First Decade*, 73.
105. Laurent, "NATO and the European Union," 152–3.
106. Cornish, *Partnership in Crisis*, 71.
107. Quinlan, *European Defense Cooperation*, 26.
108. van Ham, *Europe's New Defense Ambitions*, 5–6.
109. Rearden, "Post-Cold War Strategy," 77.
110. Mark Oates, "Common European Security and Defence Policy: A Progress Report," House of Commons Research Paper 00/84, 31 October 2000; van Ham, *Europe's New Defense Ambitions*, 9–21. Also page 36: In the process, the EU answered Secretary of State Henry Kissinger's question about what phone number he should dial to call "Europe": the EU situation and crisis center was at 32-2-285-500-00.
111. Menon, *Politics of Ambivalence*, 136.
112. "ESDP: Increased Capabilities for Crisis Management," European Union Factsheet, June 2001; Centre for Defence Studies, *Headline Goals*; Schake, "European Union Defense Initiatives"; Quinlan, *European Defense Cooperation*, 33–45.
113. Çakmakoğlu, *White Book Turkey 2000*, 12.
114. Bradley Graham and Robert G. Kaiser, "NATO Ministers Back U.S. Plan for Rapid Reaction Force," *The Washington Post*, 25 September 2002, A24.
115. Prague Summit Declaration of the North Atlantic Council, 21 November 2002, paragraph 4a.
116. Presidency Conclusions, Copenhagen European Council, 12–13 December 2002, Annex II.
117. Ibid., paragraphs 28–9.
118. Remarks by Javier Solana, EU High Representative for CFSP, 27 December 2002.
119. "Operation 'Concordia,' EU Military Operation in former Yugoslav Republic of Macedonia (FYROM)," European Council Press Release, http://ue.eu.int/arym/index.asp?lang = EN, as of 1 September 2003.
120. "Operation 'Artemis,' EU Military Operation in Democratic Republic of Congo (DRC)" European Council Press Release, http://ue.eu.int/pesd/congo/index.asp?lang = EN, as of 1 September 2003.
121. Judy Dempsey, "NATO Presses Europe to Take Lead in the Balkans," *Financial Times*, 11 January 2003, http://news.ft.com/world.
122. Cited in Quinlan, *European Defense Cooperation*, 50.
123. Quoted in Borawski and Young, *NATO after 2000*, 38.
124. Marc Grossman, "NATO and the EU's European Security and Defense Policy," Hearing before the Subcommittee on European Affairs of the Committee on Foreign Relations, United States Senate, 9 March 2000.
125. Barry James, "U.S. Out of Line on Global Positioning, EU Says," *International Herald Tribune*, 19 December 2001, http://www.iht.com/.
126. Ibid.
127. Menon, *Politics of Ambivalence*, 130–3.
128. Hubert Védrine, French Minister of Foreign Affairs, "Into the Twenty-First," Speech at the Opening of the IFRI Conference, Paris, 3 November 1999.
129. Quoted in Borawski and Young, *NATO after 2000*, 34.
130. Christopher Patten, External Relations Commissioner, "A European Foreign Policy: Ambition and Reality," speech to the Institut Français des Relations Internationales, 15 June 2000.

131. Rabkin, "Eurojustice," 19.

132. Quoted in Carpenter, "New Strategic Concept," 21.

133. Tony Blair, "Speech to the French National Assembly," 24 March 1998.

134. Cited in Borawski and Young, *NATO after 2000*, 38.

135. Ibid., *NATO after 2000*, 7–12.

136. "A Moment of Truth," *The Economist*, 4 May 2002, 23.

137. German Ministry of Defense officials, in discussions with the author, May 2002.

138. Chris Morris, "EU seeks progress on reaction force," *BBC*, 19 November 2001, http://news.bbc.co.uk/hi/english/world.

139. Quinlan, *European Defense Cooperation*, 46–7.

140. "Greece Threatens EU Defence deal," *BBC*, 5 December 2001, http://news.bbc.co.uk/hi/english/world.

141. Elaine Sciolino, "4-Nation Plan for Defense of Europe," *The New York Times*, 30 April 2003, http://www.nytimes.com.

142. Bush Interview with Tom Brokaw, 25 April 2003, transcript at http://usinfo.state.gov/regional/nea/iraq/text2003/0425bush.htm.

143. Carol J. Williams, "A European Amends for Stance on Iraq: France, Germany Offer to Take on More of Defense Burden in Their Region," *Los Angeles Times*, 30 April 2003, http://www.latimes.com.

144. John Vinocur, "Anti-War Powers to Join Forces," *International Herald Tribune*, 30 April 2003, http://www.iht.com.

145. Ibid.

146. Craig S. Smith, "Europeans Plan Own Military Command Post," *The New York Times*, 3 September 2003, http://www.nytimes.com.

147. Judy Dempsey, "Britain to Set Out its Limits on EU Defence," *Financial Times*, 2 September 2003, http://news.ft.com/world.

148. William Horsley, "US Raises EU Concerns at NATO," *BBC News*, 20 October 2003, http://news.bbc.co.uk/hi/english/world; Robert Graham, "France Seeks to Reassure US over NATO Commitment," *Financial Times*, 18 October 2003, http://news.ft.com/world; Judy Dempsey, "Blair Tries to Play Down Rift with US over Defence Role," *Financial Times*, 18 October 2003, http://news.ft.com/world.

149. Eric Moskowitz and Jeffrey S. Lantis, "The War in Kosovo: Coercive Diplomacy," in *Contemporary Cases*, ed. Carter, 65–6.

150. Leurdijk and Zandee, *From Crisis to Crisis*, 23–31; Glenny, *Balkans*, 652.

151. Moskowitz and Lantis, "The War in Kosovo," 70–2; Leurdijk and Zandee, *From Crisis to Crisis*, 33; David Travers, "The UN: Squaring the Circle," in *Kosovo Crisis*, ed. Weymouth and Henig, 249–53.

152. Sabrina P. Ramet and Phil Lyon, "Germany: The Federal Republic, Loyal to NATO," in *Kosovo Crisis*, ed. Weymouth and Henig, 84–102; Umberto Morelli, "Italy: The Reluctant Ally," in *Kosovo Crisis*, ed. Weymouth and Henig, 59–72; Stanley Henig, "Britain: To War for a Just Cause," in *Kosovo Crisis*, ed. Weymouth and Henig, 40–55; Moskowitz and Lantis, "The War in Kosovo," 78–82; Leurdijk and Zandee, *From Crisis to Crisis*, 34–45; Hampson et al., *Madness in the Multitude*, 144.

153. Leurdijk and Zandee, *From Crisis to Crisis*, 36–7, 75–87; Clark, *Waging Modern War*, 177–274, 42; Travers, "The UN," 257.

154. Duignan, *NATO*, 96–106; Peter J. Anderson, "Air Strike: NATO Astride Kosovo," in *Kosovo Crisis*, ed. Weymouth and Henig, 192–5; Travers, "The UN," 257–8, 267; Bozo, "Continuity or Change," 68.

155. Keith B. Richburg, "NATO Launches Macedonia Force," *The Washington Post*, 23 August 2001, A19.
156. J.D. Ramirez and M. Szaprio, "The EU: Old Wine from New Bottles," in *Kosovo Crisis*, ed. Weymouth and Henig, 125–7.
157. Henig, "Britain," 45–9.
158. Clark, *Waging Modern War*, 116–20, 135, 154; Moskowitz and Lantis, "War in Kosovo," 69; Smith, *First Decade*, 159–61.
159. Ramirez and Szaprio, "The EU," 129–32; Leurdijk and Zandee, *From Crisis to Crisis*, 137.
160. "U.S. Peacekeeping Contributions"; "The European Union and South Eastern Europe," EU Presidency Factsheet, December 2000.
161. Leurdijk and Zandee, *From Crisis to Crisis*, 118–24; Michta, "What has Changed?" 39.
162. Brenner and Parmentier, *Reconcilable Differences*, 63.
163. Anderson, "Air Strike," 196; Clark, *Waging Modern War*, 427; Ramirez and Szaprio, "The EU," 134–5; Tonelson, "NATO Burden-Sharing," 50–1; Andrew Michta, "NATO After the Kosovo Campaign and the KFOR Peacekeeping Operations: What has Changed?" in *NATO Enlargement*, ed. Crisen, 38; van Ham, *Europe's New Defense Ambitions*, 8.
164. Clark, *Waging Modern War*, 430.
165. Ibid., 426.
166. Sabrina P. Ramet, "The USA: To War in Europe Again," in *Kosovo Crisis*, ed. Weymouth and Henig, 175–6.
167. Jolyon Howorth, *Oxford Analytica Daily Brief*, 13 November 2001.
168. Conclusions and Plan of Action of the Extraordinary European Council Meeting on 21 September 2001.
169. EU Response to the 11 September: European Commission Action, Memo 02/122, 3 June 2002, 2, 9.
170. Colum Lynch, "Britain to Lead Peacekeeping Force," *The Washington Post*, 20 December 2001, A33.
171. Operation Fingal, UK Ministry of Defence, www.operations.mod.uk/fingal.
172. "NATO in Afghanistan (ISAF 4)," NATO Press Release, http://www.nato.int/issues/afghanistan/index.htm, 22 August 2003; Daniel Dombey and Hugh Williamson, "NATO to Command Afghan Mission," *Financial Times*, 16 April 2003, http://news.ft.com/world.
173. Richard Bernstein, "Germany Offers to Expand Afghan Force if the U.N. Approves," *The New York Times*, 27 August 2003, http://www.nytimes.com.
174. *Face the Nation*, 23 September 2001.
175. Howorth, *Oxford Analytica Daily Brief*; "Guess who wasn't Coming to Dinner?" *The Economist*, 8 November 2001, http://www.economist.com.
176. Martin Fletcher and Michael Evan, "No10 Fury as EU Claims Afghan Role," *The Times (London)*, 15 December 2001, http://www.thetimes.co.uk.
177. Paul Reynolds, "Washington Readies for War," in ed. *Counterattack on Terrorism*, Baxter and Downing, 91–2.
178. Andrew Marr, "Blair Steps Forward," in ed. *Counterattack on Terrorism*, Baxter and Downing, 176–85.
179. "Presidential Pique," *The Economist*, 4 May 2002, 50.
180. Robert Graham, "French Show Delight at U.S. Shift on Baghdad," *Financial Times*, 8 November 2002, http://news.ft.com/world.

181. Philip Stephens, "White House Warmongers Making Life Tough for Blair," *Financial Times*, 31 August 2002, 1.

182. "Excerpts: Interview With Gerhard Schröder," *The New York Times*, 5 September 2002, http://www.nytimes.com.

183. Transcript of Press Conference at http://usinfo.state.gov/topical/pol/arms/03030600.htm.

184. Elaine Sciolino, "France Will Use Veto, Chirac Says," *The New York Times*, 11 March 2003, http://www.nytimes.com.

185. Quoted from the version printed as " 'The Transatlantic Bond is Our Guarantee of Freedom': Declaration of Eight European Leaders in Support of United States on Iraq," *Washington Post*, 30 January 2003, http://www.washingtonpost.com.

186. Keith B. Richburg, "EU Unity on Iraq Proves Short-Lived," *Washington Post*, 19 February 2003, http://www.washingtonpost.com/; Rory Watson, "Chirac's Outburst Met with Disdain by EU Applicants," *The Times (London)*, 19 February 2003, http://www.thetimes.co.uk.

187. Richard Bernstein with Steven R. Weisman, "NATO Settles Rift Over Aid to Turks in Case of a War," *The New York Times*, 17 February 2003, http://www.nytimes.com.

188. "Poles Take Over in Central Iraq," *BBC News*, 3 September 2003, http://news.bbc.co.uk/hi/english/world.

189. Gregory Crouch, "Dutch Send 1,100 Troops to Iraq, Relieving as Many U.S. Marines," *The New York Times*, 31 July 2003, http://www.nytimes.com.

7 Conclusions

1. Samantha Power, "The United States and Genocide Law: A History of Ambivalence," in *National Security and International Law*, ed. Sewall and Kaysen, 173.

2. Power, "History of Ambivalence," 172.

3. Moravcsik, "Taking Preferences Seriously," 525–8, would call this the ideational variant of liberalism, since it links state preferences to social identities and values. Leading works on the development of national identity include Gellner, *Nations and Nationalism*; Smith, *Ethnic Origins of Nations*; Hobsbawm, *Nations and Nationalism*; and Anderson, *Imagined Communities*.

4. Haas, *Uniting of Europe*, 5–16. This is a further step beyond the functionalism of Mitrany, *Working Peace System*. Further discussion can be found in Moravcsik, "Preferences and Power"; Keohane and Hoffmann, ed., *New European Community*; and Geoffrey Garrett, "International Cooperation and Institutional Choice: The EC's Internal Market," in *Multilateralism Matters*, ed. Ruggie, 365–98.

5. Lepgold, "Collective Action Problem," 86–96. For a deeper description of collective goods, see Olsen, *Logic of Collective Action*; Sandler, *Collective Action*; or Barkin and Shambaugh, *Anarchy and the Environment*. Also see Patrick M. Morgan, "Multilateralism and Security: Prospects in Europe," in *Multilateralism Matters*, ed. Ruggie, 327–64.

6. Cronin, *Community Under Anarchy*, 4. He uses the Social Identity Theory described in Mercer, "Anarchy and Identity."

7. Among those who have advocated this view are Jeffrey Gedmin (Director of Aspen Institute Berlin), in discussion with the author, May 2002, and Beinart, "Euro Cheek."

8. Senior State Department official, in discussion with the author, June 2002.

9. "EU Reacts To Bush Speech On Climate Change," Press Release by the European Commission Delegation in the United States, 12 June 2001.

10. "In Ratifying Climate Pact, EU Asks U.S. to Reconsider," *The Los Angeles Times*, 1 June 2002, http://www.latimes.com.

11. William Drozdiak, "Bush Faces Pressure On Global Warming," *The Washington Post*, 16 July 2001, A01.

12. "Bush Climate Plan Gets Cold Shoulder," *The Washington Post*, 16 February 2002, A22.

13. Suzanne Daley, "Europeans Give Bush Plan on Climate Change a Tepid Reception," *The New York Times*, 15 February 2002, www.nytimes.com.

14. Krenzler and Wiegand, "More Than Trade Disputes?" 173.

15. It would require a page to identify all those who have argued this. Some of the more academic treatments include Gordon, "Bridging the Atlantic Divide"; Hirsch, "Bush and the World"; Patrick, "Beyond Coalitions of the Willing"; and Talbott, "From Prague to Baghdad."

16. Gunnar Wiegand (Spokesman for External Relations, European Commission), in discussion with the author, June 2002.

17. Kupchan, "After Pax Americana," 43–61. More details on the effect the EU's presence has on its regional neighbors can be found in Johansson, *Subregionalization*.

18. Carr, *Twenty Years' Crisis*, 132–45.

19. Legro and Moravcsik, "Is Anybody Still a Realist?" 49–50.

20. Javier Solana, "A Partnership with Many Missions," speech at the German Marshall Fund Peter Weitz Awards Dinner, Washington, 20 May 2002.

21. Christopher Patten, "Comment and Analysis," *The Financial Times*, 15 February 2002.

22. Christopher Patten, "A European Foreign Policy: Ambition and Reality," speech to the Institut Français des Relations Internationales, Paris, 15 June 2000.

23. For the classic discussion, see Massie, *Dreadnought*.

24. Thomas L. Friedman, "Our War With France," *The New York Times*, 18 September 2003, http://www.nytimes.com.

25. Kagan, "Power and Weakness," and Kagan, *Paradise and Power*, attribute the European preference for multilateralism to their relative weakness. Dunn, "Bush Administration and Iraq," and Wilkie, "Fortress Europa," share his basic view.

26. Mowle, "Dysfunctional Spillover."

27. Wiegand, discussion.

28. John Washburn (Convenor, American Non-Governmental Organizations Coalition for the ICC), Tom Malinowski (Advocacy Director, Human Rights Watch), and several U.S. government officials, in discussion with the author, June 2002.

29. Wiegand, discussion.

30. Bush, 30.

31. Hopkinson, *Enlargement*, 25–8. In addition to articles mentioned earlier in this book, other perspectives on the United States and NATO include Kupchan, "Defense of European Defense"; Rodman, *Drifting Apart*; Sloan, *The United States and European Defense*; and Layne, *Death Knell for NATO?*

32. Jeffrey Gedmin, "Europe and NATO: Saving the Alliance," in *Present Dangers*, ed. Kagan and Kristol, 189.

33. Christopher Layne, "U.S. Hegemony and the Perpetuation of NATO," in *NATO Enters the 21st Century*, ed. Carpenter, 77.

34. *Economist* cited by Kori Schake, "NATO's 'Fundamental Divergence' over Proliferation," in *NATO Enters the 21st Century*, ed. Carpenter, 111; Huntington, "Lonely Superpower," 42.

35. William Kristol and Robert Kagan, "Introduction: National Interest and Global Responsibility," in *Present Dangers*, ed. Kagan and Kristol, 12, 24.

36. Ibid., 22.

37. Ibid., 13.

38. John Van Oudenaren, "Europe as Partner," in *Partnership for a New Era*, ed. Gompert and Larrabee, 115.

39. Ted Galen Carpenter, "NATO's New Strategic Concept: Coherent Blueprint or Conceptual Muddle?" in *NATO Enters the 21st Century*, ed. Carpenter, 24.

40. Layne, "U.S. Hegemony," 66–70.

BIBLIOGRAPHY

Allison, Graham T. *Essence of Decision*. Boston: Little, Brown, 1971.

Alston, Philip and James Crawford, eds. *The Future of UN Human Rights Treaty Monitoring*. Cambridge: Cambridge University Press, 2000.

Amnesty International. *NATO/Federal Republic of Yugoslavia: "Collateral Damage" or Unlawful Killings? Violations of the Laws of War by NATO during Operation Allied Force*. New York: Amnesty International, 2000.

———. *United States of America: Worlds Apart: Violations of the Rights of Foreign Nationals on Death Row—Cases of Europeans*. New York: Amnesty International, 2000.

Anderson, Benedict. *Imagined Communities: Reflections on the Origin and Spread of Nationalism, rev. ed.*, London: Verso, 1991.

Asmus, Ronald D. *Opening NATO's Door: How the Alliance Remade Itself for a New Era*. New York: Columbia University Press, 2002.

Baker III, James A. *The Politics of Diplomacy*. New York: J.P. Putnam's Sons, 1995.

Baldwin, David A., ed. *Neorealism and Neoliberalism: The Contemporary Debate*. New York: Columbia University Press, 1993.

Ball, Howard. *Prosecuting War Crimes and Genocide: The Twentieth-Century Experience*. Lawrence: University Press of Kansas, 1999.

Banner, Stuart. *The Death Penalty: An American History*. Cambridge: Harvard University Press, 2002.

Barkin, J. Samuel and George E. Shambaugh. *Anarchy and the Environment: The International Relations of Common Pool Resources*. Albany: State University of New York Press, 1999.

Baxter, Jenny and Malcolm Downing, eds. *The BBC Reports: On America, Its Allies and Enemies, and the Counterattack on Terrorism*. Woodstock, NY: Overlook Press, 2002.

Bedau, Hugo Adam, ed. *The Death Penalty in America: Current Controversies*. New York: Oxford University Press, 1998.

Beinart, Peter. "Euro Cheek." *The New Republic* (2 June 2001): 10–11.

———. "New Life." *The New Republic* (27 May 2002): 6.

Bergsten, C. Fred. "America and Europe: Clash of the Titans?" *Foreign Affairs* 78 (March/April 1999): 20–34.

Bert, Wayne. *The Reluctant Superpower: United States' Policy in Bosnia, 1991–95*. London: Macmillan, 1997.

Bertele, Manfred and Holger H. May. "Unilateralism in Theory and Practice." *Comparative Strategy*, 17 (April–June 1998): 197–207.

Bidwai, Praful and Achin Vanaik. *New Nukes: India, Pakistan and Global Nuclear Disarmament*. New York: Olive Branch Press, 2000.

Blainey, Geoffrey. *The Causes of War, 3rd Ed.* New York: The Free Press, 1988.

Bonser, Charles F., ed. *Security, Trade, and Environmental Policy: A US/European Union Transatlantic Agenda*. Boston: Kluwer Academic Publishers, 2000.

Borawski, John and Thomas-Durell Young. *NATO after 2000: The Future of the Euro-Atlantic Alliance*. Westport, Conn.: Praeger, 2001.

Bothe, Michael, Natalino Ronzitti, and Allan Rosas, eds. *The New Chemical Weapons Convention—Implementation and Prospects*. The Hague: Kluwer Law International, 1998.

Brecher, Michael, Blema Steinberg, and Janice Stein. "A Framework for Research on Foreign Policy Behavior." *Journal of Conflict Resolution* 13 (March 1969): 75–101.

Brenner, Michael J. and Guillaume Parmentier. *Reconcilable Differences: U.S.-French Relations in the New Era*. Washington: Brookings Institution Press, 2002.

Bronstone Adam. *European Union-United States Security Relations: Transatlantic Tensions and the Theory of International Relations*. Houndmills, England: MacMillan Press Ltd., 1997.

Brooks, Stephen G. "Dueling Realisms." *International Organization* 51 (Summer 1997): 445–77.

Brown, James, ed. *Arms Control in a Multi-polar World*. Amsterdam: VU University Press, 1996.

Burg, Steven L. and Paul Shoup. *The War in Bosnia-Herzegovina: Ethnic Conflict and International Intervention*. Armonk, N.Y.: M.E. Sharpe, 2000.

Burniaux, Jean-Marc and Paul O'Brien. *Action Against Climate Change: The Kyoto Protocol and Beyond*. Paris: Organisation for Economic Co-operation and Development, 1999.

Bush, George W. *The National Security Strategy of the United States of America*. Washington: The White House, September 2002.

Butler, Richard. *The Greatest Threat: Iraq, Weapons of Mass Destruction, and the Crisis of Global Security*. New York: Public Affairs, 2000.

Çakmakoğlu, Sabahattin. *White Book Turkey 2000*. Ankara: Ministry of National Defense, 2000.

Calleya, Stephen C., ed. *Regionalism in the Post-Cold War World*. Aldershot, Hampshire: Ashgate, 2001.

Cameron, Maxwell A., Robert J. Lawson, and Brian W. Tomlin, eds. *To Walk Without Fear: The Global Movement to Ban Landmines*. Oxford: Oxford University Press, 1998.

Caporoso, James A. "International Relations Theory and Multilateralism: The Search for Foundations." *International Organization* 46 (Summer 1992): 599–632.

Carr, Edward Hallett. *The Twenty Years' Crisis: 1919–1939*. New York: Harper & Row, 1939.

Carpenter, Ted Galen, ed. *NATO Enters the 21st Century*. London: Frank Cass, 2001.

Carter, Ralph G., ed. *Contemporary Cases in U.S. Foreign Policy: From Terrorism to Trade*. Washington, D.C.: CQ Press, 2002.

Centre for Defence Studies. *Achieving the Helsinki Headline Goals*. London: Centre for Defence Studies, 2001.

Chafer, Tony and Brian Jenkins, eds. *France: From the Cold War to the New World Order*. Houndmills, Basingstoke, Hampshire: Macmillan Press, 1996.

Chatham House. *US-European Policies in the Persian Gulf: Beyond the Friction*. London: Royal Institute of International Affairs, 1997.

Clark, Wesley K. *Waging Modern War: Bosnia, Kosovo, and the Future of Combat*. New York: Public Affairs, 2001.

Claude, Inis. *Power and International Relations*. New York: Random House, 1962.

Clément, Sophia, ed. *The Issues Raised by Bosnia, and the Transatlantic Debate.* Paris: Institute for Security Studies, Western European Union, 1998.

Clinton, Bill. *A National Security Strategy for a New Century.* Washington: The White House, December, 1999.

Cogan Charles. *Forced to Choose: France, the Atlantic Alliance, and NATO—Then and Now.* Westport, Conn.: Praeger, 1997.

Cohen, Cynthia Price and Howard A. Davidson, eds. *Children's Rights in America: U.N. Convention on the Rights of the Child Compared with United States Law.* Chicago: The American Bar Association, 1990.

Cohn, Ilene and Guy S Goodwin-Gill. *Child Soldiers: The Role of Children in Armed Conflict.* Oxford: Oxford University Press, 1994.

Cornish, Paul. *Partnership in Crisis: The US, Europe and the Fall and Rise of NATO.* London: Royal Institute of International Affairs, 1997.

Council of Europe. *The Death Penalty: Abolition in Europe.* Strasbourg: Council of Europe Publishing, 1999.

Crisen, Sabina, ed. *NATO Enlargement and Peacekeeping: Journeys to Where?* Washington: Woodrow Wilson International Center for Scholars, 2001.

Cromwell, William. *The United States and the European Pillar.* London: MacMillan, 1992.

Cronin, Bruce. *Community Under Anarchy: Transnational Identity and the Evolution of Cooperation.* New York: Columbia University Press, 1999.

Daalder, Ivo H. *Getting to Dayton: The Making of America's Bosnia Policy.* Washington: Brookings Institution Press, 2000.

Dando, Malcolm, Graham S. Pearson, and Tibor Tóth, eds. *Verification of the Biological and Toxin Weapons Convention.* Dordrecht, Netherlands: Kluwer Academic Publishers, 2000.

Deaver, Michael V. *Disarming Iraq: Monitoring Power and Resistance.* Westport, Conn.: Praeger, 2001.

Desch, Michael C. "Culture Clash: Assessing the Importance of Ideas in Security Studies." *International Security* 23 (Summer 1998): 141–70.

Dhanapala, Jayantha, ed. *Small Arms Control: Old Weapons, New Issues.* Geneva: United Nations Institute for Disarmament Research, 1999.

Dittman, David L. and David L. Dawkins. *Deliberate Force: NATO's First Extended Air Operation: The View from AFSOUTH.* Alexander, Va.: Center for Naval Analyses, 1998.

Downs, George W., David M. Rocke, and Peter N. Barsoom. "Managing the Evolution of Multilateralism." *International Organization* 52 (Spring 1998): 397–419.

Doyle, Michael W. "Liberalism and World Politics." *American Political Science Review* 80 (December 1986): 1151–69.

———. *Ways of War and Peace.* New York: W.W. Norton and Company, 1997.

Drell, Sidney D., Abraham D. Sofaer, and George D. Wilson, eds. *The New Terror: Facing the Threat of Biological and Chemical Weapons.* Stanford: Hoover Institution Press, 1999.

Drew, S. Nelson. *NATO from Berlin to Bosnia: Trans-Atlantic Security in Transition.* Washington: Institute for National Strategic Studies, 1995.

Drinan, Robert F. *The Mobilization of Shame: A World View of Human Rights.* New Haven: Yale University Press, 2001.

Dugard, John. *Recognition and the United Nations.* Cambridge: Grotius Publications, 1987.

Duignan, Peter. *NATO: Its Past, Present, and Future*. Stanford, Calif.: Hoover Institution Press, 2000.

Duke, Simon. *The Elusive Quest for European Security: From EDC to CFSP*. New York: Palgrave, 2000.

Dunn, David. "Myths, Motivations, and 'Misunderestimations:' the Bush Administration and Iraq." *International Affairs* 79 (March 2003): 279–97.

Easton, David. *The Political System: An Inquiry into the State of Political Science*. New York: Alfred A. Knopf, 1953.

Eliassen, Kjell A., ed. *Foreign and Security Policy in the European Union*. London: SAGE Publications, 1998.

Elman, Colin. "Horses for Courses: Why *Not* Neorealist Theories of Foreign Policy?" *Security Studies* 6 (Autumn 1996): 7–53.

Fierke, Karin and Antje Wiener. *Constructing Institutional Interests: EU and NATO Enlargement*. San Domenico, Italy: European University Institute, 1999.

Fischer, David and Harald Müller. *United Divided: The European at the NPT Extension Conference*. Frankfurt/Main: Peace Research Institute Frankfurt, 1995.

Fottrell, Deirdre, ed. *Revisiting Children's Rights: 10 Years of the UN Convention on the Rights of the Child*. The Hague: Kluwer Law International, 2001.

Florini, Ann, ed. *The Third Force: The Rise of Transnational Civil Society*. Tokyo: Japan Center for International Exchange, 2000.

Gaddis, John Lewis. "The Long Peace: Elements of Stability in the Postwar International System." *International Security* 10 (Spring 1986): 99–142.

———. "International Relations Theory and the End of the Cold War." *International Security* 17 (Winter 1992): 5–58.

Gallagher, Nancy W., ed. *Arms Control: New Approaches to Theory and Policy*. London: Frank Cass, 1998.

Gardner, J.P., ed. *Human Rights as General Norms and a State's Right to Opt Out: Reservations and Objections to Human Rights Conventions*. London: The British Institute of International and Comparative Law, 1997.

Gehring, Thomas. *Dynamic International Regimes: Institutions for International Environmental Governance*. Frankfurt am Main; New York: P. Lang, 1994.

Gellner, Ernest. *Nations and Nationalism*. Ithaca: Cornell University Press, 1983.

Gholz, Eugene, Daryl G. Press, and Harvey M. Sapolsky. "Come Home America: The Strategy of Restraint in the Face of Temptation." *International Security* 21 (Spring 1997): 5–48.

Glaser, Charles. "Realists as Optimists: Cooperation as Self-Help." *International Security* 19 (Winter 1994/95): 50–90.

Glenny, Misha. *The Fall of Yugoslavia: The Third Balkan War*. New York: Penguin Books, 1992.

Goldblat, Jozef and Thomas Bernauer. *The Third Review of the Biological Weapons Convention: Issues and Proposals*. New York: United Nations, 1991.

Goldman, Raphael and Ann Chih Lin. *Capital Punishment*. Washington: CQ Press, 2002.

Gompert, David C. and F. Stephen Larrabee, eds. *America and Europe: A Partnership for a New Era*. Cambridge: Cambridge University Press, 1997.

Goonesekere, Savitri. *Women's Rights and Children's Rights: The United Nations Conventions as Compatible and Complementary International Treaties*. Florence: UNICEF International Child Development Centre, 1992.

Gordon, Michael R. and Bernard E. Trainor. *The Generals' War: The Inside Story of the Conflict in the Gulf*. Boston: Little, Brown, 1995.

Gordon, Philip G. "Europe's Uncommon Foreign Policy." *International Security* 22 (Winter 1997): 74–100.

———. "Bridging the Atlantic Divide." *Foreign Affairs* 82 (January/February 2003): 70–83.

Graham-Brown, Sarah. *Sanctioning Saddam: The Politics of Intervention in Iraq.* London: I.B. Tauris, 1999.

Grieco, Joseph. "Anarchy and the Limits of Cooperation: A Realist Critique of the Newest Liberal Institutionalism." *International Organization* 42 (Summer 1988): 485–507.

———. "The Maastricht Treaty, Economic and Monetary Union and the Neo-realist Research Programme." *Review of International Studies* 21 (January 1995): 21–40.

———. "State Interests and Institutional Rule Trajectories: A Neorealist Interpretation of the Maastricht Treaty and European Economic and Monetary Union." *Security Studies* 5 (Spring 1996): 261–306.

Guay, Terrence R. *The United States and the European Union: The Political Economy of a Relationship.* Sheffield, England: Sheffield Academic Press, Ltd., 1999.

Haas, Ernst. *The Uniting of Europe: Political, Social, and Economic Forces, 1950–1957.* Stanford: Stanford University Press, 1958.

Haas, Peter. "Introduction: Epistemic Communities and International Policy Coordination." *International Organization* 46 (Winter 1992): 1–36.

Haass, Richard, ed. *Transatlantic Tensions: The United States, Europe, and Problem Countries.* Washington: Brookings Institution Press, 1999.

Hall, Rodney Bruce. "Moral Authority as a Power Resource." *International Organization* 51 (Autumn 1997): 591–622.

Hampson, Fen Osler and Maureen Appel Molot, eds. *Leadership and Dialogue.* Toronto; New York: Oxford University Press, 1998.

Hampson, Fen Osler, with Jean Daudelin, John B. Hay, Holly Reid, and Todd Martin. *Madness in the Multitude: Human Security and World Disorder.* Don Mills, Ont.: Oxford University Press, 2002.

Harris, Paul G., ed. *Climate Change and American Foreign Policy, 1st ed.* New York: St. Martin's Press, 2000.

———, ed. *The Environment, International Relations, and U.S. Foreign Policy.* Washington, D.C.: Georgetown University Press, 2000.

Hellmann, Gunther and Reinhard Wolf. "Neorealism, Neoliberal Institutionalism, and the Future of NATO." *Security Studies* 3 (Autumn 1993): 3–43.

Helm, Dieter, ed. *Environmental Policy: Objectives, Instruments, and Implementation.* Oxford; New York: Oxford University Press, 2000.

Hirsch, Michael. "Bush and the World." *Foreign Affairs* 81 (September/October 2002): 18–43.

Hobbes, Thomas. *Leviathan,* ed. Michael Oakeshott. New York: Collier Macmillan, 1974.

Hobsbawm, E.J. *Nations and Nationalism Since 1780.* New York: Cambridge University Press, 1990.

Holbrooke, Richard C. *To End a War, rev. ed.* New York: Modern Library, 1999.

Holland, Martin. *European Union Common Foreign Policy: From EPC to CFSP Joint Action and South Africa.* London: Macmillan Press, 1995.

Hopf, Ted. "The Promise of Constructivism in International Relations Theory." *International Security* 23 (Summer 1998): 171–200.

Hopkinson, William. *Enlargement: A New NATO.* Paris: Institute for Security Studies, Western European Union, 2001.

Huntington, Samuel. "The Clash of Civilizations?" *Foreign Affairs* 72 (Summer 1993): 22–49.

———. "The Lonely Superpower." *Foreign Affairs* 78 (March/April 1999): 35–49.

Hyde-Price, Adrian G.V. *Germany and European Order: Enlarging NATO and the EU.* Manchester: Manchester University Press, 2000.

Jervis, Robert. "Cooperation Under the Security Dilemma." *World Politics* 30 (June 1978): 167–214.

———. "The Future of World Politics: Will It Resemble the Past?'" *International Security* 16 (Winter 1991): 39–73.

———. "A Political Science Perspective on the Balance of Power and the Concert." *American Historical Review* 97 (June 1992): 716–24.

———. "Realism, Neoliberalism, and Cooperation: Understanding the Debate." *International Security* 24 (Summer 1999): 42–63.

Johansson, Elisabeth. *Subregionalization in Europe's Periphery: The Northern and Southern Dimensions of the European Union's Foreign Policy.* Barcelona: Institut Universitari d'Estudis Europeus, 2000.

Jopp, Mathias and Hanna Ojanen, eds. *European Security Integration: Implications for Non-Alignment and Alliances.* Helsinki: Ulkopoliittinen Instituutti, 1999.

Jørgensen, Knud Erik, ed. *European Approaches to Crisis Management.* The Hague: Kluwer Law International, 1997.

Jupille, Joseph. "The European Union and International Outcomes." *International Organization* 53 (Spring 1999): 409–25.

Kagan, Robert. "Power and Weakness." *Policy Review* 113 (June/July 2002).

———. *Of Paradise and Power: America and Europe in the New World Order.* New York: Alfred A. Knopf, 2003.

Kagan, Robert and William Kristol, eds. *Present Dangers: Crisis and Opportunity in American Foreign and Defense Policy.* San Francisco, Calif.: Encounter Books, 2000.

Kaplan, Lawrence F. "Surrender: France 1, America 0," *New Republic* (20 November 2000).

Kaplan, Morton. *System and Process in International Politics.* New York: John Wiley & Sons, 1957.

Katzman, Kenneth. *Iraq: International Support for U.S. Policy.* Washington: Congressional Research Service, 19 February 1998.

Kaysen, Carl. "Is War Obsolete? A Review Essay." *International Security* 14 (Spring 1990): 42–64.

Kegley, Charles W., Jr. ed. *Controversies in International Relations Theory: Realism and the Neoliberal Challenge.* New York: St. Martin's Press, 1995.

Kegley, Charles W., Jr. and Gregory A. Raymond. *A Multipolar Peace? Great-Power Politics in the Twenty-first Century.* New York: St. Martin's Press, 1994.

Keohane, Robert O. *After Hegemony: Cooperation and Discord in the World Political Economy,* Princeton: Princeton University Press, 1984.

———. "Reciprocity in International Relations." *International Organization* 40 (Winter 1996): 1–28.

———, ed. *Neorealism and Its Critics.* New York: Columbia University Press, 1986.

———. "Multilateralism: An Agenda for Research." *International Journal* 45 (Autumn 1990): 731–64.

Keohane, Robert O. and Stanley Hoffmann, eds. *The New European Community: Decisionmaking and Institutional Change.* Boulder: Westview Press, 1991.

Kilkelly, Ursula. *The Child and the European Convention on Human Rights.* Aldershot, UK: Ashgate, 1999.

Kocs, Stephen A. "Explaining the Strategic Behavior of States: International Law as System Structure." *International Studies Quarterly* 38 (December 1994): 535–56.

Krasner, Stephen D., ed. *International Regimes.* Ithaca: Cornell University Press, 1982.

Krauthammer, Charles. "The Unipolar Moment." *Foreign Affairs* 70 (Winter 1990/1): 23–33.

———. "The Bush Doctrine: ABM, Kyoto, and the New American Unilateralism." *The Weekly Standard* (4 June 2001): 21–5.

Krenzler, Horst G. and Gunnar Wiegand. "EU-U.S. Relations: More than Trade Disputes?" *European Foreign Affairs Review* 4 (Summer 1999): 153–80.

Kupchan, Charles A. "After Pax Americana: Benign Power, Regional Integration, and the Sources of a Stable Multipolarity." *International Security* 23 (Fall 1998): 40–79.

———. "In Defense of European Defense: An American Perspective." *Survival* 42 (Summer 2000): 16–32.

Labs, Eric J. "Beyond Victory: Offensive Realism and the Expansion of War Aims." *Security Studies* 6 (Summer 1997): 1–49.

Lakatos, Imre and Alan Musgrave, eds. *Criticism and the Growth of Knowledge.* Cambridge: Cambridge University Press, 1970.

Lake, Anthony. "Confronting Backlash States." *Foreign Affairs* 73 (Spring 1994): 45–55.

Lake, David A. "Powerful Pacifists: Democratic States and War." *American Political Science Review* 86 (March 1992): 24–36.

Lantos, Tom. "The Durban Debacle: An Insider's View of the UN World Conference Against Racism." *The Fletcher Forum of World Affairs* 26 (Winter/Spring 2002): 31–52.

Larsen, Jeffrey A. and Gregory J. Rattray, eds. *Arms Control: Toward the 21st Century.* Boulder: Lynne Rienner, 1996.

Layne, Christopher. "The Unipolar Illusion: Why New Great Powers Will Rise." *International Security* 17 (Spring 1993): 5–51.

———. *Death Knell for NATO? The Bush Administration Confronts the European Security and Defense Policy.* Policy Analysis 394, Cato Institute, 4 April 2001.

LeBlanc, Lawrence J. *The United States and the Genocide Convention.* Durham: Duke University Press, 1991.

———. *The Convention on the Rights of the Child: United Nations Lawmaking on Human Rights.* Lincoln: University of Nebraska Press, 1995.

Lee, Roy S., ed. 1999. *The International Criminal Court: The Making of the Rome Statute—Issues, Negotiations, Results.* The Hague: Kluwer Law International.

Legro, Jeffrey W. and Andrew Moravcsik. "Is Anybody Still a Realist?" *International Security* 24 (Fall 1999): 5–55.

Lepgold, Joseph. "NATO's Post-Cold War Collective Action Problem." *International Security* 23 (Summer 1998): 78–106.

Le Prestre, Philippe G., John D. Reid, and E. Thomas Morehouse, eds. *Protecting the Ozone Layer: Lessons, Models, and Prospects.* Boston: Kluwer, 1998.

Leurdijk, Dick A. and Dick Zandee. *Kosovo: From Crisis to Crisis.* Aldershot, Hampshire, England: Ashgate, 2001.

Litfin, Karen. *Ozone Discourses: Science and Politics in Global Environmental Cooperation.* New York: Columbia University Press, 1994.

Litwak, Robert. 2000. *Rogue States and U.S. Foreign Policy: Containment after the Cold War.* Washington: Woodrow Wilson Center Press.

Lowi, Theodore. "American Buisness, Public Policy, Case Studies, and Political Theory." *World Politics* 16 (July 1964): 677–715.

Luterbacher, Urs and Detlef F. Sprinz, eds. *International Relations and Global Climate Change.* Cambridge, Mass.: MIT Press, 2001.

Machiavelli, Niccolo. *The Prince and The Discourses.* New York: Modern Library, 1950.

Magaš, Branka, and Ivo Žanić, eds. *The War in Croatia and Bosnia-Herzegovina, 1991–1995.* London: Frank Cass, 2001.

Maoz, Zeev and Russett, Bruce. "Normative and Structural Causes of Democratic Peace, 1946–1986." *American Political Science Review* 87 (September 1993): 624–38.

March, James G. and Johan P. Olsen. "The New Institutionalism: Organizational Factors in Political Life." *American Political Science Review* 78 (September 1984): 734–49.

Maresca, Louis and Stuart Maslen, eds. *The Banning of Anti-Personnel Landmines: The Legal Contribution of the International Committee of the Red Cross.* Cambridge: Cambridge University Press, 2000.

Marshall, Johsua Micah. "Death in Venice." *The New Republic* (31 July 2000): 12–14.

Martin, Lisa L. "Interests, Power, and Multilateralism." *International Organization* 46 (Autumn 1992): 765–92.

Massie, Robert K. *Dreadnought: Britain, Germany, and the Coming of the Great War.* New York: Random House, 1991.

Mastanduno, Michael. "Preserving the Unipolar Moment: Realist Theories and US Grand Strategy after the Cold War." *International Security* 21 (Spring 1997): 49–88.

Mattox, Gale A. and Arthur R. Rachwald, eds. *Enlarging NATO: The National Debates.* Boulder: Lynne Rienner Publishers, 2001.

McRae, Rob. and Don Hubert, eds. *Human Security and the New Diplomacy: Protecting People, Promoting Peace.* Montreal: McGill-Queen's University Press, 2001.

Mearsheimer, John J. "Back to the Future: Instability in Europe After the Cold War." *International Security* 15 (Summer 1990): 5–56.

———. "The False Promise of International Institutions." *International Security* 19 (Winter 1995): 5–49.

———. "The Future of the American Pacifier." *Foreign Affairs* 80 (September/October 2001): 46–61.

———. *The Tragedy of Great Power Politics.* New York: W.W. Norton and Company, 2001.

Menon, Anand. *France, NATO and the Limits of Independence, 1981–97: The Politics of Ambivalence.* Houndmills, Basingstoke, Hampshire: Macmillan, 2000.

Mercer, Jonathan. "Anarchy and Identity." *International Organization* 49 (Spring 1995): 229–52.

Miskowiak, Kristina. *The International Criminal Court: Consent, Complementarity and Cooperation.* Copenhagen: DJØF, 2000.

Mitchell, Hayley R., ed. *The Death Penalty.* San Diego: Greenhaven Press, 2001.

Mitrany, David. *A Working Peace System.* Chicago: Quadrangle Press, 1966.

Moore, Thomas Gale. *In Sickness or in Health: The Kyoto Protocol Versus Global Warming.* Stanford, Calif.: Hoover Institution on War, Revolution and Peace, 2000.

Moravcsik, Andrew. "Preferences and Power in the European Community: A Liberal Intergovernmentalist Approach." *Journal of Common Market Studies* 31 (December 1993): 473–82.

———. "Taking Preferences Seriously: A Liberal Theory of International Politics." *International Organization* 51 (Autumn 1997): 513–53.

Morgenthau, Hans. *Politics Among Nations, 6th Ed*, rev. Kenneth Thompson. New York: McGraw-Hill, 1985.

Morel, Benoit and Kyle Olson, eds. *Shadows and Substance: The Chemical Weapons Convention*. Boulder: Westview Press, 1993.

Morlot, Jan Corfee. *National Climate Policies and the Kyoto Protocol*. Paris: Organisation for Economic Co-operation and Development, 1999.

Morris, Madeline, ed. *The United States and the International Criminal Court*. Durham, N.C.: Duke University School of Law, 2001.

Mowle, Thomas S. "Dysfunctional Spillover: The Present and Future of Transatlantic Relations." Policy paper, Institute for National Security Studies, 2002.

———. "Worldviews in Foreign Policy: Realism, Liberalism, and External Conflict." *Political Psychology* 24 (September 2003): 561–92.

Mueller, John. *Retreat from Doomsday: The Obsolescence of Major War*. New York: Basic Books, 1989.

Nacos, Brigitte Lebens, Robert Y. Shapiro, and Pierangelo Isernia, eds. *Decisionmaking in a Glass House: Mass Media, Public Opinion, and American and European Foreign Policy in the 21st Century*. Lanham, Md.: Rowman & Littlefield Publishers, 2000.

Nesi, Giuseppe and Mauro Politi, eds. *The Rome Statute of the International Criminal Court: A Challenge to Impunity*. Aldershot: Ashgate, 2001.

Niblock, Tim. *"Pariah States" & Sanctions in the Middle East: Iraq, Libya, Sudan*. Boulder, Co.: Lynne Rienner Publishers, 2001.

Niou, Emerson N.S. and Peter C. Ordeshook. "Realism versus Neoliberalism: A Formulation." *American Journal of Political Science* 35 (May 1991): 481–511.

Nordling, Eric. *On the Autonomy of the Democratic State*. Cambridge: Harvard University Press, 1981.

Nye, Joseph S., Jr. "Neorealism and Neoliberalism." *World Politics* 40 (January 1988): 235–51.

Oberthür, Sebastian and Hermann Ott. *The Kyoto Protocol: International Climate Policy for the 21st Century*. New York: Springer, 1999.

Olsen, Mancur. *The Logic of Collective Action*. New York: Schocken, 1968.

Owen, David. *Balkan Odyssey*. New York: Harcourt Brace & Company, 1995.

Papacosma, S. Victor, Sean Kay, and Mark R. Rubin, eds. *NATO After Fifty Years*. Wilmington, Del.: Scholarly Resources, 2001.

Paris, Roland. "Peacebuilding and the Limits of Liberal Internationalism." *International Security* 22 (Fall 1997): 54–89.

Patrick, Stewart. "Beyond Coalitions of the Willing: Assessing U.S. Multilateralism." *Ethics & International Affairs* 17 (Spring 2003): 37–54.

Pearson, Graham S. *The UNSCOM Saga: Chemical and Biological Weapons Non-Proliferation*. London: Macmillan Press, 1999.

Pelletiere, Stephen C. *Managing Strains in the Coalition: What to Do about Saddam?* Carlisle Barracks, Pa.: Strategic Studies Institute, 1996.

Peterson, John and Elizabeth Bomberg, eds. *Decision-Making in the European Union*. New York: Palgrave, 1999.

Peterson, John and Helene Sjursen. *A Common Foreign Policy for Europe? Competing Visions of the CFSP*. London: Routledge, 1998.

Pilat, Joseph F. and Robert E. Pendley, eds. *1995: A New Beginning for the NPT?* New York: Plenum Press, 1995.

Posen, Barry R. and Andrew L. Ross. "Competing Visions for U.S. Grand Strategy." *International Security* 21 (Winter 1996): 5–53.

Potter, William C. "Issue Area and Foreign Policy Analysis." *International Organization* 34 (Summer 1980): 405–27.

Powell, Robert. "Anarchy in International Relations Theory: The Neorealist-Neoliberal Debate." *International Organization* 48 (Spring 1994): 313–44.

Prados, Alfred B. *Iraq Crisis: U.S. and Allied Forces.* Washington: Congressional Research Service, 2 September, 1998.

Putnam, Robert D. "Diplomacy and Domestic Politics: The Logic of Two-Level Games." *International Organization* 42 (Summer 1988): 427–60.

Quinlan, Michael. *European Defense Cooperation: Asset or Threat to NATO?* Washington: Woodrow Wilson Center Press, 2001.

Rabkin, Jeremy. "Eurojustice: An Exercise in Posing and Preening." *The Weekly Standard* (10 September 2001): 19–25.

Rauchhaus, Robert W, ed. *Explaining NATO Enlargement.* London: Frank Cass, 2001.

Regelsberger, Elfriede, Philippe de Schoutheete, and Wolfgang Wessels, eds. *Foreign Policy of the European Union: from EPC to CFSP and Beyond.* Boulder: Lynne Rienner, 1997.

Renner, Michael and Jane A. Peterson. *Small Arms, Big Impact: The Next Challenge of Disarmament.* Washington: Worldwatch Institute, 1997.

Rieff, David. *Slaughterhouse: Bosnia and the Failure of the West.* New York: Simon & Schuster, 1995.

Ripley, Tim. *Operation Deliberate Force: The UN and NATO Campaign in Bosnia 1995.* Lancaster: CDISS, 1999.

Ritter, Scott. *Endgame: Solving the Iraq Problem—Once and for All.* New York: Simon & Schuster, 1999.

Roberts, Brad, ed. *Ratifying the Chemical Weapons Convention.* Washington: Center for Strategic & International Studies, 1994.

Robertson, Geoffrey. *Crimes against Humanity: The Struggle for Global Justice.* New York: New Press, 2000.

Rodman, Peter. *Drifting Apart: Trends in U.S.-European Relations.* Washington: The Nixon Center, 1999.

Rohde, David. *Endgame: The Betrayal and Fall of Srebrenica, Europe's Worst Massacre since World War II.* Boulder, Colo.: Westview Press, 1998.

Rose, Gideon. "Neoclassical Realism and Theories of Foreign Policy." *World Politics* 51 (October 1998): 144–72.

Ruggie, John Gerard. "Multilateralism: The Anatomy of an Institution." *International Organization* 46 (Summer 1992): 561–98.

———, ed. *Multilateralism Matters: The Theory and Practice of an Institutional Form.* New York: Columbia University Press, 1993.

———. "The Past as Prologue? Interests, Identity and American Foreign Policy." *International Security* 21 (Spring 1997): 89–126.

Russett, Bruce. *Grasping the Democratic Peace.* Princeton: Princeton University Press, 1993.

Sadat, Leila Nadya. *The International Criminal Court and the Transformation of International Law: Justice for the New Millennium.* Ardsley, N.Y.: Transnational Publishers, 2002.

Sandler, Todd. *Collective Action: Theory and Applications.* Ann Arbor : University of Michigan Press, 1992.

Schabas, William. *The Abolition of the Death Penalty in International Law, 2nd ed.* Cambridge: Cambridge University Press, 1997.

Schake, Kori N. "Do European Union Defense Initiatives Threaten NATO?" *Strategic Forum,* 184, August 2001.

Scheffer, David J. "The United States and the International Criminal Court." *American Journal of International Law* 93 (January 1999): 12–21.

Schimmelfennig, Frank. "The Community Trap: Liberal Norms, Rhetorical Action, and the Eastern Enlargement of the European Union." *International Organization* 55 (Winter 2001): 47–80.

Schreurs, Miranda A. and Elizabeth Economy, eds. *The Internationalization of Environmental Protection.* Cambridge; New York: Cambridge University Press, 1997.

Schweller, Randall L. "Domestic Structure and Preventive War: Are Democracies More Pacific?" *World Politics* 44 (January 1992): 235–69.

———. "Bandwagoning for Profit: Bringing the Revisionist State Back In." *International Security* 19 (1994): 72–107.

———. "Neorealism's Status Quo Bias: What Security Dilemma?" *Security Studies* 5 (Spring 1996): 90–121.

Serfaty, Simon. *Stay the Course: European Unity and Atlantic Solidarity.* Westport, Conn.: Praeger, 1997.

Sewall, Sarah B. and Carl Kaysen, eds. *The United States and the International Criminal Court: National Security and International Law.* Lanham, Md.: Rowman & Littlefield Publishers, 2000.

Shelton, Dinah, ed. *International Crimes, Peace, and Human Rights: The Role of the International Criminal Court.* Ardsley, N.Y.: Transnational Publishers, 2000.

Shogren, Jason F. *The Benefits and Costs of the Kyoto Protocol.* Washington, D.C.: AEI Press, 1999.

Singer, Max and Aaron Wildavsky. *The Real World Order: Zones of Peace, Zones of Turmoil.* Chatham, N.J.: Chatham House, 1993.

Sloan, Stanley R. *The United States and European Defense.* Chaillot Paper 39, Institute for Security Studies of the Western European Union, April 2000.

Smith, Anthony D. *The Ethnic Origins of Nations.* Oxford: Basil Blackwell, 1986.

Smith, Hazel. *European Union Foreign Policy and Central America.* New York: St. Martin's Press, 1995.

Smith, James M. and Gwendolyn M. Hall, eds. *Milestones in Strategic Arms Control 1945–2000: United States Roles and Outcomes.* Montgomery, Ala.: Air University Press, 2002.

Smith, Karen E. and Margot Light, eds. *Ethics and Foreign Policy.* Cambridge: Cambridge University Press, 2001.

Smith, Martin A. *NATO in the First Decade after the Cold War.* Dordrecht: Kluwer Academic Publishers, 2000.

Smith, Martin A. and Graham Timmins. *Building a Bigger Europe: EU and NATO Enlargement in Comparative Perspective.* Aldershot, Hants, England: Ashgate, 2000.

Smith, Michael. *Western Europe and the United States: The Uncertain Alliance.* London: George Allen and Unwin, 1985.

Snow, Donald and Eugene Brown. *International Relations. The Changing Contours of Power.* New York: Longman, 2000.

Snyder, Glenn H. and Paul Diesing. *Conflict Among Nations: Bargaining, Decision Making and System Structure in International Crises.* Princeton: Princeton University Press, 1977.

Snyder, Jack. "Averting Anarchy in the New Europe." *International Security* 14 (Spring 1990): 5–41.

———. *Myths of Empire: Domestic Politics and International Ambition.* Ithaca, N.Y.: Cornell University Press, 1991.

Social Learning Group. *Learning to Manage Global Environmental Risks, Vol. 1.* Cambridge, Mass.: MIT Press, 2001.

———. *Learning to Manage Global Environmental Risks, Vol. 2.* Cambridge, Mass.: MIT Press, 2001.

Soetendorp, Ben. *Foreign Policy in the European Union: Theory, History, Practice.* London: Longman, 1999.

Sperling, James, ed. *Two Tiers or Two Speeds? The European Security Order and the Enlargement of the European Union and NATO.* Manchester: Manchester University Press, 1999.

Stein, Arthur. "Coordination and Collaboration: Regimes in an Anarchic World." *International Organization* 36 (Spring 1982): 294–314.

Susskind, Lawrence, Esther Siskind, and J. William Breslin, eds. *Nine Case Studies in International Environmental Negotiation.* Cambridge, Mass.: Program on Negotiation at Harvard Law School, 1990.

Talbott, Strobe. "From Prague to Baghdad: NATO at Risk." *Foreign Affairs* 81 (November/December 2002): 46–58.

Taliaferro, Jeffrey W. "Security Seeking Under Anarchy: Defensive Realism Revisited." *International Security* 25 (Winter 2000/1): 128–61.

Taylor, Michael. *The Possibility of Cooperation.* Cambridge: Cambridge University Press, 1987.

Taylor, Paul and John Groom, eds. *International Organizations: A Conceptual Approach.* London: Frances Pinter, 1978.

Telò, Martin, ed. *European Union and New Regionalism: Europe and Globalization in Comparative Perspective.* Aldershot, Hampshire: Ashgate, 2001.

Tertrais, Bruno. *Nuclear Policies in Europe. Adelphi Paper 327.* Oxford: Oxford University Press for the International Institute for Strategic Studies, 1999.

Tewes, Henning. *Germany, Civilian Power and the New Europe: Enlarging NATO and the European Union.* New York: Palgrave, 2002.

Thucydides. *History of the Peloponnesian War,* trans. Rex Warner. New York: Penguin Books, 1982.

Trapp, Ralf. *Verification under the Chemical Weapons Convention: On-site Inspection in Chemical Industry Facilities, SIPRI Chemical & Biological Warfare Studies, No. 14.* Oxford: Oxford University Press, 1993.

Udovički, Jasminka and James Ridgeway, eds. *Burn This House: The Making and Unmaking of Yugoslavia, rev. ed.* Durham, N.C.: Duke University Press, 2000.

Van Evera, Steven. "Primed for Peace: Europe After the Cold War." *International Security* 15 (Winter 1990/1): 7–57.

———. "Offense, Defense, and the Causes of War." *International Security* 22 (Spring 1998): 5–43.

van Ham, Peter. *Europe's New Defense Ambitions: Implications for NATO, the US, and Russia.* Garmisch-Partenkirchen, Germany: The George C. Marshall European Center for Security Studies, 2000.

van Ham, Peter and Richard L. Kugler. *Western Unity and the Transatlantic Security Challenge.* Garmisch-Partenkirchen, Germany: The George C. Marshall Center, 2002.

van Leeuwen, Marianne, ed. *The Future of the International Nuclear Non-proliferation Regime.* Dordrecht, Netherlands: Martinus Nijhoff Publishers, 1995.

Vanke, Jeff. "An Impossible Union: Dutch Objections to the Fouchet Plan, 1959–62." *Cold War History* 2 (October 2001): 95–112.

Vasconcelos, Alvaro and George Joffé, eds. *The Barcelona Process: Building a Euro-Mediterranean Regional Community.* London: Frank Cass, 2000.

Vasquez, John. "The Realist Paradigm and Degenerative vs. Progressive Research Programs: An Appraisal of Neotraditional Research on Waltz's Balancing Proposition." *American Political Science Review* 91 (December 1997): 899–912.

Verhellen, Eugeen. *Convention on the Rights of the Child: Background, Motivation, Strategies, Main Themes, 2nd ed.* Leuven, Belgium: Garant, 1997.

Victor, David G. *The Collapse of the Kyoto Protocol and the Struggle to Slow Global Warming.* Princeton: Princeton University Press, 2001.

Vlahos, Michael. "Culture and Foreign Policy." *Foreign Policy* 82 (Spring 1991): 59–78.

Vogel, Frederick J. *The Chemical Weapons Convention: Strategic Implications for the United States.* Carlisle Barracks, Pa.: Strategic Studies Institute, U.S. Army War College, 1997.

Vogler, John and Mark Imber, eds. *The Environment and International Relations.* London; New York: Routledge, 1996.

Wallace, William. "The Sharing of Sovereignty: The European Paradox." *Political Studies* 47 (Special Issue 1999): 503–21.

Walt, Steven M. *The Origins of Alliances.* Ithaca, N.Y.: Cornell University Press, 1987.

———. "International Relations: One World, Many Theories." *Foreign Policy* 110 (Spring 1998): 29–46.

Waltz, Kenneth. *Man, the State, and War.* New York: Columbia University Press, 1959.

———. *Theory of International Politics,* Reading, Mass.: Addison-Wesley, 1979.

———. "America as a Model for the World? A Foreign Policy Perspective." *PS: Political Science and Politics* 24 (December 1991): 667–70.

———. "The Emerging Structure of International Politics." *International Security* 18 (Fall 1993): 44–79.

Weale, Albert, Geoffrey Pridham, Michelle Cini, Dimitrios Konstadakopulos, Martin Porter, and Brendan Flynn. *Environmental Governance in Europe: An Ever Closer Ecological Union?* Oxford; New York: Oxford University Press, 2000.

Weiss, Edith Brown and Harold Karan Jacobson, eds. *Engaging Countries: Strengthening Compliance with International Environmental Accords.* Cambridge, Mass.: MIT Press, 1998.

Wendt, Alexander. "Anarchy is What States Make of It: The Social Construction of Power Politics." *International Organization* 46 (Spring 1992): 391–426.

Weymouth, Tony and Stanley Henig, eds. *The Kosovo Crisis: The Last American War in Europe?* London: Reuters, 2001.

White, Paul K. *Crises after the Storm: An Appraisal of U.S. Air Operations in Iraq since the Persian Gulf War.* Washington: Washington Institute for Near East Policy, 1999.

Wiener, Jarrod, ed. *The Transatlantic Relationship.* New York: St. Martin's Press, 1996.

Wilkie, Robert. "Fortress Europa: European Defense and the Future of the North Atlantic Alliance." *Parameters* 32 (Winter 2002/3): 34–47.

Williams, Geoffrey Lee and Barkley Jared Jones. *NATO and the Transatlantic Alliance in the 21st Century: The Twenty-Year Crisis.* New York: Palgrave, 2001.

Winslow, Anne, ed. *Women, Politics, and the United Nations.* Westport, Conn.: Greenwood Press, 1995.

Winslow, Philip C. *Sowing the Dragon's Teeth: Land Mines and the Global Legacy of War.* Boston: Beacon Press, 1997.

Wittkopf, Eugene. "On the Foreign Policy Beliefs of the American People: A Critique and Some Evidence." *International Studies Quarterly* 30 (1986): 425–66.

———. "Elites and Masses: Another Look at Attitudes Toward America's World Role." *International Studies Quarterly* 31 (1987): 131–60.

Wohlforth, William C. "The Stability of a Unipolar World." *International Security* 29 (Summer 1999): 5–41.

Woolett, Gillian R. and Sara Radcliffe. "Bioweapons, Bioterrorism, and the New Threats of the 21st Century." *Regulatory Affairs Focus* (March 2002): 7–10.

Wurmser, David. *Tyranny's Ally: America's Failure to Defeat Saddam Hussein.* Washington: AEI Press, 1999.

INDEX